zero entropic zone - random drifts

MODE [4]

VERSAL ORIGINATION POINT.
(ARY)

APOCRYPHA

APOCRYPHA

THE ART OF
DENNIS EVANS

MATTHEW KANGAS

INTERVIEW WITH PATTERSON SIMS

UTOPIAN HEIGHTS STUDIOS

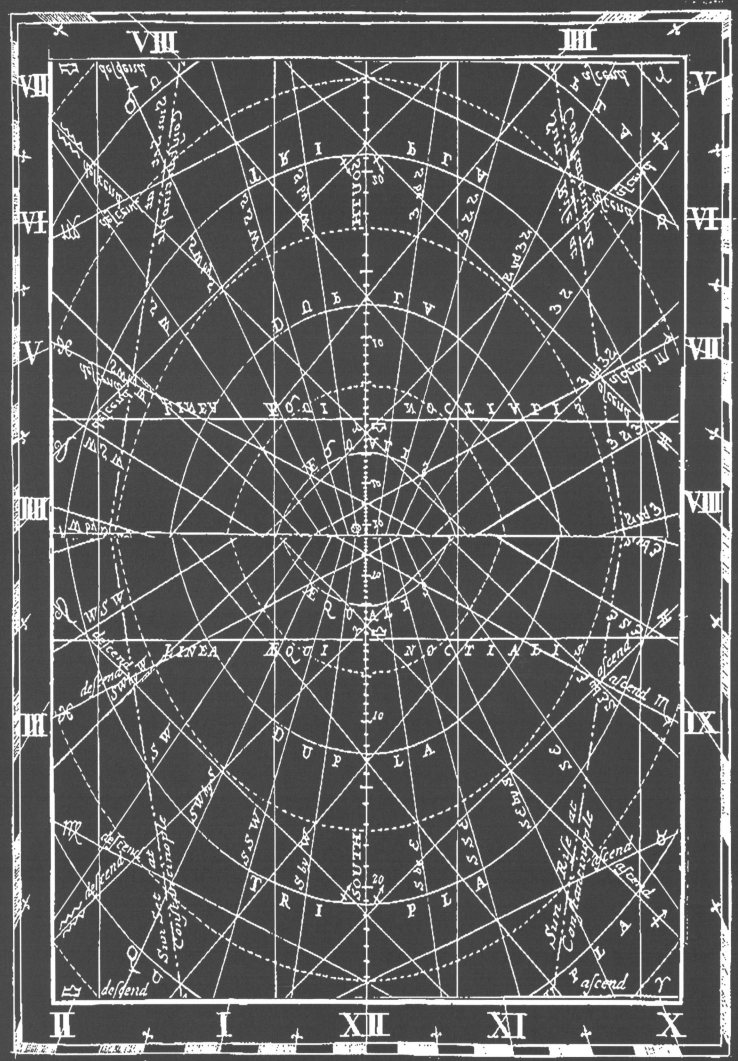

*At the end of y*ᵉ *Tenth*

CONTENTS

Dennis Evans performing *Geographic Acupuncture* at University of Washington Center for Urban Horticulture, Seattle, 1976

INTERVIEW WITH PATTERSON SIMS

EARLY LIFE

PATTERSON SIMS: What or who in your early life, family and circle of friends signaled or set you on your path to creativity and being an artist?

DENNIS EVANS: I was born in Yakima, Washington, in 1946, in the aftermath of World War II. My father was a meat cutter, and my mother was a housewife. We were an ordinary blue-collar Catholic family.

Though I didn't realize it until much later, being raised in a French Catholic family was a profound influence. We celebrated the liturgical year with our food, our home decorations, and our unquestioning devotion. We lived five doors down from the town's Catholic cathedral. I was an altar boy there and assisted in the celebration of masses, funerals and weddings, which were all performed in Latin. The liturgical seasons and the liturgical calendar were very influential in my daily life. The vestments, the rituals, the fire, the accessories in the Catholic church all left an indelible mark on my psyche.

I went to a Catholic school grades one through eight and then a Jesuit boys' school, Marquette, in Yakima. I graduated with a Classical Diploma, having studied Latin for four years and read the classics. There were no art programs at the school.

I was also a Boy Scout who wanted nothing more than to acquire every merit badge that had to do with making things. I painted awesome posters for school dances and edited the school yearbook so I could design its covers.

I was the first member of my family to attend college. My parents had high expectations for me. I went to Seattle University for a year, studying Liberal Arts. I then transferred to the University of Washington and entered the pre-med program, studying chemistry, with all intentions of going to medical school.

ADULTHOOD

In 1969, President Richard Nixon established a lottery system to assist in selecting young men for the draft. My number was 21, and so I had 21 days to be drafted. I entered the US Marine Corps and spent the majority of my time at Camp Lejeune in North Carolina, with no service in Vietnam. During that time, I began filling drawing books with ideas and sketches about art. To this day I have no idea from where this impulse had come. I had zero art education to that point in my life.

I know I was born to be an artist but, growing up in my family, art was not considered anything worthwhile. But I was a natural "bricoleur," continually building things in my father and grandfather's shops. There was no material that I did not incorporate into something artful, including carving little figures from Ivory soap bars and making suits of armor out of soup cans. At twelve years old, I built an eight-foot pram/boat in my back yard and then fashioned a trailer for my bicycle so I could transport it to water. It all freaked out my parents, as I was then and still am a poor swimmer.

I was one hundred per cent untrained, but I now realize I was born with the heart, desire and talent to be an artist.

PS: How did you begin your formal art education?

DE: Returning to Yakima after Marine service, I began to study ceramics with an elderly woman potter who after six months strongly suggested I go back to the University of Washington and study art. To quote her, "Dennis, you are a true artist, go fulfill that gift." So I enrolled at Central Washington State University in Ellensburg, where I studied sculpture for a year with Christos Papadopoulos. He, too, took me aside and recommended I go back to UW and get a degree in art.

In 1971, I returned to UW and entered the BFA program in ceramics. In 1973, I began an MFA program in film and video and print media. Bill Ritchie was my initial graduate adviser and he was very influential in my interest in live-time performance work. It was at that time that I began the work that resulted in my early performances. Art school at the University of Washington was heaven on earth. I had already satisfied the University requirements with my four years of chemistry studies, so I was afforded the opportunity to study art full-time. Because of my more rigorous science training, I wanted to study art in a more rigorous way. I wanted to know everything about art history and historical precedents. Thus, I spent endless afternoons in the art library pouring over international journals and books about artists and movements.

PS: You have always lived and worked in the Northwest. Artists like Morris Graves, Joseph Cornell, Adolf Wölfli and certain conceptualists appear to me to be influences on your aesthetic. Are these significant figures for you or are there other artists or practices that importantly inform what you do? To what extent does the Northwest's fabled history, mystique and landscape shape your artistic practice?

DE: Besides studying with Bill Ritchie, my graduate work was massively influenced by the Dutch-American art historian, curator and museum administrator Jan van der Marck. His seminars featured his extensive knowledge of Dada, Art Povera and Fluxus and he had a deep familiarity with art by artists like Marcel Duchamp, Alfred Jarry (especially the Ubu plays), John Cage, George Macunias and Joseph Beuys. He brought artists like Christo and art historians like Germano Celant to Seattle, acquainting and familiarizing us with European art culture. Specific artists like Piero Manzoni, Ben Vautier, Jannis Kounellis, Mario Merz and other European Conceptual artists had a profound impact on what I considered significant and meaningful art.

My undergraduate major had been in ceramics and my main teacher and adviser was Howard Kottler. Howard used ceramic plates as vehicles to explore very conceptual, witty and ironically inspired ideas. With my intense interest in Cage's music, Beuys's performances and Dada, I began trying to unite all those factors in my own body of work.

At that point, I began making musical instruments using porcelain and many other substances like sponges, tuned stones and dryer lint. I collected rain water at specific times of the year and used it as part of my percussive instruments. I built beautiful lacquered boxes for these instruments and began performing with them. I wrote scores and diagrammatic/cosmic choreographies for the performances. My cosmic/absurdist performances were implemented by my alter ego Ubu Waugh, based on the character in the play by Alfred Jarry titled *Ubu Roi*. My performance events, which soon moved outside, were very much inspired by Dada and Fluxus.

My continuing education and influences veered off to the French Structuralists Claude Lévi-Strauss and Jacques Derrida. I also was drawn to the writings on semiotics by Umberto Eco. My study of the Western alchemy of Carl Jung and Joseph Campbell became the basis of much of my art at this time, as I conjoined Dadaism, alchemy and re-enactments of creation myths from around the world. Provincial Catholicism, alchemy, European Conceptualism and an abundance of creation myths checkered my early education and contributed to my tool box as a young artist. The fabled mystical artistic tradition of the American Northwest had zero influence on my work. My primary influences were European art and artists.

PS: Most of the attention on and exhibition of your work has occurred in the Northwest, but at the start of your career in the late 1970s and early 1980s your work was seen in group shows at the American Craft Museum, the Whitney Biennial, and at the New Museum in New York, with one inclusion at the Museum of Modern Art in a drawings show in 1996. How has that early history and attention impacted you and your art?

DE: After some performances and exhibitions, galleries and museums as far away as New York began taking notice of my work, I was included in the 1978 Whitney Biennial in the section entitled "Private Mythologies." At that point, I was introduced to many major New York art dealers. I met with the likes of Leo Castelli, Holly Solomon and Ronald Feldman, who all took and sold many of my diagrammatic scores and drawings. It was the time, career-wise, to pack my bags and relocate. New York had shown me a lot of what I thought I wanted from my art life, but it had also shown me the very steep price one would pay for that life. I was reading Carl Jung and Joseph Campbell, which also triggered a major existential question: "What is this existence all about?"

I had purchased in 1976 a small house in Seattle that I was slowly converting into a great studio. I was in love with another artist, Nancy Mee, and we wanted an artistic life together. We were realistic as to what the cost of moving to New York would be. We decided to stay in Seattle, and I have never regretted that decision. Nancy and I married in 1980 and continued our lives as professional artists. I taught art part-time at the Bush School and Nancy had an art-framing business. Like most young artists, we needed a day job to support ourselves. I luckily got a job teaching art in a small private k-thru-12 progressive school. Nancy had worked as picture framer in college and formed her own business. We both continued to work and show and struggled to make a living. Our goal was to quit our day jobs and survive on our art work. In 1988, Nancy closed her business and, in 1990, I quit my teaching job. Since then we have supported ourselves with our art.

PS: Like the sequence and content of your specialist library spaces, your sensibility and the artistic embodiments of your knowledge and insights are often inoperable, impenetrable, and unreadable—more about sculpture than inscribed words and thoughts. Is it your intention for your art to be esoteric and definitively un-interpretable?

DE: Yes. This has probably been the most difficult question for me and my audience with which to come to terms. I would not ask that question about my entire body of work, because my intentions have changed as my work has changed over fifty years. I think it is a fair and apt question about my early work. My early work was influenced by the Dada and Fluxus movements. So many of my actions were meant to be absurdist and seemingly irrational, and perhaps for some, impenetrable. My "music" and instruments were heavily influenced by the works of John Cage and chance and random systems. I believe that in the context of those movements my works had an internal logic.

The landscape performances were impacted by Lévi-Strauss's work *The Raw and the Cooked*. This work and my twelve-hour performance, *A Passion Play,* were results of my assimilation of the ideas of structural anthropology that Lévi-Strauss elucidated. The installation work of the eighties plumbed the depths of [Carl Jung's] *The Science of Mythology*.

Besides Lévi-Strauss, Mircea Eliade and Joseph Campbell were my main mentors and spirit guides. I knew my work required heavy lifting for my audience but I knew at the core there existed deep rewards, and truth. And as an art lover as well as an artist, the art I most loved required me as the viewer to do some work. Joseph Beuys's installations and performances come to mind. I have always and still feel true reward comes from some deep work by the viewer.

I have never been a deep enthusiast of retinal art. Marcel Duchamp, another artist whose ideas influence my work, once said, "Painting shouldn't be exclusively retinal or visual; it should have to do with the gray matter, with our urge for understanding. . . . I am interested in the intellectual side."

I believe some of my work had taken this idea too far. As Duchamp so aptly put it, "I was interested in ideas—not merely in visual products. I wanted to put painting once again at the service of the mind. I felt that as a painter it was much better to be influenced by a writer than by another painter. . . . This is the direction in which art should turn: to an intellectual expression, rather than to an animal expression. I'm sick of the expression *"bête comme un peintre"*—"stupid as a painter."

PS: Your work is exquisitely and impeccably constructed. How does your studio operate? Do you do all your work alone or do you have assistants?

DE: We began hiring assistants on a steady basis around 1990. They were often recent graduates from area art schools who had particular skills we needed. Some

lasted for short periods, but a few came and stayed. André Gene Samson, my current special assistant, began helping me with installation work in 1982 and still remains in our employ. He is now more of a family member than an employee and he is irreplaceable. At a certain point, Nancy moved her studio space home, and we began sharing spaces and assistants. The assistants who lasted learned many skills, and their work was raised to the level of perfection we demanded. They help us make our art, but they never are what we refer to as "the hand of the artist."

PS: Please discuss the history of Utopian Heights and what it has become in your and Nancy's lives.

DE: Slowly, as our art practice grew and we began exhibiting outside of Seattle, our business grew and our need for more space became evident. We bought property in our neighborhood and converted the buildings into studio spaces. We built outdoor Japanese gardens to display and sell my own and Nancy's outdoor sculpture. I designed our neighbors' gardens and fences. I planted forty-five ornamental plum trees in all four directions up and down the nearby streets to give Utopian Heights a uniform and well-designed look. These outdoor spaces have benches and decks that encourage people to linger, have lunch, read and meditate. Bronze plaques with wise proverbs were placed in the gardens and on the benches. We have sought to create a spiritual space for art and people.

We named our compound of studio and domestic structures Utopian Heights, an homage to the artist Joseph Cornell's lifetime residence and studio on Utopia Parkway in New York's borough of Queens. In 2002, we named our neighborhood Utopian Heights, and our neighbors use it to refer to the part of Seattle they live in. I became the mayor of Utopian Heights, and remain so.

PS: Have you travelled? If so, where and when? To what extent has that changed your perspectives and art?

DE: In the 1990s we began traveling. Our objective was that these trips should be "mind altering." They first took us to Indonesia, and then Bali, Sulawesi, Java and later to Japan, Turkey, Greece and India. Each trip altered my perception about what constituted art and what the function of art might be. Utopian Heights was one of the results of those trips. One year upon returning from a trip to Japan, I built a Shinto shrine on the corner of our property under the "Welcome to Utopian Heights" sign. I put a stack of small paper and pencils out and let humanity take over. Over time, hundreds of prayers and wishes and affirmations began to appear. As a result, on holy days, solstices, equinoxes and Catholic cross-quarter days we gather with like-minded people and burn the prayers. We get approximately 1000 prayers every six months. The burning of prayers is a highlight for many who come, connect and engage. The gardens of Utopian Heights have become a spiritual destination for many, a repository for the ashes of dear and departed friends (our Garden of Souls) and the site for several weddings and other significant events. It has become what I consider the perfect cauldron for how art should function in society.

PS: How has living with Nancy Mee and marriage to and collaborations with her impacted your life and art?

DE: Nancy and I have shared studios and studio assistants for a long time; though our artworks are quite different, they cohabitate very well. We share openly what we are thinking about in terms of our ideas. At some point, the idea of working on a project together came up and we acted upon it. *Imagine—After the Deluge* was the first result. It was a highly successful enterprise, received well. We imagined that if one was to rebuild a society or utopia, who would be the essential characters: a Physician, an Architect, a Holy Man, an Astronomer and so forth.

We then attempted to give life to each of them in each of our own particular styles. We continued for several more years, collaborating and showing very elaborate installations. We intend to work together but not at the exclusion of pursuing trajectories of thought that appeal to us individually.

PS: What is the role of the Gallerie C.E.N. in your artistic production?

DE: On July 4, 2012, the ATLAS and CMS experiments at the Large Hadron Collider at CERN [the European Organization for Nuclear Research] announced they had each observed a new particle in the mass region around 125 GeV. [Mass at subatomic levels is given in electron volts, eV. It is standard in physics that GeV represents one billion electron volts.] This was a sign that the Higgs boson particle that had been predicted by the Standard Model does exist. This finding threw the scientific community into a frenzy and for whatever existential reason did the same for my work.

This event signaled the beginning of my interest in cosmology. It became my sole field of interest. I began consuming every bit of information about the origin of the universe, the discovery of elementary particles and the search for new elementary particles at CERN.

This current inquiry into the origins of the Universe and what comprises Matter has led me to the questions:

Where did the Universe come from?

How did it begin and how will it end?

What is the place for Homo sapiens in this universe?

These have become all-consuming questions for me and are now the primary generating factors in my art activities.

Gallerie C.E.N. on the grounds of Utopian Heights is my exhibiting gallery/laboratory for all my cosmological artistic inquiries. I continue doing large-scale installations and paintings with the thirteen billion-year evolution of the Universe as my query.

The myths that drove my work for forty years are now dead to me. My artistic mind, which once groped for understanding through myths, now wonders about the place art has in the history of Time. In a way, my journey and my artistic trajectory have circled back to my days as a young student scientist. The strategy of a scientist and an artist are very similar. We find questions and attempt to find answers for them by doing experiments. The grand question now confronting humankind is to look back, perhaps thirteen and a half billion years, and wonder. At this autumnal point in my journey, I feel the only project left is to immerse myself into what has been eloquently expressed by Carl Sagan when he said, "The size and age of the Cosmos are beyond ordinary human understanding. Lost somewhere between immensity and eternity is our tiny planetary home. . . . I believe our future depends on how well we know this Cosmos in which we float like a mote of dust in the morning sky."

Dennis Evans working in the studio, 2019

Lance Corporal Dennis Evans with *Seven Land Interventions,* Yakima Firing Center of the US Army, Yakima, WA, 1971

INTRODUCTION Planting the World

I'd like to orchestrate nature.

—Dennis Evans, as Ubu Waugh, interview, *Le Jardin du Monde*, 1977[1]

A bit of a magician and a bit of a fraud, Evans wants to reinterpret and revitalize nature.

—Regina Hackett, "She Strives for 'Pure' Response in Her Work," 1980[2]

The mind, that ocean where each kind
Does straight its own resemblance find,
Yet it creates, transcending these,
Far other worlds, and other seas;
Annihilating all that's made
To a green thought in a green shade.

—Andrew Marvell, "The Garden," 1681[3]

The notion of growing or planting the world could be a metaphor for the artistic practice of American artist Dennis Evans (b. 1946): placing things in earth and water, like the farmer forefathers of his childhood, and watching them grow into art. However, as we shall see, this only covers half of his lifetime interest in unconventional responses to the question, "What is a work of art?" Besides exploring and "orchestrating" nature, the other half of his studio activities involves charting the universe and examining its origins. Addressing all this over a sixty-year period has granted Evans the expansion of parameters necessary to encompass such a vast set of aesthetic pursuits.

The artist's relationship to Earth preoccupied many American and European artists of the 1960s and 1970s. Fortunately, Evans's sole exploration of Earth Art, the predominant trend of the era, ended quickly after he was apprehended in 1971 for digging a long trench that echoed *Double Negative,* a pair of huge trenches in the Nevada desert created in 1969 by Michael Heizer. More pertinently, ecology in the form of a holistic embrace of the organic, the seasonal and, above all, the temporal aspect of life on the planet would permeate Evans's consciousness, expressing itself in a decade of musical compositions, theatrical performances on land and water, and settings as far flung as

remote rain forests and a peninsula in the Guerrero state of Mexico near Acapulco.

These activities accumulated as a sequence of events that combine ecological content with ceremonial and ritualistic forms, oblique spin-offs of christenings, baptisms and bodily immersions. The gradual shift from active participant—composer, musician and conductor to maker-fabricator, craftsman and fabulist—comprises the first phase of his art, nearly one-third of his career. Before examining such steps, his *gradus ad Parnassum*—movement toward aesthetic enlightenment—it is worth briefly exploring his early education in order to understand how crucial the path was, so formative that it prepared him to become not only a visual artist of great subtlety and wit, but one imprinted with cultural practices originating in Europe, especially France, rather than the more widely dispersed Scandinavian and Northern European influences of mid-twentieth-century Pacific Northwest. The influence of Asian art came later, after his performative persona Ubu Waugh developed.

My biggest lesson from the nuns was how to learn.
Dennis Evans, interview, 2021[4]

Dennis Evans performing *Transversals to a Flow* at Los Muertos Beach, Sayulita, Mexico, 1977

Even before he became aware of his remarkable similarities to French writers and creative figures of the late-nineteenth and early-twentieth centuries, Evans shared their origins in the French provinces and their sporadic forays into the city. Evans's Paris—Seattle, Washington—offered an escape from his rural home in Yakima, the state's fourth largest city and largest agricultural center. Both sides of Evans's family, the paternal Irish-immigrant Evanses and the maternal La Framboises from France, settled in the Yakima Valley early in the twentieth century because it was conducive to the growth of hops for the ale and beer they were familiar with in Ireland and France.

Neither working class nor Protestant elite, the Evanses and La Framboises sent their children to local parochial schools operated by Dominican nuns and Jesuit priests. Such highly developed educational methods provided young Dennis Eugene with a precocious knowledge of mathematics and sciences such as chemistry, but little or nothing of the visual arts. These arts he inadvertently discovered on his own, playing in the family garage, building small boats or cars from the ground up.

Evans family in front of the family home, Yakima, WA, 1956. From left: Terry Evans, Dennis Evans, Cecelia Evans, Maurice Evans holding Susan Evans

(below) Annual Retreat of Marquette High School and St. Joseph Catholic School, Yakima, 1965

Incorporating Roman Catholic doctrine and dogma into strict academic curricula, the Sisters of St. Dominic (founded in 1215) concentrated on educating children. Evans's instruction by an all-female faculty (except for athletic coaches) encompassed kindergarten through eighth grade and included English grammar, arithmetic, history and geography with other elementary school subjects. For high school, Evans left St. Paul Cathedral School for Marquette High School, a few blocks away from the family home. Father Jacques Marquette (1637–1675) was the first European missionary to explore North America. A member of the Society of Jesus, or Jesuits, founded in 1534 by Ignatius of Loyola, his travels covered the entire Mississippi River Valley and beyond. The Jesuits, with their global network of monasteries and, eventually, secondary and university-level educational institutions, have been referred to as "entrepreneurs of the soul," so influential was their participation in the settling of North, South and Central America. Unlike other monastic orders, for the Jesuits "humanist classicism turned out to have many uses . . . the classically educated soon proved that their training in the arts of . . . writing made them effective and articulate."[5] For the early pupils, as for Evans, Ignatius, who "soon committed himself to providing classical literary training as well as theology for young Jesuits,"[6] provided an important model. Four years of Latin and some ancient Greek were foundational secondary-school subjects. Small classroom size reinforced "carefully regulated progress through increasingly difficult subjects and meticulously expurgated classical readings."[7] Over the ensuing 400 years of the Society of Jesus, the

growth of Jesuit-run "schools and churches, revival meetings, and missions mattered only as a part of an effort to impose the hegemony of the written over the oral, the disciplined over the spontaneous, and the modern over the archaic."[8]

It is these polarities and potential contradictions that partially explain the appearance of so many text elements in Evans's subsequent art, as well as his rebellion against such rigid precepts: spontaneity would battle with discipline; archaic forms and rituals would seek to overcome modernizations such as the Mass recited in English. Later, these guidelines, obtained as a child and adolescent, would subside or be complemented by competing medieval and Renaissance ideologies that challenged the all-knowing faith of the Jesuits: alchemy—which became science—and science—which became cosmology, astronomy and physics. Finished with reenacting ritual and ceremony as artistic inspirations by the late 1990s, Evans began to adapt non-theological explanations of astronomy, cosmology and spirituality through empirical observation, the use of numerical measurements and the study of physics, leading him to the incorporation of material inquiries like those that had preoccupied the early alchemists. This complex approach opened a new world for the rigorously trained Jesuit-school alumnus. Instead of embracing faith in the miracles of the sacraments, such as the transubstantiation of the Host (the change of communion wine and wafer into the blood and body of Christ), Evans borrowed the vocabulary of these procedures to create his own religious paraphernalia and reenact them as possible spoof, satire or heretical parody.

In the process, Evans contributed to a growing body of contemporary art in the 1980s and 1990s that addressed Christian and Catholic dogma. This was evidenced in the boxes resembling Eucharist containers, the chalices and the reenactment of Mass-like customs transposed to equally hermetic gestures of the artist. They appeared as Roman Catholic references in the steps and actions of the many performances which included the artist holding and wearing the sculptures. Though he went unacknowledged as part of that movement, and was not included in the leading monograph on the topic, *Postmodern Heretics: The Catholic Imagination in Contemporary Art* (2004) by critic Eleanor Heartney,[9] another Catholic art critic, Regina Hackett, summarized his interface: "From Catholicism he got his love of ritual and mystery. . . . From his family, Evans got an ingrained association between seasonal changes, crop rotation and religious ceremonies."[10] Hackett further argued in her 1989 interview with the artist that his intentions are more instructive than rebellious: "[He] wants people late in the twentieth century to care about what he sees as the demise of an essentially medieval religion and the disappearance of the farmer, the man of nature."[11]

Evans undertook a considerable range of studio activities after he left high school in Yakima. He proceeded to Seattle University, a Jesuit school, and transferred after one year to the University of Washington (UW) pre-med program, where he majored in chemistry, in 1966. After graduating, but before serving in the US Marine Corps (1969–71), he spent half a year at Central Washington University in Ellensburg (1967–68). Before his arrival on the UW campus, the School of Art was already aligned with the School of Paris. Founding deans Ambrose Patterson (1877–1966) and Walter F. Isaacs (1886–1964) and their students, Wendell Brazeau (1910–1974) and Spencer Moseley (1925–1998), both of whom studied with Fernand Léger (1881–1955), all had lived in Paris and exhibited in the *Salons des indépendants* while there. Returning to Seattle, they taught at the School of Art in high-windowed, École des Beaux Arts-style atelier classrooms with close supervision, regular student exhibitions and graduation requirements in the form of rigorous faculty critiques. Returning to the university to pursue a

Alfred Jarry, 1896

Dennis Evans, 1997

degree in art, Evans, with his French-American background, perhaps more than any other artist associated with the University of Washington School of Art, absorbed its French aesthetics into his art.

Rather than seeking nonexistent progenitors from Asia or the sympathetic members of the Northwest School (the "École du Pacifique," as it was called in Paris)—Mark Tobey (1890–1976), Morris Graves (1910–2001), Kenneth Callahan (1906–1986) and Guy Irving Anderson (1906–1998)—Evans emerged as a delayed chrysalis from the late-nineteenth and early-twentieth centuries. An influence most explicitly avowed by Evans was Alfred Jarry (1873–1907). Jarry's extensive influence in Europe was like a time bomb, exploding in 1896 with the production of his avant-garde play *Ubu Roi.* Interest in his anarchist work reignited after World War II, when examples of rebellion and freedom were sought to replace stuffy French dramatists, some of whom had collaborated with German occupiers.

Evans's confession about the importance of Jarry's cultural influence occurred at age thirty-one; he noted

in a 1977 interview, "Alfred Jarry is the sort of spirit I have reincarnated in Ubu Waugh. . . . The new Ubu Roi, in a sense. The Americanized, the profane Ubu Waugh, and the spirit is the spirit of absurdity."[12] With the reference to absurdity, Evans may have been alluding as well to Theatre of the Absurd and the dramas of the 1960s by playwrights such as Samuel Beckett, Eugene Ionesco, Howard Pinter, Edward Albee, and others.

The emergence and efflorescence of Ubu Waugh, Evans's chosen alter ego, developed out of his admiration for two seemingly disparate literary figures: the outrageous, anti-establishment raconteur and poseur Jarry and the British novelist Evelyn Waugh (1903–1966). Jarry, a child prodigy, was feted by the very aristocrats and intellectuals he scorned. Waugh was both a Catholic convert and a mercilessly funny critic of modern society in works such as *Decline and Fall* (1928) and *The Loved One* (1948). It was the author of these early works, rather than the one represented by the post-conversion novel *Brideshead Revisited* (1944), that Evans evoked with his pseudonym.

But perhaps Jarry loomed largest for Evans, not least because of many seemingly parallel experiences. During their early formative years, unbridled, if unfocused creativity of both Evans and Jarry first bloomed. Jarry, like Evans, was educated in Catholic schools, but moved from one convent or boarding school to another due to his unruly behavior as a boy. Rebelling against the Jesuit administrators and lay instructors, he concocted plays starring a character based on one of his teachers, Monsieur or Père Hebé—*voil*à, Père Ubu and Ubu Roi. For Evans, his Ubu—Ubu Waugh—was a pun on "king": the French *roi* in English is "king," as in the English title of the play, *King Ubu*.[13] By the end of Jarry's *lycée*, he was ready for a change: he went off to Paris, where he found his métier and planted his world. *Ubu Roi* premiered in 1896; Jarry was twenty-three.

Jean Bouise in *Ubu Roi*

In Evans's case, he returned to Seattle after a two-year stint in the Marine Corps and Reserve and six months studying pottery in Yakima with Lorene Samuelson (1924–1994), a former student of Richard Fairbanks (1929–1989) at Central Washington University.[14] At her suggestion, Evans attended Central Washington University as an art major, learning bronze-casting, among other foundry skills, from Professor Christos Papadopoulos. In contrast, Jarry had several returns to home after his debut in Paris to recover from his youthful debauchery. His parents were always there for him and continued to send money to him in the City of Light until his father's death in 1895.[15]

The great *succès d'estime* of Jarry's *Ubu Roi* was a surprise; for many, it was offensive and boring, with its scabrous plot of royalty and conspiracy, not to mention its variable length. Five decades later, Evans's twelve-hour-long *A Passion Play* (1980) challenged the audience's patience and taste, too. Action occurred on an hourly basis beginning at eight o'clock in the morning. Activities moved from area to area, all surrounding

a freshwater lagoon of sorts, which necessitated the artist wading in hip boots, taking the "plot" further into nature, water, plant life and reverential interactions with Mother Nature.

Evans's work was created during a fertile period of American avant-garde theatre, much of which involved sustained productions created by Robert Wilson, the Living Theatre and La Mama Experimental Theater Club, among other companies. Evans and these troupes took inspiration from Jarry and his concepts of time. Duration and temporality became unstable elements, linked to chance operations, spontaneous improvisations and unscripted passages.

These inspirations informed the three-hour-long performance of Evans's *The Theory of Non-Enigmatic Geometricities* (1976), which took place at the home of Seattle department-store heiress Illsley Ball Nordstrom, in The Highlands north of Seattle. Presented in the formal gardens at Nordstrom's Merrill House, replete with reflection pools and extensive rose gardens, Evans's tongue-in-cheek choreography was observed by members of the Henry Gallery Association, the

Dennis Evans (in water) in the performance *A Passion Play, 12th Hour*, 1980.

Mary Ann Peters, Dennis Evans (in fountain), Andrew Bateman performing *Part Twelve: Southern Cross—The High to Low* from *Twelve Field Us(e)ages/A Passion Play*, 1982, at Merrill House, Seattle

Dennis Evans in the performance *The Theory of Non-Enigmatic Geometricities* at the home of Mrs. Illsley Ball Nordstrom, The Highlands, WA, 1976

Dennis Evans performing with Mary Ann Peters at Seattle Art Museum Seattle Center Pavilion

board of the state's oldest art museum, the University of Washington's Henry Art Gallery. Amused and perplexed, they watched formally attired performers carry black-box sculptures, which seemed a cross between Japanese bento boxes and orthodox Jewish tefillin (head ornaments worn during prayer).[16]

While Jarry's achievements continued to live by legend and cast a shadow over later performers, including Merce Cunningham (1909–2009) and John Cage (1912–1992) with their similar mixes of Jarry-esque banality and impertinence, Seattle's professional art critics seemed to be unnerved or outraged by Evans's comparable antics. As we shall see in Chapter Five, the art critics' responses to Evans will tell us about their circumstances and their earnest attempts to unravel meaning. What the French poet Henri de Régnier (1864–1936) wrote of Jarry could also be applied to Evans, dressed up in tuxedo, tails and sport-fishermen's hip-boot waders: "The author's singularly bizarre intellect in which hermeticism was mixed with buffoonery [is] by turns satisfying and preposterous."[17]

Central to Jarry and totally assimilated by Evans is Jarry's absurdist philosophy of Pataphysics, a playful take-off on the Jesuit systems of learning and the organization of knowledge. How could a philosophy of inconsistency and grandiose claims be expressed in a way that might, if only for a moment, fool and entertain

the listener, the audience, the viewer, the teacher, the interlocutor—and a priest? According to one of Jarry's biographers, Alistair Brotchie, "Pataphysics is the science of imaginary solutions, which symbolically attribute the properties of objects."[18] Taking pains to explain Jarry's elusive philosophy, Brotchie quoted Jarry's 1897 claims for "unexceptional exceptions . . . a science of the particular despite the common opinion that the only science is the general."[19] Pataphysics is an acceptance of the unknowable in the cloak of specific knowledge; this is a good approach to the art of Dennis Evans. Alertness to the phony-baloney, Jarry-esque terminology and his punning, fol-de-rol verbiage helps the viewer unpack layered references as one explores, examines and "reads" an Evans assemblage or sculpture, free to stop and look or listen, resuming inspection at leisure.

There are other parallels. Evans's affluent early patrons and hosts were Mrs. Nordstrom and Mr. and Mrs. William Street of Lakewood, Washington, near Tacoma, who offered the sites where Evans's first important performances occurred. For young Jarry, two couples, one French and the other British, loved and supported the recalcitrant teenager. Alfred and Marguerite Vallette,[20] owned their own magazine, *Mercure de France*, while his adoring London fans, Maggie Boehmer-Clark and William Mollard, used the eccentric young man to enhance their own *réclame* in the *haute monde* of Paris by underwriting several productions. For the four patrons, the fact that irony and humor could coexist in serious art works like *Ubu Roi* or Jarry's later, increasingly obscene and incoherent novels like *Messalina* (1901) and *Supermale* (1902), carried great appeal. Evans's *The Theory of Non-Enigmatic Geometricities* was similarly both intellectually titillating and intriguing. Building on Jarry's pretentious-professor persona giving an incomprehensible lecture, Evans stood at an easel to lecture to his audience, then continued his instructions by taking to

Dennis Evans performing *Sound Studies: An Impact-Significant Deep-Water Event* at the home of Mr. and Mrs. William Street, Lakewood, WA, 1976

the lake in a rowboat to make further gestures, such as lifting chalices and dropping stones into the lake for their "sounding."

Though his short life may have been a slow train wreck, Jarry's example of wide-ranging pursuits included a thorough knowledge of Asian art, another aspect he shares with Evans. Brotchie commented on how the deep interest Jarry had in theological speculations "lay in the modalities and aesthetics of their structure rather than in their supposed meaning," a vital and enduring observation that equally applies to Evans.[21] With Jarry's excision of faith from religion, "Catholicism furnished a scheme of codes and symbols, a system of representation that could be subjected to aesthetic and logical manipulation."[22] This is an uncannily apt and, for our purposes, perspicacious viewpoint for our explorations of the art of Dennis Evans. By shifting focus to sacred interactions with nature and the earth, Evans gradually used Christian mythology to reconnect to pre-Christian, pagan and animistic nature worship. This was awe-inspiring to some and shocking to others. Using Jarry's Ubu as a model for a character, Evans created his own artistic persona, Ubu Waugh, alternately a veil and an introduction to a bizarre new world.

NOTES

1   Dennis Evans, as Ubu Waugh [with Charles Grimes], "Interview with Ubu Waugh," *Le Jardin de Monde: The Journal of International Casafundada* (Summer 1977): 33.
2   Regina Hackett, "She Strives for 'Pure' Response in Her Work," *Seattle Post-Intelligencer* (May 11, 1980): G6.
3   Andrew Marvell, "The Garden," Poetry Foundation, https://www.poetryfoundation.org/poems/44682/the-garden-56d223dec2ced
4   Dennis Evans, interview with author, June 17, 2021.
5   Anthony Grafton, *Worlds Made by Words: Scholarship and Community in the Modern West* (Cambridge, MA: Harvard University Press, 2009), 168–69.
6   Grafton, *Worlds Made by Words*, 169.
7   Grafton, *Worlds Made by Words*, 169.
8   Grafton, *Worlds Made by Words*, 164.
9   Eleanor Heartney, *Postmodern Heretics: The Catholic Imagination in Contemporary Art* (New York: Midmarch Arts Press, 2004).
10   Regina Hackett, "Artist Eulogizes Ritual He Knew as a Catholic Farm Boy," *Seattle Post-Intelligencer* (January 14, 1989): C1.

11   Hackett, "Artist Eulogizes Ritual," C3.
12   "Interview with Ubu Waugh," 33.
13   Cyril Connolly and Simon Watson Taylor, translators. *The Ubu Plays* (New York: Grove Press, 2007).
14   See my *Richard Fairbanks: American Potter* (Seattle: University of Washington Press, 1993).
15   Alistair Brotchie, *Alfred Jarry: A Pataphysical Life* (Cambridge, MA: MIT Press, 2011), 87.
16   Barbara Taylor, "Report," *Insight: Journal of the Henry Gallery Association* (Summer, 1980), n.p.
17   Brotchie, *Alfred Jarry*, 87.
18   Brotchie, *Alfred Jarry*, 30.
19   Brotchie, *Alfred Jarry*, 30.
20   Madame Vallette used the pseudonym Rachilde and was a popular cross-dressing novelist, author of *Monsieur Vénus* (1884).
21   Brotchie, *Alfred Jarry*, 68.
22   Brotchie, *Alfred Jarry*, 336.

Dennis Evans working in the studio at the Ravenna house, 1993

CHAPTER ONE Campus Crucible

Because of my science training, I wanted to study art in a more rigorous way. I wanted to know everything about art history and historical precedents. Thus, I spent endless afternoons in the [School of] Art library poring over international journals and books about artists and movements.

—Dennis Evans, Interview with Patterson Sims, 2021[1]

When Dennis Evans arrived back on the University of Washington campus to study ceramics after brief sojourns at other schools and his apprenticeship with Mrs. Samuelson in Yakima, the School of Art was already among the most developed and respected on the West Coast. Officially established in 1935 with the encouragement of President Henry Suzzallo (1875–1933), the Department of Painting, Sculpture and Design (as it was later called) had firm ties with European art schools, conservatories and private ateliers. This was important for the development of the young ex-Marine. It nestled him in an environment that was open to international developments abroad. Ambrose Patterson, an Australian Post-Impressionist, set up the school along French art-school lines, comprising studios, classrooms and lecture halls, and offering quarterly critique sessions among faculty and students. In addition, Patterson had exhibited widely in Paris in annual juried shows, where he also came across other non-European artists, including Walter F. Isaacs, a former student of Arthur Wesley Dow (1857–1922) at Columbia University.

Isaacs had also studied in Paris, with Charles Guérin (1875–1939). Hired by Patterson in the early 1920s, he helped set up curriculum plans and pedagogical methods encouraging innovative, avant-garde activities while gaining classical École des Beaux-Arts training in life classes, still-life drawing and painting. Isaacs's tutelage under Dow in New York also lent him sympathy for other arts such as ceramics, glass, textiles, printmaking and graphic design. This was reflected in his and Patterson's first- and second-generation faculty hires, which included potters, weavers, printmakers and metals artists and demonstrated precepts similar to those of the Bauhaus in Germany, where all the arts were considered equal. Thus, aspects of the French academic system were combined with a more modern perspective.

Over a thirty-year period, when Patterson and Isaacs were unable to travel back and forth to Europe as regularly as they would have liked, they generously invited Europeans to join them in Seattle for guest professorships. Perhaps surprisingly for a city so small and an art department so young, modern art luminaries as varied as Alexander Archipenko (1887–1964),

Amédée Ozenfant (1886–1966), Chilean-American muralist Pablo O'Higgins (1904–1983), Swiss ceramic designer Paul-Ami Bonifas (1893–1967), former secretary to Le Corbusier (1887–1965) and Bauhaus painter Johannes Molzahn (1892–1965), among others, were hired, some for repeat residencies. This atmosphere benefited Evans, who easily switched from ceramics, his undergraduate subject, to printmaking and video for his Master of Fine Arts degree. Following a custom begun by Patterson and Isaacs, former Bonifas student Robert Sperry (1927–1998) succeeded Bonifas as ceramics head, but began to make avant-garde films alongside his large-scale ceramic murals, setting an example for clay students who wanted to try other things. Before that, the deans (Isaacs succeeded Patterson) sent their two best students, Wendell Brazeau and Spencer Moseley, to study privately with the noted Cubist Fernand Léger in Paris. Upon their return, they utilized the sophisticated teaching methods they had absorbed, of which Evans became a willing beneficiary. Completing the faculty circle, Moseley succeeded Isaacs as director after Isaacs's retirement in 1956.

Off campus, Seattle's art world was developing, too, but at a slower pace than at the UW. Mark Tobey, Morris Graves and Guy Irving Anderson had never attended a higher institution of learning to acquire their art skills, and Kenneth Callahan attended the UW only briefly, leaving before his first quarter ended. As a result, developments in art criticism and commentary was largely left to journalists, the best of whom was Margaret Bundy Callahan (1904–1961), Kenneth Callahan's wife. By the time Evans left school and began exhibiting, the quality and quantity of writing about the visual arts had ebbed, despite the two daily newspapers, the *Seattle Times* and *Seattle Post-Intelligencer*, assigning reviews to full-time reporters on a regular basis, sometimes providing even weekly coverage. As we shall see in Chapter 5, their responses to Evans's art over

a long period of time give us a fascinating glimpse into the evolution of art writing in smaller population centers outside of New York, Chicago and San Francisco.

Curator and museum director Jan van der Marck

Another event that occurred only two years before Evans's arrival was the 1969 exhibition *557,087* at the Seattle Art Museum Seattle Center Pavilion, a converted Seattle World's Fair building. At the fair itself, held in 1962, several exhibitions arranged by European curators brought major twentieth-century artists and newer, postwar European artists to the Pacific Northwest, some for the first time. Stedelijk Museum director Willem Sandberg (1897–1984) was invited to organize the international section of *Art Since 1950* at the fair and was assisted in another exhibition at the Vancouver Art Gallery by a younger Dutchman, Jan van der Marck (1929–2010), who became a crucial figure in Evans's development once he was hired as a curator at the Henry Art Gallery, the University of Washington's art museum. His hiring led to an extended feud over programming among van der Marck, acting director LaMar Harrington (1917–2005), and the Henry's board of trustees, which included Anne Gerber (1910–2005) and budding New York School-collector Virginia Bloedel Wright (1929–2020). On top of that, the School of Art faculty was historically entitled to periodic exhibitions of their work; all this was to unravel as van der Marck battled with Harrington. Evans became caught between the two—and benefited from both.

Before Evans's encounter with van der Marck, however, the exhibition *557,087* (titled after Seattle's population in 1968) had a significant impact on him. The show was the first occurrence of postmodern art in

557,087

an exhibition organized by lucy r. lippard for the contemporary
art council of the seattle art museum at the seattle art museum
pavilion from september 5 to october 5 1969; version titled
955,000 to vancouver art gallery 1970.

Cover of exhibition catalogue *557,087*, 1970. Collection of
Matthew Kangas

Author, art critic and art historian
Lucy Lippard in New York, 1993

Seattle, held at the Seattle Art Museum in 1970. Land Art, Earth Art, Process Art, Minimal Art, Conceptual Art, Fluxus and all their variants were included by curator Lucy R. Lippard. As Gerber pointed out in a 1983 interview, Lippard had been recommended by the New York dealer Xavier Fourcade (1927–1987): "He got me her telephone number and I called her up when I got back to the hotel. In a day or two we met for lunch. And she was really keen about it! She started right out making a list of artists she was going to get and then, over the whole year, she got it together."[2]

Among the artists whose works were exhibited were Vito Acconci (1940–2017), Carl Andre, Hans Haacke, Dennis Oppenheim (1938–2011), Walter de Maria (1935–2013) and Adrian Piper. Many of the artworks consisted of index cards with details for possible construction of the pieces; some of these were realized, others remained unfulfilled plans. Among the exhibiting artists Evans heard about later were Joseph Kosuth, Robert Smithson (1938–1973), Edward Kienholz (1927–1994), and Daniel Buren. A full calendar of artist's films was also shown during the exhibition's one-month run. Although he never saw the exhibition, *557,087* was a turning point for Evans and his generation of younger artists, as well as for Seattle. With the

coming of age of the postwar baby-boom generation, the number of visitors the exhibition drew proved there was a reliable audience for contemporary art, but there were very few places (one being the Henry Art Gallery) that showed it regularly.

Just six years later, Evans and Lippard would cross paths when she included his work in her second Northwest survey, *In Touch: Nature, Ritual and Sensuous Art*, at the Portland Center for the Visual Arts in 1976.[3] In Portland, Evans's well-attended musical performance badly backfired, causing him injury, but not stopping the performance. By then, the Seattle artist was well along in his growing career as a New Music artist—making works both with and without sound, and sometimes even without music.

The contemporary avant-garde music scene in Seattle preceded the contemporary art scene by several years. John Cage left The Cornish School in the late 1930s, and it was not until 1962 that another avant-garde music group, New Dimensions in Music, was founded by the composer Joan Franks Williams (1930–2003). Lasting until 1971, when Williams moved with her family to Israel, NDM hosted many composers, including Stefan Wolpe (1902–1972) and Ursula Mamlok (1923–2016). Conventional musical-instrument scores were accompanied by electronic tapes and given West Coast premieres, including works by composers Morton Subotnick, Mario Davidovsky (1934–2019) and Vladimir Ussachevsky (1911–1990). Evans was unable to attend any of these concerts but their programming grounded future audiences who were exposed to his compositions and performances. Both NDM and Ubu Waugh retained an atmosphere of playfulness that contrasted with the often serious-sounding or perplexing events they witnessed.

Dennis Evans the artist is inconceivable without the intervention and tutelage of van der Marck. The curator had an illustrious career even before arriving in Seattle (as well as after), and his situation at the Henry Art Gallery had a momentous impact on the students attending his informal graduate seminar. They included Evans, Norie Sato, Sherry Markovitz and Carl Chew. As Sato mentioned in an interview:

> [Van der Marck] would just chat and talk, tell us stories. We all got excited; he was definitely instrumental, moving us beyond conventional thinking to Conceptual art and helping us think more broadly about what art was and what it could be. [The seminar] really inspired us away from medium-based work and to question institutions and structures. I remember Dennis moved into a house in Ravenna before [he lived in] his house in Bryant. We had some art sales and shows. We were already thinking of setting up our own structures to help us.[4]

Two other teachers were important to the group: Bill Ritchie, a printmaking teacher who was exploring video art, and Howard Kottler (1930–1989), a ceramist with a PhD from Ohio State University who is now considered the godfather of conceptual ceramics. Both were encouraging to Evans, urging him to go beyond the materiality of clay technique into a realm of meaning and inference.

Evans first learned of performance art and postwar European sculpture by artists such as Piero Manzoni (1933–1963) and Joseph Beuys (1921–1986)

in van der Marck's seminar, where the curator also introduced the graduates to the legend of Alfred Jarry. Sato heard "[a] lot about Dada and Surrealism; we learned much more from van der Marck than anyone else."[5] It is unlikely van der Marck realized he was fomenting the interest of so many younger contemporary artists with his wide-ranging classroom discussions. An adviser to Evans during his graduate studies, van der Marck brought firsthand experiences and anecdotes about all the major postwar European art movements, including Arte Povera and Fluxus, and New Music events occurring in the shadow of

Bill Ritchie

Howard Kottler posing as Mississippi ceramic artist George E. Ohr

a former Seattle composer John Cage, whose redefinition of music—"There is no such thing as silence"[6]— would have significant ramifications for Evans. Not content with sharing documents, catalogues and anecdotes, van der Marck invited friends like the Italian art

Piero Manzoni, *Artist's Shit No. 014*, 1961. Metal, paper, "artist's shit," 1⅞ x 2½ in. Museum of Modern Art, New York, 4.1999. Gift of Jo Carole Lauder and Ronald S. Lauder

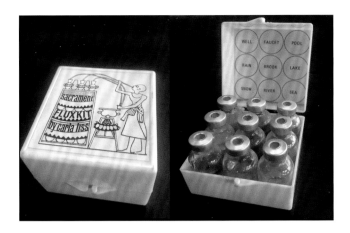

Carla Liss, *Sacrament Fluxkit,* 1969. Plastic box with two offset labels containing nine vials of liquid, 2¹⁄₁₆ x 2⅝ x 2¹⁵⁄₁₆ in. Collection of Nancy Mee and Dennis Evans

George Brecht, *Water Yam,* 1963. Cardboard box with offset printing containing sixty-nine offset-printed cards, 5⅞ x 6⁵⁄₁₆ x 1¾ in. Collection of Nancy Mee and Dennis Evans

Dennis Evans, *Box for Seasonally Collected Rain Water, Skirr, Sponge and Bowl,* 1976. Mixed media, 15 x 12 x 8 in. Collection of the artist

critic and a founder of Arte Povera Germano Celant (1940–2020) and Bulgarian-born sculptor Christo (1935–2020) to meet with students and faculty. (Later, van der Marck supervised and assisted in Christo's *Running Fence* [1972–76] in California.) With classroom references to artists such as Jannis Kounellis (1936–2017) and Mario Merz (1925–2003), both Arte Povera artists, and Fluxus member Ben Vautier, Evans incorporated their sense of displaced and dispersed

compositions into his later installations, appropriating their strategies of anti-monumentality and deployment of humble everyday materials. Many of his works at the time echoed to a greater degree those by the Fluxus artists, one of whom, George Maciunas (1931–1978), Evans would meet and host in Seattle in 1977.

Evans did not become a performance artist overnight, nor did his art evolve in an orderly fashion; instruments often morphed into sculptures that would be shown later in galleries and museums, unaccompanied by music or any other type of performance. He became a composer first. With Seattle's considerable history of avant-garde music, dating back to Cage's concerts at The Cornish School (where he invented the prepared piano in 1935), there was a receptive audience for Evans's transgressions of musical boundaries. A special concert series that continued throughout Evans's student days, "New Dimensions in Music," brought important composers of chance music, electronic music and twelve-tone serial music to Seattle. The organization was noted for world premieres and the custom of repeating a new work for the audience's second, more focused, hearing.

Evans had been exposed to the immateriality of Conceptual Art, but was trained as a ceramist and conventional sculptor. During the van der Marck

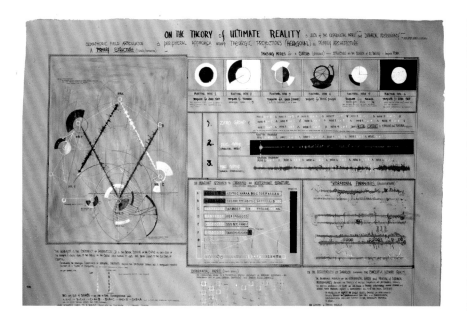

On the Theory of Ultimate Reality, 1978. Ink on rice paper,
27 x 38 in. Collection of the artist

Dennis Evans performing at the Concert for New Music,
Evergreen State College, 1975

Evans had an epiphany of sorts. As he later told curator
and museum director Patterson Sims: "It was at this
point that I began making musical instruments out of
porcelain and many other substances; e.g., sponges,
tuned stones, dryer lint. I collected rain water at specific times of the year and used it to be part of my percussive instruments."[7]

As with Cage, percussion, rather than melody or
harmony, was crucial for Evans's music. After all, Cage's
inability to find enough room on stage at The Cornish
School for all of his percussion instruments led to his
one-instrument percussion "ensemble," the prepared
piano. Tapping, hitting, screwing and rubbing piano
hammers, rubber erasers and mallets against piano
strings created different sounds. The Cageian interface
between object and sound was similar to Evans's early
explorations; his found riverbed and beach stones contained pitches of their own to be activated during musical performances. Unlike Cage, though, as a sculptor
Evans put equal emphasis on the musical-instrument
containers: "[The] beautiful lacquered boxes for these
instruments. . . . [I] began performing using these cre-
ations. I wrote scores and diagrammatic/cosmic choreographies for the performances. My cosmic/absurdist

performances were implemented by my alter ego Ubu
Waugh. . . . These events were very much Dada and
Fluxus-inspired."[8]

Leaving campus in 1975, Evans merged into the
Seattle art scene equipped to transform it altogether
with his former MFA fellows. Not only did they further their own careers, they established four essential
centers for Seattle's contemporary art scene in the final
quarter of the twentieth century. The first, Triangle
Studios in Pioneer Square, was the birthplace of local
contemporary art and video art in the city in 1975.[9]
Then, in 1976 came <u>and/or</u>, a multipurpose site for
visiting artists and exhibitions and performances by
local artists. Next was the gallery opened by Linda
Farris (1945–2005) in 1971 in Pioneer Square, where,
as Sherry Markovitz put it, "It was a new experience.
It was like the graduate-program studio moved into
the Linda Farris Gallery. She had a nose."[10] The fourth,
Center on Contemporary Art (CoCA), an outgrowth
of <u>and/or</u>, was founded by Evans, Parks Anderson,
Mary Ann Peters, Anne Focke and others in 1980. Its
bylaws hold that it must feature living artists, never
own a permanent space, and never form a collection.
In one stroke, for the first time since its new building

Linda Farris at Linda Farris Gallery with Dennis Evans's *Soundings*, 1977

opened in 1933 in Volunteer Park, Seattle Art Museum seemed slightly irrelevant, losing much of its prestige and power to the local art community. CoCA continues today in Pioneer Square, as does a transformed, vigorous contemporary art community and many exhibition venues.

The art of Dennis Evans was accumulating, formulating itself into an amalgam of crafted functional objects, such as musical instruments, enigmatic performances, charts and maps of possible worlds, and faux chronologies of fantasy worlds and places.

NOTES

1   Dennis Evans, in "Interview with Patterson Sims," in this volume, 8.
2   Interview with Anne Gerber, February 24–April 21, 1983, Northwest Art Oral History Project, Archives of American Art, Smithsonian Institution. https://www.aaa.si.edu/collections/interviews/oral-history-interview-anne-gerber-13276
3   Lucy R. Lippard, *In Touch: Nature, Ritual and Sensuous Art* (Portland, OR: Portland Center for the Visual Arts, 1976).
4   Norie Sato, interview with author, February 24, 2021.
5   Sato, interview.
6   John Cage, *Silence: Lectures and Writings* (Middletown, CT: Wesleyan University Press, 1961), 1.
7   Evans, in "Interview with Patterson Sims," in this volume, 8.
8   Evans, in "Interview with Patterson Sims," in this volume, 8.
9   Other artists at Triangle Studios who became noted professionals include Jeffrey Bishop, Carl Chew, Carolyn Law, Nancy Mee, Mary Ann Peters and Bill Ritchie.
10   Sherry Markovitz, interview with author, February 12, 2021.

Dennis Evans performing in *Transversals to a Flow*, 1977, Los Muertos Beach, Sayulita, Mexico

CHAPTER TWO

Soundings: Music, Performance
and Ritual Objects

Just about everything [John Cage] stands for changed my life.... Also Marcel Duchamp.... Cage taught me
time and Duchamp taught levels of meaning.

—Dennis Evans, as Ubu Waugh, interview, *Le Jardin du Monde*, 1977[1]

Here at the fountain's sliding foot,
Or at some fruit tree's mossy root,
Casting the body's vest aside,
My soul into the boughs does glide;
There like a bird it sits and sings,
Then whets, and combs its silver wings;
And, till prepar'd for longer flight,
Waves in its plumes the various light.

—Andrew Marvell, "The Garden," 1681[2]

Winding things up at the University of Washington School of Art, Dennis Evans was making art out of clay, making money by selling pottery and teaching at a local private elementary and secondary school, the Helen Bush School. Altogether, he became a full-time artist. Employing the ceramic skills he gained in undergraduate school, he exhibited regularly and sold handmade pottery at the Pacific Northwest Arts and Crafts Fair in the upscale suburb of Bellevue, Washington, with the help of an artist he had met in the Bill Ritchie printmaking classes, Nancy Mee, originally from Sacramento, California. Accepted for the prestigious Henry Art Gallery crafts-biennial exhibition in 1975, Evans won a top award and thereby was granted a solo exhibition, his first, and in the state's most prestigious academic art museum, rather than a commercial gallery, as can be the case with emerging artists. LaMar Harrington, the Henry's curator, made sure Evans's award-winning sculpture *Splints* (1975) was acquired for the Henry's permanent collection. It was his first art-museum acquisition, one of many to come, including acquisitions by the Metropolitan Museum of Art and the Museum of Modern Art, New York.

As he told the interviewer for *Le Jardin du Monde*, "[The Henry] said I could do anything I wanted.... And were they sorry! No one understood anything about my exhibit."[3]

Such bemused confoundings and misunderstandings would become standard responses to Evans,

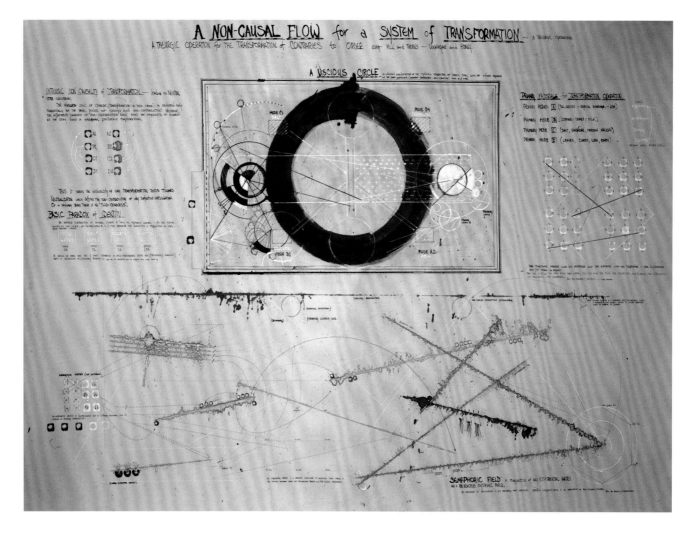

Drawing for *A Non-Causal Flow for A System of Transformation*, 1977. Ink on paper, 27 x 38 in. Collection of the artist

alternately puzzling and delighting members of the public who happened upon his art in the coming years. But, before the gallery and museum exhibitions, there was Dennis Evans, New Music artist. Listening to a local nonprofit, subscriber-supported radio station (one of the first in the U.S.), KRAB-FM, and attending occasional live concerts, Evans responded by creating his own musical instruments, fashioning his own performance attire and performing "compositions" on the articles and paraphernalia he made of wood, porcelain, metal and paper. Explanatory "scores" accompanied each "composition." Drawing inspiration from the calligraphic scores of Cage, Evans made his own diagrams, often with impenetrably obtuse instructions and explanations. In this sense, he became part of the midcentury New Music movement before he became a contemporary artist, expanding the purview of what music could be, even without notes, sounds, tones or silent intervals.

His musical performances were evanescent experiences, different each time, dependent upon circumstances, whims and the spontaneity of the performer. As he told *Le Jardin du Monde*: "I don't even play the scores myself. That's part of the contradiction. They are totally absurd. They can be played and they can't be played. Everything I do has this quality."[4]

At the opening of his museum debut at the Henry, the artist was approached by a student from Evergreen State College in Olympia (TESC, founded by the state legislature in the early 1970s as an experimental four-year college concentrating on ecology and Indigenous studies), who wanted to perform on Evans's musical instruments at an upcoming concert. Balking at the idea, Evans insisted he perform the music by himself.

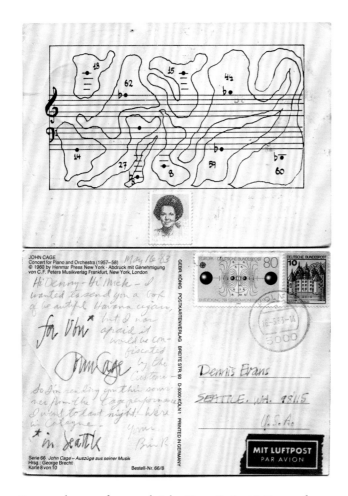

Recto and verso of postcard: John Cage, *Series 66, Concert for Piano and Orchestra*. Collection of the artist. Signed and dedicated to Ubu by Cage. Sent by Bill Ritchie to Evans in Seattle.

His subsequent debut as musician, composer and performer occurred at TESC in 1975. As he recalled in an interview: "I thought, what did I get myself into? I already had a tuxedo and tails, which I wore to dinner parties as a joke. The pieces proceeded from the instruments in a way: each piece had its own instrument. With the microphones, amplified sounds of the water and wet sponges emerged from particular instruments. Stones would have sounds like a tap, but in rhythm."[5]

Not long after Ubu Waugh's debut concert, Lucy Lippard, who had curated the pathbreaking *557,087* for Seattle Art Museum, was contacted by the Portland Center for Visual Arts (PCVA) to organize another epoch-making exhibition, this one covering the entire region. She organized *In Touch: Nature, Ritual and Sensuous Art*.[6] It was on this occasion that the

Marcel Duchamp, *Three Standard Stoppages*, 1914. Wood box 11⅛ x 50⅞ x 9 in. with three threads 39⅜ in. glued to three painted canvas strips, 5¼ x 47¼ in., each mounted on a glass panel 7¼ x 49⅜ x ¼ in.; three wood slats, each 2½ x 43 x ⅛ in., shaped along one edge to match the curves of the threads. Museum of Modern Art, New York. Katherine S. Drier Bequest 149.1953 a-i

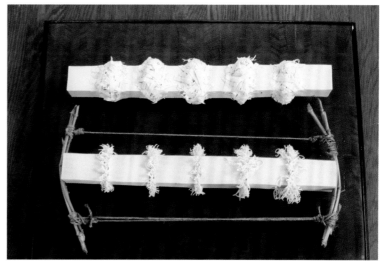

Splints, 1975. Hand-built porcelain with paper tape, sticks, weeds, twine, kelp, fabric, Plexiglas box, 3¼ x 15½ x 2 ¾ in. without Plexiglas box. Seattle Art Museum. This work won the Northwest Craftsmen's Exhibition Purchase Award in 1975.

artist premiered his *Box for Bow, Skirr and Target Score* (1976), lasting approximately one-half hour. Evans shot "skirrs," or long white porcelain "arrows," from his handmade wooden bow and, in so doing, sliced into his fingers and arm, but kept performing until the end of the piece. At that point, he was taken to a nearby hospital emergency room for treatment.

Installation view of *Musical Instruments and Scores*, 1977. Henry Art Gallery, University of Washington, Seattle

Dennis Evans performing at the Concert for New Music, Evergreen State College, 1975

Lippard was present, and she may have been surprised at the unpredictable outcome. In the catalogue, she revealed that "Dennis Evans's sculptures are actually musical instruments and his drawings are scores. Wands, arrows, slender bows, mallets, sponges, bowls and wind and percussion instruments are made of wood, porcelain and beeswax. The making of these objects, and the esoteric and sensuous rites in which they are used, are part of a single process. Sometimes, the materials are collected or the pieces played only at certain times—an equinox or a solstice. Wind, rain, stones and silence are also elements."[7]

Lippard was the first critic and curator to recognize both the ritualistic and sensuous aspects of Evans's work. She was also the first to explain his motives and intentions as a composer: "In his intentions to move toward increasing fragility and ephemerality, Evans sees the score as a target and the music as the shooting. . . . Trying to 'stay irrational, foot in cheek' (as he put it), alter ego Ubu Waugh combines Dada and Zen to dress in top hat and tux when the music is performed. Perhaps this is the active counterpart to the visual contradiction that occurs when these beautiful

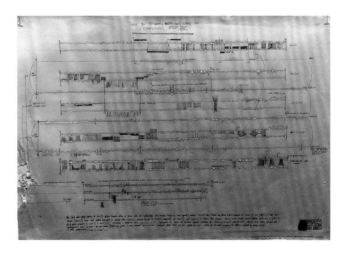

Drawing for *Musical Score for Skirrs, Mallets and Water*, 1975. Ink on rice paper, 22 x 27 in.

Dennis Evans performing *The Slaying of the World Parents*, Portland Center for the Visual Arts, Portland, OR, 1977

Dennis Evans performing *Box for Moon Bowls and Bar*, Portland Center for the Visual Arts, Portland, OR, 1977

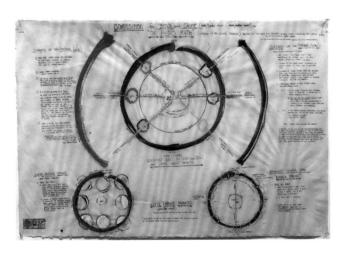

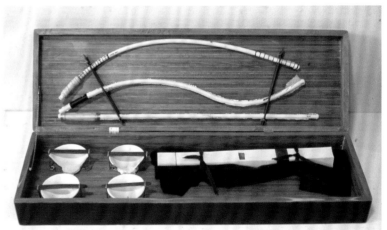

(above) *Composition for Bow and Skirr, The Hero's Myth*, 1977. Ink on rice paper, 22 x 27 in. Collection of the artist

(above right) *Instrument Box for Moon Bowls and Bar*, 1977, Porcelain, wood, 10 x 24 x 8 in. Collection of the artist

(right) *Box for Bow, Skirr and Target Score*, 1976. Porcelain, wood, ink on paper, cloth, 12 x 68 x 5 in. Collection of the artist

objects, before their destruction, are presented as precious items, nestled luxuriously in lined boxes under Plexiglas."[8]

The only part the New York art critic got wrong was the contention or assumption that the musical instruments were eventually destroyed. This strategy would have fit in snugly with a definitive theoretical defense of Conceptual Art, chronicled in her influential 1973 book, *Six Years: The Dematerialization of the Art Object from 1966 to 1972*.[9] *Au contraire*: in a long series of art-gallery and museum exhibitions over the next several years, the instruments remained "precious items, nestled luxuriously in lined boxes," but fewer under Plexiglas.

The intense, exciting atmosphere in a Seattle discovering contemporary art—local, national and international—was bound to give birth to a number of nonprofit alternative spaces, and Evans benefited from all of them. Above all, at and/or his exposure (and eventual participation) involved a heady, continuous mixture of concerts, lectures, exhibitions and film and video series, along with ingeniously low-cost publications, monographs and even a critical journal for fledgling art critics, *and/or Notes*. Founded in 1974 by former Berkeley, California, resident Anne Focke, and/or was collaborative, cross-disciplinary and do-it-yourself from the beginning. Having worked at the Seattle Art Museum and the Seattle Arts Commission, Focke knew how to run a not-for-profit operation, how to fund it (writing newly available government grant applications), and how to frame it as artist-directed. When CoCA was founded in 1980, it followed the example of and/or: no collection, no permanent real estate, and programming that followed the interests and advice of the artist board members rather than curators. When curators were hired, they followed the directions of well-engaged board members, not collectors.

Self-effacing to a fault, Focke nevertheless was a genius at gently galvanizing groups of people to

substantive actions that got results; her approach was, perhaps, a product of her witness of the Free Speech Movement at the University of California. With composer David Mahler guiding the music program and Rolon Bert Garner (1940–2015), former assistant to Seattle Art Museum founding director Richard E. Fuller (1897–1976), overseeing the exhibitions from art selection to display and lighting, visiting and exhibiting artists were exposed to the highest museological standards available. The and/or people knew how things should look, if not always how to pay for them. In a brief seven-year period (1974–81) highlighting music, video, theatre, monologists, performance art, sculpture, painting, drawing and photography, all of the vaunted new pluralism of the 1970s went on view, week after week, including for our purposes Evans's appearance at the 1977 FluxFest. The festival was a wide-ranging sequence of events that was held for one week in September, celebrating the amusing, if confounding, international art movement begun in Europe after World War II, Fluxus.[10]

To call and/or a fertile incubator for new artistic talent would be an understatement, but the metaphor might not be inappropriate when we examine and/or's links to another significant cultural and social phenomenon of the period, feminism. To read critic Roberta Wilkes's analysis of the organization at the time is to see the tight interface between women, women artists and what became known as feminist art. and/or was at the center of all this, operating from its simple, nondescript storefront on Tenth Avenue. As Wilkes noted: "Since [the 1976 Women in the Arts Festival], a number of . . . women and others . . . have gotten together to form their own association. Based at and/or gallery on Tenth Avenue, the Women Artists Group has evolved from a series of informal meetings into a formal, ongoing organization of about fifty women. The group is sponsoring organized events and is beginning to define some goals and a long-term program."[11] Wilkes continued: "and/or director Anne Focke was instrumental in forming the group and the membership overlaps to a great extent with that of the gallery."[12]

Taking the link a step farther, the Women Artists Group raised money from an auction and undertook the funding of a Judy Chicago exhibition at and/or in May 1976. Not mentioned by Wilkes or other interviewees is the fact that it was a two-person show: Judy Chicago and her then-husband Lloyd Hamrol, a public-art sculptor soon to become responsible for *Gyro Jack* (1979), a cast-concrete, tilting spiral on the corner of a downtown Seattle park. Chicago and Hamrol were given equal time at the public discussion of their exhibition, transcribed in an issue of the house journal, *Hindsight*. Foreshadowing issues of gender in Dennis Evans's early performance pieces and Nancy Mee's earliest etched-glass sculptures, Chicago answered a question about vaginal imagery, "our vagina, our cunt, is a metaphor for us, identifies us in the same way men identify themselves with their cocks."[13]

Responding to a parallel query about masculine identity in his work, Hamrol pleaded: "I am not primarily concerned with formal values, which I see as being male.... I am making an effort to make the work softer, literally softer, as the sand-bag *Soft Wall* [at and/or] is."[14]

Chicago and Hamrol's attempts at aesthetic, sexual and professional reconciliation did not outlast their marriage, but the duality as such must have appealed to Evans on a number of levels. His 1980 marriage to Nancy Mee cemented preexisting studio collaborations that had been simmering for several years and foreshadowed the male/female subjects that both Evans and Mee would deal with in their art in the coming years. In Evans's case, male and female components in several sculptures were also a nod to the veiled sexuality of Duchamp's works. With Mee, depictions of women's spinal malformations went beyond

Nancy Mee with her sculptures from *Support*, 1980

Nancy Mee and Dennis Evans at their wedding, June 2, 1980

Dennis Evans performing in Flux Fest with David Mahler at and/or, Seattle, 1977

Dennis Evans performing in Flux Fest with Susan MacCleod at and/or, Seattle, 1977

Chicago's blunt literalness, but did present an aspect of self-identification.

Chicago and Hamrol were trying to offer a model for how artist couples can succeed and co-exist professionally over a longer period of time, but they failed. Evans and Mee's collaborations on public-art projects and in temporary installations would grow and mutually enhance each other's talent, creating a hybrid entity with increasingly blurred gender presences.

The dizzying schedule of events at and/or between May 1977 and April 1978 alone included spectacles and happenings both on and off Tenth Avenue, such as a walking tour of Belltown conducted by Buster Simpson, a University of Michigan transplant who moved to Seattle in 1974 with his girlfriend, artist Pat Oleszko. The toast and sensation of the Seattle Women Artists Group, wearing her body suit decked with stuffed fabric penises, Olesko soon rose to prominence as an erotic-performance artist on the national circuit.

Similarly conveying startlingly explicit feminist content, Sherry Markovitz, another Evans MFA classmate, gained national recognition in *Heresies* (a leading radical feminist journal) with her and/or photography exhibit, *Women: Body, Space and Personal Ritual*. Another Simpson comrade Chris Jonic premiered her evening-long costumed extravaganza, *Women of the Whirl*, a feminist dance fable for especially tall women.

Anne Grosshans, head of and/or publications at age twenty-two, remembered concerts by Robert Ashley (1930–2014, another Ann Arbor cohort), Laurie Anderson, Meredith Monk, Terry Riley and Charlemagne Palestine. Her memory of Evans's and/or debut at the 1977 FluxFest is that it was "more visual than aural. First [at and/or], we had the music groups and then we had performance art groups. For me, it was always the performance art category with Dennis. They were not so improvisatory as ritualistic. He was Catholic to me; I am Lutheran, so the elegance of his gestures, the lifting up of the objects like they were the Host—but was really a chiseled rock!—this resonated to me."[15]

Discussing the link between and/or and the Jan van der Marck group (some of whom joined the Linda Farris Gallery stable), Norie Sato stressed that the classmates

had created a strong bond that made us
want to stay together rather than leave

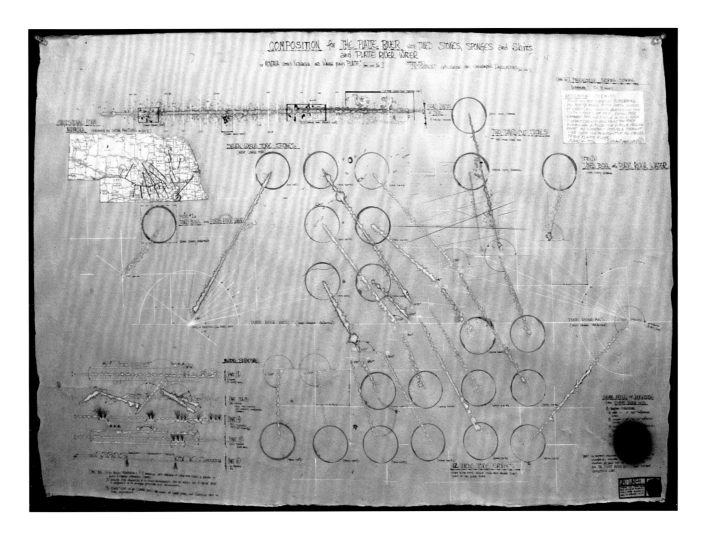

Composition for the Platte River with Tuned Stones, Sponges and Skirrs and Platte River Water, 1977. Ink on paper, 27 x 38 in. Collection of the artist

town, the way most MFA grads had. Our class stayed in Seattle because that's what we found: the beginning of the [contemporary] art community in Seattle. It was us. So we all wanted to do stuff. I had met Anne Focke and worked at <u>and/or</u> doing all the video programming. The people who visited or had shows were amazing: Shigeko Kubota and Nam June Paik, Hans Haacke, Martin Puryear, Suzanne Lacy and Mierle Laderman Ukeles.[16]

Despite so many firsts, in typically low-profile and ambiguous Anne Focke fashion, <u>and/or</u> became legendary before it had barely been open long enough to attain such status. (It closed in 1981 and Focke moved on to other less challenging tasks at the National Endowment for the Arts and elsewhere.) Nevertheless,

the 1977 FluxFest hosted by <u>and/or</u> (September 27– October 2) was a high point for the fluid, uncategorizable institution (it wasn't even really an institution, Focke told everyone) and especially for Evans, whose performance involved FluxScience, FluxGames, Fluxus Films, Fluxus Sports & Games Night and FluxStore selling Fluxus artist objects.[17]

Reports vary widely as to the occurrences and the art works (which included a mobile public toilet and clinic), their locales and their purposes; this is perfectly appropriate for the most deliberately confusing and ambiguous postwar art movement. Resistant to gallery commodification (as was the Italian movement Arte Povera), Fluxies were enraptured by the banal, but loaded their works with subversive meaning (another

Dennis Evans and George Maciunas at Flux Fest at and/or, Seattle, May 1997

Fluxus, *Fluxkit*, 1965. Suitcase with contents by Fluxus artists, assembled by George Maciunas, 12 x 17½ x 5 in. Getty Research Institute, Los Angeles. Jean Brown papers (890164)

inheritance from Alfred Jarry). Who could say what Fluxus was? Sato nearly succeeded: "Fluxus was an upside-down way of thinking about art, willing to embrace everything from ordinary gestures to extraordinarily crafted things. It wasn't painted. Always more: let's do something funny and unexpected. Fluxus toilets; Fluxus ping-pong paddles, unusable, of course. Then, musical instruments that didn't work, toys that were broken, and smashed pianos, way beyond Cage."[18]

Evans's performance at and/or was assisted by David Mahler and artist Susan McLeod (1948–2017), who inspired Evans to acquire water samples from the Platte River in North Dakota and Nebraska, crucial to the composer's desire for a widened topographical and hydrologic sound base. Mahler assisted with technical volume and speaker and microphone placement, and acted as creative consultant in his role as director of and/or's music programs. In the first part, "The Collective Significance of Gravity," musical instruments included amplified "tuned stones," skirrs and "tuned sponges." In the second part, porcelain "moon bowls" and Mahler's "Insertion Principle" were featured. Detailed maps of North Dakota and Nebraska were altered by McLeod and mounted on the surrounding walls. All this in the presence of Fluxus

founder George Maciunas, whose unsigned *Hindsight* obituary seven months later noted: "He developed a different way of looking and categorizing the arts and was working on charting them. His way of thinking about systems and the way things worked influenced many artists and enabled him to carry out projects for many artists besides himself. . . . He left an energy behind, and, for those who were fortunate enough to have been in contact with him, a feeling that his view of the world, the arts and society, has affected ours."[19]

Before his Fluxus epiphanies, Evans performed his concerts indoors and out, emphasizing ties to nature, water and air. *Sound Studies: An Impact-Significant Deep Water Event* (1976) presented at the home of Seattle Art Museum Contemporary Art Council members Mr. and Mrs. William Street in Lakewood, Washington, mimicked Jarry's pseudo-professorial talks with Evans's own easel, diagrams

Dennis Evans performing *Sound Studies: An Impact-Significant Deep-Water Event* at the home of Mr. and Mrs. William Street, Lakewood, WA, 1976

(right, from top to bottom)
Mary Ann Peters and Dennis Evans performing *Part Twelve: Southern Cross—The High to Low* from *Twelve Field Us(e)ages/A Passion Play*, Merrill House, Seattle, 1982
Mary Ann Peters and Dennis Evans performing *Part Seven: Romance of Reciprocation* from *Twelve Field Us(e)ages/A Passion Play*, University of Washington Urban Horticulture Center, Seattle, 1980
Mary Ann Peters and Dennis Evans performing *Part Eight: Churn a Rotary Romance* from *Twelve Field Us(e)ages/A Passion Play*, University of Washington Urban Horticulture Center, Seattle, 1980
Dennis Evans performing *Part 5 A Both: The Fulcrum of Between* from *Twelve Field Us(e)ages/A Passion Play*, University of Washington Urban Horticulture Center, Seattle, 1980

and demonstrations. Ridiculing academia, both artists posed as teachers, lecturing on absurd topics to highly educated and wealthy patrons.

Also water-immersive and connected to the land, *Rain Bowls, Skirrs and Sounding Stones: Transversal to a Flow Enactment* (1976) followed. Evans's *The Theory of Non-Enigmatic Geometricities* (1976), also set outdoors in Nordstrom's formal gardens in The Highlands,

borrowed a Seattle Symphony musician to act as an acolyte of sorts to Evans's priest-like leader in tux and tails. Audiences followed performers who carried musical instruments in boxes and occasionally played above, near and on a platform over a pond in the garden. In the highly formal setting, the sounds took on a distinguished, more serious character, amusingly at odds with the mock-seriousness of the straight-faced actors. Despite its musical nature, this work drew attention to the musical instruments as sculptures, and invited admiration and inquiry as to their function. The audience was appreciative, if politely confused, not that different from the sophisticated audiences in Paris that alternately praised and pilloried the plays of Jarry.

Part Seven from *A Passion Play* (1978–80) was commissioned by the Henry Gallery Association and acknowledged in their quarterly magazine *Insight*. Performed in the Nordstroms' gardens, the colonnaded pergola, fountain and oval pool provided background for four performers, including Evans, and

Detail of *100 Discrete Tuned Sounding Stones for Puget Sound*, 1978. Stones, wood, copper, 4 x 48 feet. Collection of Nancy Mee

served as components in an elaborate stage set for the transmission, dedication and reconciliation of binary opposites, male and female, alive and/or dead. Wearing leather-strapped, black-lacquered wooden chest packs, the white-shirted performers bowed and followed one another, acting on, behind, before and in the cupid-topped fountain. As a backdrop for *Part Seven*, Merrill House offered a Neoclassical container for an event based on fracturing seriousness and idealism, substituting jabs at the sacred and stolid sanctimony. Syllogistic, solipsistic and self-contained, *Part Seven* reveled in an orderly symmetry but played more to the aleatoric, or chance, aesthetic of Cage. Music and sound took supportive ancillary positions and the movements and the instruments, particularly the chest packs, became the signifying elements. One eyewitness, Barbara Taylor, Evans's colleague in the English department at Helen

(top) Dennis Evans performing *100 Discrete Tuned Sounding
Stones for Puget Sound*, Puget Sound, WA, 1978

(above) Installation view of *100 Discrete Tuned Sounding Stones
for Puget Sound,* 1978, Linda Farris Gallery, Seattle. Tray holding
100 stones and 100 photographs of 100 soundings

Bush School, reported on the event in *Insight*, the Henry Art Gallery magazine:

In *A Passion Play: Act Seven*, Evans performed a ceremony that was like a wedding; only it was a wedding of parts of himself as represented by two "actors," a male and a female, both dressed like Evans in a white shirt and tuxedo pants. At the front of the performing area was an altar-like table on which sat the focus of the piece about to be performed: a square, blue lacquered box with the square center portion cut out. Evans separated the box into two L-shaped halves and presented the contents of each: one male, containing stones, the other female, containing copper vessels. Then Evans lit his cigar and walked the two actors over a mound of salt to their positions on large copper and steel squares placed on the lawn, first facing each other across the central axis and then to plates in various quadrants around the pond. He placed a small altar in the pond and waded into the waist-deep water. Using his hat to transport salt and stones, Evans took the male actor's stones and placed them first upon a mound of salt on one altar and then moved them to another altar in front of the woman. At the same time he filled the woman's copper vessels, and she poured the waters from both of them through a "turbelone" [*sic*] or funnel banded to her head, splashing the water over the stones. This activity was repeated until all the male's four stones were used. When that was completed, Evans ended the performance by returning the actors to their initial places and putting the pieces of the box back together.[20]

With the culminating drama of *Part Seven* from *A Passion Play*[21] Evans reached a point of potential reconciliation between musical instruments and sculptures. With this new understanding, he took *Box for 100 Discrete Sounding Stones for Puget Sound* onto Puget Sound and suspended the chiseled rocks ("tuned stones," as the artist called them) in the water, along with sensitive microphones and recording materials. Constituting a triple pun, this was both a baptismal and a memorial ceremony of sorts. As he explained to *Le Jardin du Monde*: "This piece can be played by itself. It doesn't need a performance because the rain event can be the evening you decide to go out and enjoy the rain. This . . . is a discrete rain event. It is composed of one hundred discrete rain events and is to be played throughout the year. These are the lunar cycles."[22]

As the transition from composer to conceptual sculptor occurred, two exhibitions that included works by Evans were seen in New York that same year, 1979: *The Harmonious Craft: American Musical Instruments* at the American Craft Museum and *Sound: An Exhibition of Sound Sculpture, Instrument Building and Acoustically Tuned Spaces* at P. S. 1. Originating at the Renwick Gallery of the Smithsonian American Art Museum, *The Harmonious Craft* exhibition was curated by Renwick director Lloyd E. Herman and James Weaver (1938–2020), curator of musical instruments at the National Museum of History and Technology. The *Sound Sculpture* exhibition came from LAICA, the Los Angeles Institute of Contemporary Art, and was organized by curator Richard Armstrong, composer Ivan Darreg (1917–1994) and critic Peter Frank. Attempting a valiant effort at explanation, the American Craft Museum's press release for the Smithsonian show mentioned Evans, and his alter ego Ubu Waugh, and the *Box for 100 Discrete Sounding*

Stones for Puget Sound, which contained "small stones tuned to echo sounds when thrown into water."[23]

In Seattle, the cumulative effect of both shows, which were presented in Los Angeles, Washington, DC and New York, was to raise Evans's reputation substantially—so much so that *Seattle Post-Intelligencer* art critic R.M. Campbell (1942–2017) announced in 1978: "He is undoubtedly one of the most important artists of the day."[24]

In time, with regard to Evans, art critics agreed with one another, disagreed with one another, misunderstood him, and persistently struggled to communicate the meaning of his art to their readers. The task would not be easy for them—or for the artist.

Dennis Evans performing *Sound Studies: An Impact-Significant Deep-Water Event* at the home of Mr. and Mrs. William Street, Lakewood, WA, 1976

NOTES

1   Dennis Evans, as Ubu Waugh [with Charles Grimes], "Interview with Ubu Waugh," *Le Jardin du Monde: The Journal of International Casafundada* (Summer 1977): 37.
2   Andrew Marvell, "The Garden," Poetry Foundation, https://www.poetryfoundation.org/poems/44682/the-garden-56d223dec2ced
3   Evans, "Interview with Ubu Waugh": 36.
4   Evans, "Interview with Ubu Waugh": 35.
5   Dennis Evans, interview with author, June 17, 2021.
6   See the exhibition catalogue Lucy R. Lippard, *In Touch: Nature, Ritual and Sensuous Art* (Portland, OR: Portland Center for Visual Arts, 1976).
7   Lippard, *In Touch.*
8   Lippard, *In Touch.*
9   Lucy R. Lippard, *Six Years: The Dematerialization of the Art Object from 1966 to 1972* (New York: Praeger Publishers, 1973).
10   Marcia Reed, *Fluxus Means Change: Jean Brown's Avant-Garde Archive* (Los Angeles: Getty Research Institute, 2020).
11   Roberta Wilkes, "Women Artists," *CHAOS* (September 16–October 3, 1976): 28.

12   Wilkes, "Women Artists": 28.
13   Judy Chicago and Lloyd Hamrol, "Q & A," *Hindsight I* (1976): 18.
14   Chicago and Hamrol, "Q & A."
15   Anne Grosshans, interview with author, May 28, 2021.
16   Norie Sato, interview with author, April 1, 2021.
17   "Fluxus Events," *Hindsight II* (1978): 30.
18   "Fluxus Events." Other artists associated with Fluxus include Joseph Beuys, George Brecht, Anna Banana (Ann Lee Long), Robert Filliou, Ray Johnston, Joe Jones, Alison Knowles, Shigeko Kubota, John Lennon, Charlotte Moorman, Yoko Ono, Nam June Paik, Dieter Roth, Takako Saito, Mieko Shioni, Ben Vautier and Robert Watts.
19   "George Maciunas 1931–1978," *Hindsight II* (1978): 31.
20   Barbara Taylor, "Dennis Evans," *Insight: A Journal of the Henry Gallery Association* (Spring 1980): n.p.
21   The play was not performed in its entirety until 1980.
22   Evans, "Interview with Ubu Waugh": 36.
23   American Craft Museum, "A Celebration of Musical Instruments and Their Makers," press release, October 1979. Dennis Evans archive, Seattle.
24   R.M. Campbell, "Art Pavilion Show—Small is Beautiful," *Seattle Post-Intelligencer*, March 15, 1978: D13.

Dennis Evans performing *The Mysterium Conjunctionis: The Union of Opposites* at the wedding of Sheila Klein and Ries Niemi,
Seattle, 1984

CHAPTER THREE
The Absurd Meets the Sensuous: Performative Objects

I believe your question concerning . . . my art to be esoteric and uninterpretable might refer to work of this time. It was a conjunction of Dadaism and alchemy and re-enactments of creation myths from around the world.

—Dennis Evans, interview with Patterson Sims, February, 2021[1]

I redo a myth in my own terms.

—Dennis Evans as Ubu Waugh, interview, *Le Jardin du Monde*, 1977[2]

A long with gradual greater recognition in the art world beyond the New Music community, invitations continued to come to Dennis Evans. His studio practices evolved away from music toward performances using the objects for their own sake, as sculptural props, rather than as tuned or pitched instruments. This transition was another result of the artist's wide reading beyond John Cage. Among them, Claude Lévi-Strauss (1908–2009), the structural anthropologist who, among other achievements, advocated that research investigate every culture, regardless of its level of industrial or mechanical development, with the same rigorous analysis. He saw culture in the expression of repeated communal rituals, the complexity of individual languages and dialects, and the employment of a wide variety of origin and fertility myths.[3] In America, Sarah Lawrence College English literature professor Joseph Campbell (1904–1987) collated and categorized what he deemed universal or widely shared myths, ideas articulated in his books, *The Hero with a Thousand Faces* (1949)[4] and *The Power of Myth* (1988).[5] Campbell took Lévi-Strauss's notion of the cumulative collectivity of all cultures much farther, arguing that particular myths or tales, e.g., the hero, the journey, the antagonists, popped up over and over across geographical and tribal lines. Lévi-Strauss called these figures "archetypes." Evans explained his interest in them this way: "Your unconscious self knows exactly what to do. I am a Jungian."[6]

In the minds of many, both Lévi-Strauss and Campbell reinforced the ideas of an equally controversial figure, Carl G. Jung (1875–1961). The Swiss psychiatrist developed a psychological theory of archetypes and was especially esteemed in the 1970s. Providing a more upbeat counterpoint to the theories of his former mentor, Sigmund Freud (1856–1939), Jung's star rose and fell on American college campuses, perhaps appealing to Evans and others for bringing diverse cultures together, which Jung did through archetypes rather than repeat Freud's emphasis on repressed sexuality and child-parent relations as the nexus of neurosis and unhappiness.

As Evans explained in *Le Jardin du Monde* in 1977, "What they are about is re-enacting myth, psychological mythology . . . myths that deal with ego development. . . . The *content* is veiled but I think that it is apparent to everyone, mostly unconsciously though."[7]

Dennis Evans performing *A Zero Entropic Driftola,* University of Washington Center for Urban Horticulture, Seattle, 1976

At the time, theories that linked myth and psychological states were widely popular, in large part stemming from Jung's influential concept of the "collective unconscious," which saw similarities among myths across disparate societies: cosmic origins, sexual roles, demons and shamans from different cultures had common elements.[8] Even after a century, and lacking scientific evidence, Lévi-Strauss, Campbell and Jung remain appealing and popular influencers of literary, dramatic, artistic and musical culture, although breakthrough studies in neuroscience and pharmaceutical therapeutics for mental illness have superseded their theories. Freud's id, ego and super-ego were never located within the brain, and Jung's well-meaning, more optimistic and unifying view of a humanity linked through shared tales that explain behaviors has since been debunked. But, at the time, Evans's beloved triumvirate of thinkers proved useful to his—and many other artists'—creative evolution and intellectual grounding.

In the case of Evans, this meant a number of nuanced shifts. First, what began indoors—the concerts—moved outdoors to better attune them to nature. Then, as the musical dimension waned or became exhausted, the events moved back indoors.

Set in university halls, art galleries, museums and even wedding ceremonies, the purpose of the artist's activities, too, changed, from the interiority of composing music to the exteriority of relating to nature, or planting the world. Horticultural settings, undeveloped natural sites within city limits and actions in a boat were reconfigured by the artist, first in the role of shaman or tribal adviser and, then, as an actor or performer overshadowing the poses of composer and musician. In a conventional sense, the theatre replaced the concert hall. More to the point, the absurdity of "playing" bowls, dishes and rocks collided with the sensuous interactions of the artist-shaman and the audience. The sculptural objects (formerly musical instruments) were merged with the natural environment in the climactic work, *A Passion Play* (1980), the twelve-hour outdoor-staged drama with Evans and Mary Ann Peters at Montlake Landfill. This was an undeveloped wildlife preserve on the southeastern edge of the University of Washington campus, bordering Lake Washington and in sight of Mount Rainier, a spectacular, though swampy backdrop for increasingly

Nota bene: In arte noſtri magiſterij nihil eſt *Secretum*
celatũ à Philoſophis excepto ſecreto artis, quod *artis*
non licet cuiquam reuelare, quod ſi fieret ille ma
lediceretur , & indignationem domini incur⸗
reret , & apoplexia moreretur.   Quare om⸗
nis error in arte exiſtit , ex eo, quod debitam .
                                              C ij

Illustration of "Philosophorum" from Arnold de Villanova, *Rosarium Philosophorum*, published in Frankfurt, Germany, 1550. Reproduced in C.C. Jung, *Mysterium Coniunctionis; An Inquiry into the Separation and Synthesis of Psychic Opposites in Alchemy*, Bollingen Series 20, 2nd ed. (Princeton: Princeton University Press, 1970).

hermetic and enigmatic activities that made use of the sculptures. Occurrences were timed throughout the day to coincide with chronological and solar events, often using the weather or the marsh's characteristics as triggers for the actors and props' movements. This was not New Music or Theatre of the Absurd; it was performance art, the leading contemporary art development of the 1970s along with Earth Art. As RoseLee Goldberg wrote in her definitive study, *Performance: Live Art 1909 to the Present*:

> Performance in the last two years of the sixties and of the early seventies reflected conceptual art's rejection of traditional materials of canvas, brush, or chisel, with performers turning to their own bodies as art material. . . . Ideas on space could just as well be interpreted in actual space. . . . [T]ime could be suggested in the duration of a performance. . . . Sculpture . . . became even more tangible in live presentation.[9]

Evans's performance art, transformed the absurdity of unmusical musical instruments and anti-theatrical theatre à la Jarry: wet and slightly uncomfortable; silent except for nature's sounds; visually dynamic, yet slow, like *kabuki*. This materially resonant action was Evans's contribution to the new genre. What was being performed involved new props—metal canisters, glass jars, and ebonized backpacks and headdresses—to be used for zany and implausible actions, wading, floating and so on. Applying his endless research to an existing body of work, Evans began exploring the history of science, which, as he discovered, began in Europe with the pursuit of alchemy, the search for making gold from other materials, like lead. Myth and ritual combined became magic. Magic, with its hidden formulae, curses and sleights of hand, merged with alchemy. And alchemy, as Evans seized upon it, became modern science. This was a rich heritage indeed, at once useful to mankind and heretical to the Catholic Church.

The inadvertent European "discovery" of porcelain and its essential ingredient (kaolin), which, when fired at the highest possible temperature then attempted, hardened the clay without breaking it to pieces, had global implications for commerce and culture. The Chinese had long taunted their lucrative Western market with this "secret ingredient," which intrigued Evans as he pursued his research. In 1710, at the Dresden court of Augustus II (1670–1733), the King of Poland, an alchemist so important he was

under *schloss*-arrest, Johann Friedrich Böttger (1682–1719) happened upon kaolin, a form of potash mined in Bohemia. When it was mixed with clay and fired, it hardened without breaking to pieces. And, thus, out of the castle kiln came porcelain, so similar to the Chinese ceramic, even though Böttger, the magician-alchemist, had predicted and had been expecting gold.

Kaolin proved far more valuable than gold. In the ensuing mania called *Porzellankrankheit* (porcelain sickness), Augustus II became helpless, so strong was his desire for goods made with the material. Soon, porcelain was considered among the first magical materials to have been discovered through alchemy. Evans took this narrative and incorporated it into his work, making a gradual shift from the mythology of magical materials like porcelain—the bowls, the skirrs, the arrows—to the materiality of the earthbound, sensuous world of *A Passion Play*. During its performance, actions throughout the long day mimicked both scientific and ritualistic procedures. Peters described it: "We paced it out. . . . [H]e had to know where the audience was so he could be seen, because it was a marshland. . . . I have a memory of sitting in the grass and of an affinity with artists dealing with the land and my becoming implanted in the earth."[10] Audience members became

Dennis Evans and Mary Ann Peters performing *Part 10, Stairstep: Ten Points* from *Twelve Field Us(e)ages/A Passion Play*, University of Washington Center for Urban Horticulture, Seattle, 1980

unwitting participants in an unspecified ceremony of nature worship, shifting location by the hour, observing closer ties to the land, the water, the mud, and the performers "seeding" of the earth with stylized gestures and objects, like the smoky censers in an outdoor cathedral. Peters, a frequent participant in Evans's events and co-exhibitor once Linda Farris took her up along with the van der Marck/Ritchie/MFA group, went on to note specifically: "[The] meaning? There was a ritualistic theatricality that could be applied to the land. He was the director [but there was] not too much directing because he liked the chance aspect. Nothing was over-planned."[11]

Other observers begged to differ in informal and published accounts. Sherry Markovitz, another MFA cohort and Linda Farris Gallery stablemate, may have been more objective, but distinctly opinionated, with her psycho-biographical reading: "[The performances] often were very elaborate, mixed-up attempts at humor. He made a science of derivative ideas. . . . He wanted to be a powerful guy. It was a different way

Andrew Bateman, Dennis Evans, Mary Ann Peters performing various parts from *Twelve Field Us(e)ages/A Passion Play*, Seattle Art Museum, 1985

of being. . . . It was [all] a cross between a clown and a deeply involved artist. He was off the charts with the costumes, quite outrageous. There was something silly about him, a playfulness, but there was no compromise with Dennis. He became more of himself."[12]

Seattle Post-Intelligencer music and art critic R.M. Campbell did not attend *A Passion Play*, but was present at a number of other events, including one at the Seattle Art Museum. As early as 1978, he explained that, "The diagrams and drawings, which are so scrupulously rendered, are guides to the performance of his pieces. . . . Evans dresses in tails . . . performs as Ubu Waugh . . . and performs rituals that are often inexplicable."[13]

Perplexity about Evans, his performances and eventually stand-alone (or hang-alone) objects may have been experienced by artists and art critics, but there was enough magic or mystery to challenge and to entertain nonspecialist viewers. After seven years of watching and listening to his art, I wrote a response in 1984 to his work in a Linda Hodges Gallery group show curated by *Artweek* contributor Ron Glowen, *Little Romances/Little Fictions*. I focused on a turning point for Evans, his attempted fusion of object and idea:

> Evans's lacquered boxes and copper-clad implements are the relics of a 12-hour performance . . . surrounding a post-modern

fertility rite of sorts. That would be hard to tell by the objects themselves, so Evans has included photo-documents of the marsh where he and Mary Ann Peters wore the boxes. Having witnessed all 12 hours (using 12 sets of boxes, etc.), I would say the things deal more with sexuality than sensuality. In fact, all Evans's art has dealt, in my opinion, with issues of bondage and confinement between opposite sexes. This comes off as mystifying because it is accompanied by a morass of playful . . . language, inscriptions. . . . We are left with more a sense of *matière* than meaning, let alone the cryptic, hermetic, or pseudo-scientific paradigms to which Evans aspires. Further, [he] attains a union of the aesthetic and material despite their narrative or mythic pretensions. That is to say . . . things hold up better than their ideas.[14]

With the hindsight of forty years, like Campbell, I recognize and justify the complexity of his undertaking, and advocate Evans to audiences of general readers. I affirm Campbell's dictum, "He is one of the most important artists of the day."[15]

Evans created three other performances, in 1981, 1988 and 1999, that merit brief comment and analysis. Two of them were actual wedding ceremonies: *The Chymical Nuptials of Soma and Agni* for artists

Dennis Evans and the groom Ries Niemi performing in *The Mysterium Conjunctionis: The Union of Opposites* at the wedding of Sheila Klein and Ries Niemi, Seattle, 1984

Sheila Klein, *Cache*, 1979. Mixed media, 36 x 29 x 4 in. Collection of Nancy Sternoff

Sheila Klein and Ries Niemi, and *The Mysterium Conjunctionis: The Union of Opposites* for architect and developer John Kucher and Linda Farris. Evans's ceremony for the Klein/Niemi marriage was only fifteen minutes long and performed outdoors before seventy-five guests around the Capitol Hill swimming

pool of Niemi's parents, prominent Seattle attorneys Preston and Janice Niemi. The couple selected their own marital attire. Klein, a rising contemporary artist but not part of the UW MFA clique, based her wedding gown on one worn by Loulou de la Falaise, a muse for fashion designer Yves Saint-Laurent. Niemi wore an all-white, three-piece suit. Neither entered the pool. According to Klein: "We had no idea of what we were to do. He probably had some idea. He often acted as master of ceremonies. So, it was 'You go here,' and 'You go there.' He was directing us."[16]

With two "transversal flotillas" familiar from his first musical performance and the Linda Farris Gallery debut in 1977, Klein eked out some intended binary, gendered content underlying the shenanigans watched by the attentive audience, including the bride's parents, remarking, "My [honey and milk] flotilla was pushed across the water and met Ries's [flotilla of] burnt sticks in the middle of the pool—and that signified our union."[17] She concluded: "Audience impression? My parents were absolutely mystified. [To observe a Jewish wedding custom] they asked him to break the [wine] glass. Which he did—and they were relieved! Everyone was delighted."[18]

The wedding ceremony for Kucher and Farris was titled *Mysterium Conjunctionis*, an "outdoor opera with twelve assistants." The groom recalled:

> "We had no idea until the day of our wedding what would happen. We had a rehearsal with the props earlier, but it was all in his head. Linda would be brought in and then me, on a throne, carrying me like a litter. We would gather before Dennis. . . . The other guys put on monk's outfits. They wore masks and carried a lance. Their job was to "slay the dragons," which was all pantomimed out in a field. We were at the opposite end of the pond. There was fire—me—and ice—Linda—in porcelain

Wedding party of Linda Farris and John Kucher, Vashon Island, WA, 1988

bowls which he lit. For Linda, there were rose petals with ice cubes. The music was the "Merry Widow" waltz. To me, it was more real than the stupid religious ones. Linda was under a "hupa." As I attempted to stand and walk toward her, the muscle relaxant zapped my upper body and I could not move [Author's note: John Kucher is partly paralyzed], but I made it, with help, all the way up with the walker. Instead of breaking the wine glass [as in Jewish custom], he had a box with a piece of glass which he smashed inside the box.[19]

Pepper Schwartz, the host and close friend of Farris, remembered:

Nancy Mee, Linda Gerrard and I, all in kimonos, were carrying boxes made by

Dennis with symbolic things, so we carried them forward. He was explaining to us what was about to happen. One thing we did in the upper arbor, so John could see and confront the "soldiers" and fight for the "maiden," Linda.

The guys in the pasture were all wearing beautiful masks and carrying big sticks that were gorgeously painted. They had a fake battle with John who fought them off and vanquished them symbolically. Dennis was narrating it all to us. Another thing he did after the battle: He wore an elaborate Himalayan headdress to symbolize his priestly role in the ceremony for John and Linda.

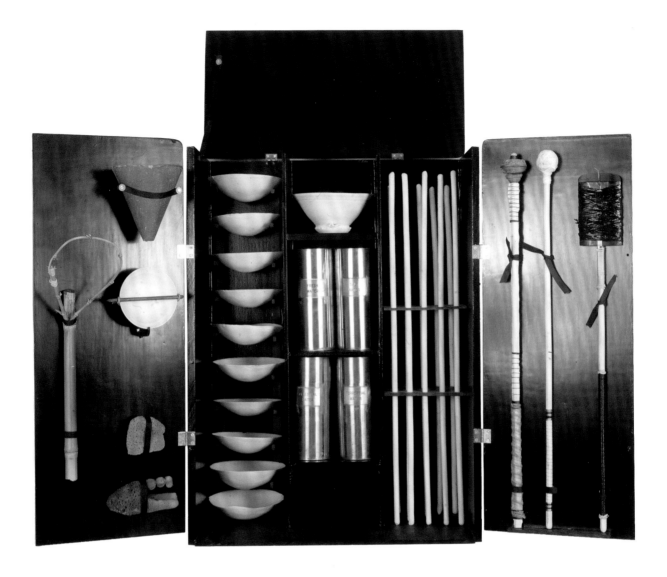

At the end, he burned something in the pond. Everyone was then taken to the lower pond and we were all given little papers to float away and bring the ceremony to an end. Linda went back onto her pallet and was carried out.

The whole thing lasted less than one hour. Dennis has always been involved with the four elements—earth, air, fire and water—and we had that, all four elements, in the marriage ceremony.[20]

Dr. Schwartz, a sociologist and sexologist, and author of two *New York Times* bestsellers,[21] was asked about Evans's relationship to two of his favorite thinkers,

An Accompanying Instrumentation Box, 1978. Lacquer, wood, porcelain, copper, 10 x 17 x 24 in. Seattle Art Museum, PONCHO 78.42.2

Lévi-Strauss and Jung. She responded: "[Like them] Dennis did help create communities; he did create good for communities and we were all in the thrall of a mixture of reality and fantasy, creating a joyous space. . . . So we had that in common, plus our shared beliefs in community strengths and celebrations. It was a magical experience in its own way."[22]

Two other events occurred in 1978, Evans's *wunderjahr*: the artist's second display at Linda Farris Gallery, which garnered unanimous critical acclaim, and *New Ideas #1*, a four-person exhibition at the

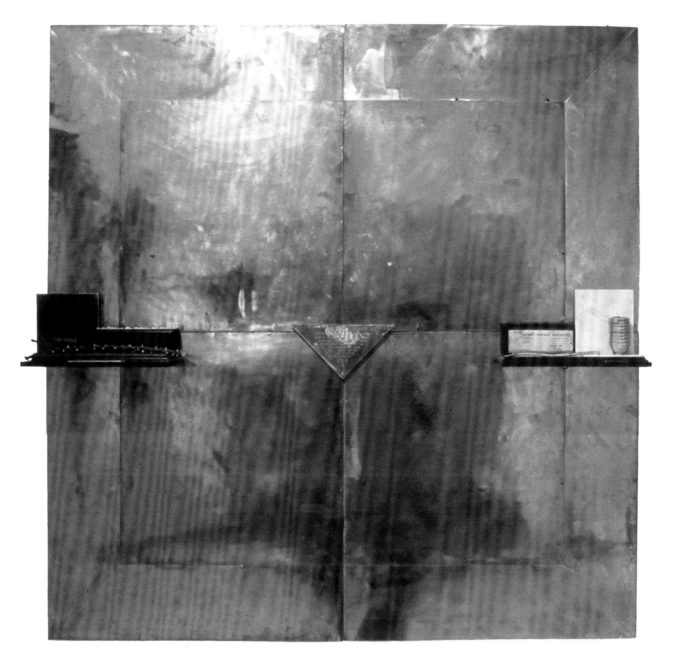

Seattle Art Museum Seattle Center Pavilion, the site of *557,087*. Keith Beckley, Jeffrey Bishop, and Charles B. Luce were also selected by the museum's first-ever modern art curator, Charles Cowles (1941–2021). All four artists were represented by Farris who, just three years earlier, told the Archives of Northwest Art interviewer that an art museum's role is "really a very complex one. I don't think the museum here [Seattle Art Museum] has quite figured out its role yet. . . . Ideally, a museum should be an integral part of the community; it should be a very stimulating place to go. . . . I really think the museum should be involved . . . in buying

Sponsa/Sponsus, 1983. Mixed media, copper, lead, wax, carbon, salt, wood, lacquer, glass, 96 x 96 x 8 in. Seattle Art Museum. Gift of the Pacific Northwest Art Council, in honor of the museum's 50th year, 83.207

works of young artists here. . . . Adding the Pavilion to do travelling shows was probably the best thing because that allows the museum to show contemporary art."[23]

By 1978, Seattle Art Museum had acquired its first Dennis Evans artwork, purchased from Farris through a local arts umbrella group, PONCHO. Beckley, Bishop and Luce each had important solo debut exhibitions

Charles B. Luce, *Cyclonic Collapse of the Tea House (Version #1)*, 1978, in the exhibition *New Ideas #1*, Seattle Art Museum Seattle Center Pavilion. Wood, canvas, mulberry paper, color-copier prints, terra-cotta roof tiles, acrylic paint, string, rubber stamps, tatami mats, painted rope, mirrors, etched glass, 240 x 240 x 240 in.

with Farris in Pioneer Square, leading Cowles to select them for his first small show of local artists, *New Ideas #1*. The former Seattle World's Fair British Pavilion, which had been taken over by the museum as an additional exhibition space and was known then as the Modern Art Pavilion, was filled to the brim with the trio's works of string, concrete blocks, graph paper, rice paper and wooden slats—and Evans's "driftola" flotillas, paintings, sculptures and assemblages.

Luce, originally from Southern California, moved after graduation from Amherst College to Seattle in 1969 to participate in Teach For America in the city's depressed Central District and became close friends with Evans. He joined Farris's gallery in 1975, after she saw his work in a group show at the Seattle Art Museum. Luce had also been part of Triangle Studios, another UW MFA spin-off founded in the Prefontaine Building in Pioneer Square by Norie Sato, other van der Marckians and ex-Bill Ritchie students interested in merging printmaking and video. Remembering

Cowles (whose only job as a curator was at Seattle Art Museum), Luce noted how "very generous and really quirky he was and always super-supportive." Luce expressed his gratitude to Evans over forty years later in an interview:

> We were both teaching at Bush School at the time. He really was influential on me in opening my eyes. I was already interested in Asian art, and was always drawn to it. My parents were travelers after they retired and would buy Asian art. Dennis was way into it. His Ubu character was already established when we met and then I created my persona: John Osaka Osawa. Somehow it was all melding together: I-Ching elements, Duchamp, psychoanalytical literature and chance elements. With all this and his clay projects, it was like conceptual crafts. I wanted to integrate that, too, in my work.[24]

Luce also commented on his installation in *New Ideas #1*: "By 1976, I was changing directions and realized how much I was influenced by and loved non-Western cultures; I had had this aesthetic since I was quite young. In *Collapsing Teahouse after a Cyclone* [the SAM piece], it was lightweight wood and meant to sway, like real Japanese architecture. But the teahouse was symbolic to me; it became a psychological vehicle as well."[25]

The year culminated in an invitation to Evans to exhibit work in the 1979 Whitney Biennial in New York City. Thanks to Charles Cowles, Barbara Haskell, one of the Whitney curators, had seen Evans's work in the 1979 *Washington Open*, which she juried at the Pavilion. With a top-tier gallery under his belt, two solo exhibitions, and the prestige of the Seattle Art Museum honor, moving to New York would have been the logical next step. As Dennis Evans would learn,

Seattle Art Museum curator of modern art (1975–79) Charles Cowles

biting the Big Apple did not mean having to uproot himself and plant a new world. Instead, it posed the question, "Can you become part of the New York art scene without having to move—and live and work successfully in Seattle?" In the course of the coming decade and four or five subsequent visits, Manhattan would be the urban backdrop for a type of apotheosis of the young artist's career: exposure, praise, museum exhibitions and gallery sales, recognition—all followed by the considerations of geographical distance, faltering memories and disappointments, a renewed appreciation of life outside New York, and the possibility of making art without the considerable sacrifice of giving up Seattle. Indeed, *Outside New York: Seattle* was the name of Evans's third New York museum invitational, an exhibition at the New Museum assembled for 1983, when the mountain in the form of a New York curator, Ned Rifkin, came to Mohammed in the Pacific Northwest, Dennis Evans, a.k.a. Ubu Waugh. Astonishingly, what was a high point for the selected artists would be largely bypassed by New York's assiduous audience for contemporary art. *Outside New York: Seattle's* irrelevance would become fatal fodder for one of Seattle's newly confident generation of art critics.

NOTES

1   Dennis Evans, excerpt from interview with Patterson Sims, February 2021.

2   Dennis Evans, as Ubu Waugh [with Charles Grimes], "Interview with Ubu Waugh," *Le Jardin du Monde: International Journal of Casafundada* (Summer 1977): 38.

3   Claude Lévi-Strauss, *The Raw and the Cooked* (New York: Harper & Row, 1969).

4   Joseph Campbell, *The Hero with a Thousand Faces* (Novato, CA: New World Library, 2008).

5   Joseph Campbell, with Bill Moyers, *The Power of Myth* (New York: Anchor Books, 1991).

6   Evans, "Interview with Ubu Waugh," 38.

7   Evans, "Interview with Ubu Waugh," 38.

8   Carl G. Jung, *The Archetypes and the Collective Unconscious*, 2nd ed, trans. R.F.C. Hull (Princeton, NJ: Princeton University Press, 1980), 1–25.

9   RoseLee Goldberg, *Performance: Live Art 1909 to the Present* (New York: Harry N. Abrams, 1979), 98.

10   Mary Ann Peters, interview with author, February 22, 2021.

11   Peters, interview.

12   Sherry Markovitz, interview with author, February 2, 2021.

13   R.M. Campbell, "Evans: It's Not Your Standard Gallery Show," *Seattle Post-Intelligencer* (September 28, 1978): 18.

14   Matthew Kangas, "Seattle: Little Romances/Little Fictions," *Vanguard* 13, no. 4 (May 1984): 41–42.

15   Campbell, "Evans: It's Not Your Standard Gallery Show," 18.

16   Sheila Klein, interview with author, July 18, 2021.

17   Klein, interview.

18   Klein, interview.

19   John Kucher, interview with author, July 29, 2021.

20   Pepper Schwartz, interview with author, July 26, 2021.

21   Pepper Schwartz, *Love Between Equals: How Peer Marriage Really Works* (New York: Touchstone, 1995), and Pepper Schwartz with Philip Blumstein, *American Couples: Money, Work, Sex* (New York: William Morrow, 1983).

22   Schwartz, interview.

23   Linda Farris, interview with Sally Swenson, February 26, 1975, Archives of Northwest Art, University of Washington, Special Collections.

24   Charles B. Luce, interview with author, May 19, 2021.

25   Luce, interview.

Linda Farris and Dennis Evans standing in front of Evans's artwork in the *1979 Biennial Exhibition*, Whitney Museum of American Art, New York

CHAPTER FOUR Manhattan Apotheosis

We were very tired, we were very merry,
We had gone back and forth all night on the ferry.
We hailed, "Good morrow, mother!" to a shawl-covered head,
And bought a morning paper, which neither of us read;
And she wept, "God bless you!" for the apples and pears,
And we gave her all our money but our subway fares.

—Edna St. Vincent Millay, "Recuerdo," 1922[1]

I had early interest [in my work] in New York and was included in the [1979] Whitney Biennial, in the section entitled "Private Mythologies." At that point I was introduced to many big name art dealers . . . New York had shown me a lot of what I thought I wanted from my art life, but it had also shown me the very steep price one would pay for that life.

—Dennis Evans, Interview with Patterson Sims, 2021[2]

In a strange turnabout, New York coming to Seattle, Dennis Evans met and learned a lot from Christopher Wilmarth (1943–1987), one of the most acclaimed younger New York artists of the 1970s and 1980s. They met, surprisingly, in Seattle at Merrill House, for the performance of *The Theory of Non-Enigmatic Geometricities*, which Wilmarth attended while visiting Seattle as a guest of Charles Cowles.[3] Three years older than Evans, Wilmarth's astronomical climb to the pinnacles of the New York art world carried a steep price. He was dead at age forty-four, a drug-overdose suicide, perhaps brought on by the pressures of success, the prospects of which were something he discussed with Evans during their long conversation at the reception following the performance. Wilmarth warned Evans about New York's sirens and sinkholes, as if Patroclus were warning Aeneas before heading off to the Trojan War. According to Evans, "He said point blank, 'They're corrupt.'"[4] All of this shook Evans considerably, prone as he was to noticing unprompted prophecies, chillingly reinforced by Wilmarth's death less than a decade later in his Brooklyn studio. This anti-epiphany for Evans, the glaring extinction of a genius, colored his subsequent interactions throughout the mid- to late 1980s, his own brief heyday or Manhattan apotheosis, a period about which he told Patterson Sims forty-five years later: "It was the time, career-speaking, to pack my bags and relocate."[5]

Leading up to that fateful decision was a rapid

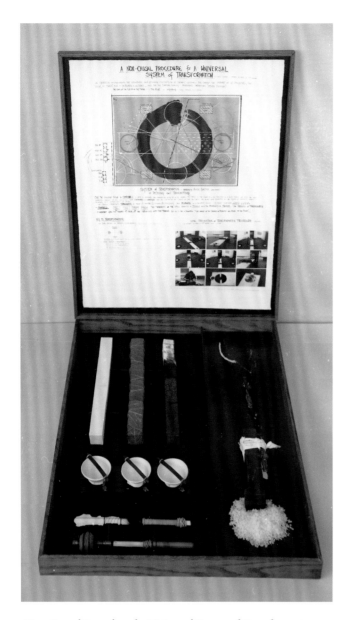

Non-Causal Procedure for Universal System of Transformation, 1977. Mixed media, 22 x 18 x 5 in. (closed). Collection of the artist

succession of New York group shows, backroom gallery sales and other artists' examples. While *The Harmonious Craft* at the American Craft Museum in New York looked valedictory at the time (good-bye, craft; hello, SoHo), in retrospect, it appears to be one bookend of a long phase of the artist's development: the rejection and restoration of the handmade art object, resulting in a fusion of idea and thing, what Charles B. Luce (who moved to New York in 1982 and embarked on his own career) kept referring to as the "informed object."[6] Nevertheless, with *Harmonious Craft* covered by the Manhattan media for its folkloric,

"fiddles of Appalachia" dimension, attendance there was overshadowed by the Whitney Biennial, Evans's true debutante ball at the Hotel Pierre of the art world, the Whitney Museum of American Art, "founded in 1930 by Gertrude V. Whitney," as proclaimed on the letterhead of the typewritten and photocopied press release and invitation for the January 13, 1979 preview.

The press release alone had Seattle's media and art worlds agog. As Linda Farris pointed out in her own assiduous echo of the New York museum release, "It is the first time an artist from Seattle has been so honored."[7]

As if that were not newsworthy enough, the presence of the other artists invited amounted to a dazzling—and dismaying—list of heavy hitters and has-beens of the near future. In the former category, Evans remembered his favorites and those who impressed him most besides Wilmarth: "Robert Arneson, Alice Aycock, Jackie Ferrara, Robert Graham, Bryan Hunt, Robert Mangold—whom I met—and Ken Price.... Lucas Samaras, Richard Serra, Michael Singer and H.C. Westermann. All great artists to be with."[8] Farris attended the opening with Evans. It was her debut, too, cementing her unquestioned stature as the foremost contemporary art dealer north of San Francisco, her childhood home.

The equivalent of a condensed, postdoctoral fellowship for Evans, a flurry of gallery, museum and dealer visits ensued. Evans's memory retains a freshness about people who now seem historical:

> Seeing Julian Schnabel's first show at
> Mary Boone blew my brains out.
>
> Castelli came out after ten minutes.
> He sat down and was so polite. He looked
> at my work and asked me good, quick-
> quiz questions and then said, "Obviously,
> this is not for me, but why don't you go
> see Ronald Feldman? Which I did.

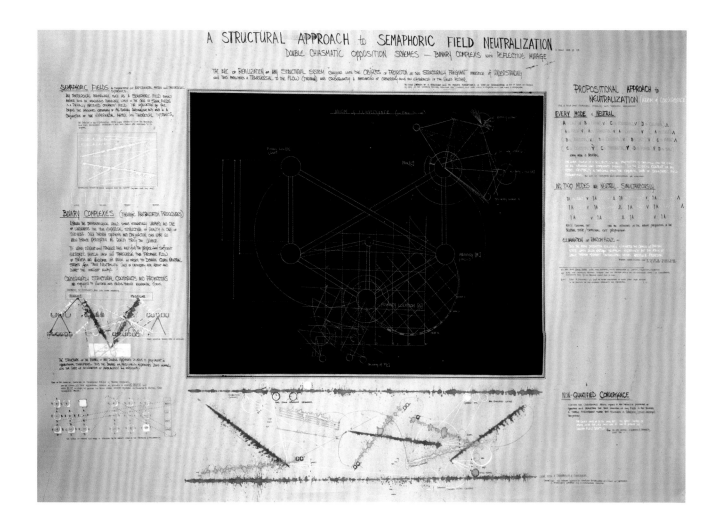

A Structural Approach to Semaphoric Field Neutralization, 1978. Mixed media on paper, 27 x 38 in. Collection of the artist. This work was included in *1979 Biennial Exhibition*, Whitney Museum of American Art, New York.

Feldman said to me, "Let me take a look!" I rolled out my [unframed] scores and he asked "Can you leave these behind?" And "How much are they?" And I said "Five to eight hundred each." Could I come back tomorrow? No problem! He'd sold five and gave me a check for four or five thousand dollars: I thought to myself, "This is how it should be!" Little did I know!

Feldman was wonderful. He sold a few more, but didn't offer me a show. It didn't matter; it was a gallery where two of my idols, Hans Haacke and Joseph Kosuth, showed. I kept rolling [works] up in tubes and shipped them to him.[9]

Another time, Evans met a woman who could have been Linda Farris's *doppelgänger*: Holly Solomon (1934–2002): "She was a lot like Linda, very upfront. She looked at my work and said, "This is really good, but it's not what I'm showing—but thank you for letting me see it.""[10]

On yet another night in the Big Apple, courtesy of Patterson Sims, the thirty-two-year-old kid from Yakima, Washington, dined with Cy Twombly (1928–2011) and Dan Flavin (1933–1996) for Twombly's birthday celebration. Evans met Sims (then a Whitney associate curator) at Sperone Westwater Gallery at 420 West Broadway, the gallery building and nerve center of SoHo. Greeted by owners Angela Westwater and Gian Enzo Sperone, who represented both Twombly and Flavin, Evans and Sims joined the small party for dinner at a nearby restaurant: "I was in a state of psychological shock. Being there with these giant figures of contemporary art and surrounded by several beautiful women whose names I never learned—it was all amazing."[11]

Despite all the encouragement and steady diet of stimulating art to see—"I lived at the Met," Evans laughed in a later interview[12]—the artist drew back from moving there the way Luce had, although other Seattle artists in Farris's stable, Jeffrey Bishop, Andrew Keating and Peter Santino, would do so. Evans explained his decision to stay: "I had just purchased a small house in Seattle, which I was slowly converting into a great studio. I was in love with another artist [Nancy Mee] and we wanted an artistic life together. But we were realistic as to what price moving to New York would cost. So we decided to stay in Seattle. I have never regretted that decision."[13]

The wisdom of that decision quickly became evident five years later when a curator, on behalf of Marcia Tucker (1940–2006), founding director of the New Museum in New York, showed up in Seattle scouting for a small Seattle-only group show. Notwithstanding the global embrace of the popular music genre, grunge, which included rock as well as torn-plaid flannel-shirt fashion, Seattle was increasingly talked about, the way unseen places or tourist locales often are. Tucker's 1977 lecture at and/or, coming on the heels of her dismissal from the Whitney Museum of American Art for her badly received Richard Tuttle retrospective, alerted her to the vibrant and varied contemporary art scene coalescing in Seattle. As Evans began to show his work with Farris, an important government incentive program opened up opportunities for him and other artists: the One Per Cent for Art program was instituted in Seattle in 1973. A municipal regulation, structured similarly to a program established in Philadelphia in 1959, dictated that one percent of all publicly funded

Former curator and assistant director of the New Museum of Contemporary Art Ned Rifkin

capital construction budgets be allocated for art. Only visual artists qualified: architects and graphic designers were banned from applying. This resulted in the formation of, among other things, artist-design teams, and artists were given equal seats at the conference table with architects and city bureaucrats and, unlike with previous public-art projects, included in planning meetings before construction began. This was revolutionary for Seattle and other cities where similar programs were eventually adopted.[14] Evans and Nancy Mee, whom he married in 1980, were substantial beneficiaries, completing fifteen public projects over their careers, including nine libraries for city, county, regional, college and university libraries. This kind of public patronage suited Evans's particular fusion of the conceptual and the practical.

Another event confirmed the wisdom of Evans's decision to stay in Seattle, the organization of an exhibition of Seattle artists at the recently opened New Museum in New York. Both director Tucker and the museum's curator Ned Rifkin made visits to Seattle to research the exhibition. Tucker made a trip first, doing research for her new institution. She was invited to lecture at the experimental exhibition space and/or. Her exposure to artists during the trip alerted her to the vibrant and varied contemporary art scene coalescing in Seattle.

(above) Installation view of *Pharmacy* in *Outside New York: Seattle* at the New Museum of Contemporary Art, New York, 1984. Mixed media, variable dimensions. Collection of the artist

(right) New Museum of Contemporary Art founding director Marcia Tucker

Rifkin made two trips to Seattle to visit artist studios and make his decisions. In addition to Evans, he selected eight artists for *Outside New York: Seattle*: photographers Paul Berger and Marsha Burns; painters Randy Hayes and Fay Jones; sculptors and multimedia artists Alan Lande, Barbara Noah and Buster Simpson. Rifkin told Regina Hackett, the art critic for the *Seattle Post-Intelligencer*, that Evans was "continuing an important legacy, investigating conceptually motivated cosmologies of a certain kind. He works out of a deep belief. What he does is intense, playful and compelling at the same time. He simply had to be included."[15]

New York reviewers did not appreciate the show; it was panned by *New York* magazine art critic Kay Larson.[16] The participating artists were disappointed and chastened by the Manhattan feedback. In Seattle, Hackett's interview with Rifkin was one of three reports she wrote on *Outside New York: Seattle*. She

Plan View for a Pharmacia, 1984. Mixed media on paper, 27 x 38 in. Collection of the artist

wrote reviews of the exhibition's showing at the Henry Art Gallery in 1983, where it traveled after being seen in New York. She did not see the original exhibition. But then, neither did R.M. Campbell, her colleague at the *Post-Intelligencer,* nor did Deloris Tarzan, the *Seattle Times* art critic. Coupled with the muted peeps from New York, Hackett's critical view undermined the significance of the show. In a damned-if-you-do, damned-if-you-don't move, in her first review, Hackett quoted Larson's put-down of *Outside New York: Seattle* as "not being unruly enough," while going on to add her own description of most of the works by the eight artists.

A week later, in a longer review, Hackett pointed out how different the Seattle show was from the one in New York, given that four of the eight artists did installations in Seattle rather than show the same individual works that had been exhibited in New York. About Evans, she claimed it was the "complex culture of his dreams" that drove his "lush and ritual-loaded art objects." Drilling down on the artist's Pavilion installation (which was not shown in New York but was included at the Henry), she argued that "the installation wants to convey states of being tuned to the seasons, to sexual dualities, materialities and types of fuel."[17] In a significant shift of opinion, Hackett expressed doubts about Evans's work that would continue for years, accusing the work of not being "rooted in his own experience" and "hence look[ing] artificial and undigested. . . . Evans has to digest his enormously ambitious mass of material before presenting it."[18]

Rifkin's catalogue essay on Evans, the first by a prominent out-of-town curator, but far from the last, combined discussions of Evans's sculpture, installation

Cover, *Ubu Roi* by Alfred Jarry (New York: New Directions, 1961)

INTERLOCKS

		DIABATICS		HERESIARCH CATAGORIES / SECTARIAN		VIRTUES & VECTORS	ANOMALIES
A	DAWN	ONE	POST 4-HEAD	1	6AM	EAST → WEST BRANCHING and GRABBING	DOUBLE (TWIN) TOP – BOTTOM
B	SLIGHT	TWO	BELLY	1+1	7AM	DISPERSAL 100% SPRAY	
C	ELSEWHERE	THREE	ORGAN	(1+1+1) or (1+2)	8AM	30°-60°-90° SPILLWAY	
D	ERUDITE	FOUR	SLIGHT CALIBERS	(1 + 2 + 3 + 4)	9AM — SCENE FIELD	(FALSE) ROMANCE	
E	PENETRATE	FIVE	IMPORTANCE	(1+2+ 3 + 2 + 1)	10AM		DOUBLE (TWIN) RIGHT LEFT
F	NOON	SIX	TOUCH	(1+2+3 2+5+1)	11AM CONDENSATION	ROMANCE	
G	NOON	SEVEN	TO TONGUE	1+2+3+4+5+6+7 =28→10 1	12AM HUMIDITY	ROMANCE	
H	HIGH	EIGHT		(4 + 4)	1PM	ROMANCE	
I	ABIDE	NINE		(3+3+3) (2+3+4) (4+4+1)	2PM ACTION:	NINE POINTS 1. LINE - NAVEL 2. ABS - RING 3. 3:4 90°:60°	DOUBLE (TWIN) FRONT — BACK
J	SHADOWS	TEN		1+2+3+4+5+6+7+8+9+10	3PM ACTION / SCENE ::	0° to 360° SPRAY ARRAY	
K	TWILIGHT	ELEVEN		(10 + 1)	4PM CARD::	NORTH 90% BLACK SENTIMENTALLY	
L	DUSK (DAWN)	TWELVE		SEPARATION	5PM CARD::	SOUTH CLEAR 0%	

Interlocks, Diagram for Twelve Field Us(e)ages from the catalogue *The Twelve Field Us(e)ages*, 1980. Ink on paper, 8½ x 11 in. Collection of the artist

and esoteric content. With his background in the semiotics of film (he had written a learned analysis of the 1964 film *Red Desert* by Michelangelo Antonioni (1912–2007), Rifkin positioned Evans in the West Coast tradition of the artist-persona that descended from Marcel Duchamp (1887–1968) in Pasadena to William T. Wiley (1937–2021) and others. In a remarkably concise history of Evans's musical instruments, through the performances (with the first scholarly reference to Alfred Jarry in relationship to Evans), and on to Duchampian puns and word games, Rifkin was predisposed to understand Evans, seeing him as a French or European artist. He took the artist's linguistic tropes and analogies farther than any critic at the time. He listed the artist's intellectual pursuits:

"Western dialectics . . . comparative religions . . . Jungian psychology [and] numerology."[19] *A Passion Play*, which he referred to as "Twelve Field Us(e)ages, Utopian Desires towards a Passion Play. Analects from the Book of Revealed and Concealed Banalities,"[20] was discussed at length. In addition, he noted that Evans's use of language elevated a discourse grounded in verbal obfuscations, double talk and tongue-in-cheek to a high art form.[21] Rifkin concluded by throwing the responsibility for interpretation back at the viewer: "the artist merely provides situations for people 'to hold [themselves] between.'"[22] By stressing audience involvement, Rifkin bolstered the links between

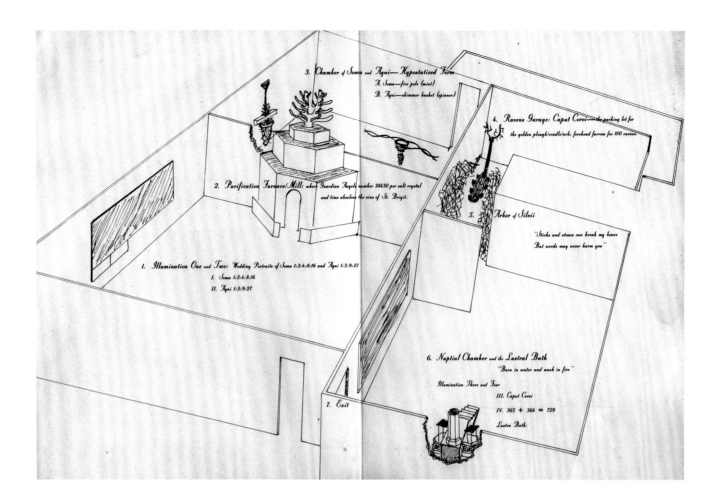

Inside the diagram:

3. *Chamber of Soma and Agni—Hypostatized Form*
A. *Soma—fire pole (mint)*
B. *Agni—shimmer basket (spinner)*

4. *Ravens Garage: Caput Corvi—the parking lot for the golden plough/cradle/ark; forehead furrow for 100 ravens.*

2. *Purification Furnace/Mill: where Guardian Angels number 38430 per salt crystal and time absolves the sins of St. Brigit.*

5. *Arbor of Sileii*
"Sticks and stones can break my bones But words may never harm you"

1. *Illumination One and Two: Wedding Portraits of Soma 1:2:4:8:16 and Agni 1:3:9:27*
I. *Soma 1:2:4:8:16*
II. *Agni 1:3:9:27*

6. *Nuptial Chamber and the Lustral Bath*
"Burn in water and wash in fire"
Illumination Three and Four
III. *Caput Corvi*
IV. $365 + 364 = 729$
Lustra Bath:

7. *Exit*

earlier theatrical-event audiences and contemporary art audiences.

In other words, thanks partly to Rifkin, the performative Ubu Waugh was sidelined in favor of the viewer, who becomes the physical executant and creator of meaning—tilted by the artist's complex hints, but no longer dependent upon watching Ubu for clues to content. This Manhattan imprimatur of objecthood or "informed objecthood," coupled with the responsibility of the viewer to engage and shape content and meaning from a personal viewpoint, became central to

Diagram of the installation *The Chymical Nuptials of Soma and Agni*, 1981, Linda Farris Gallery, Seattle. Ink on paper, 11 x 17 in. Collection of the artist

Evans's subsequent studio practice. Ubu Waugh was dead; long live Ubu Waugh; long live the King. To paraphrase a famous stage direction from Shakespeare's *The Winter's Tale,* after New York, Ubu was directed to "Exit, pursued by a bear."[23]

Installation view of *The Nuptial Chamber and Lustral Bath from the Chymical Nuptials of Soma and Agni,* 1981, at Linda Farris Gallery, Seattle. Mixed media, size variable. Installation no longer extant.

NOTES

1   Edna St. Vincent Millay, "Recuerdo," *Poetry: A Magazine of Verse* 14. no. 11 (May 1919), 68.

2   Dennis Evans, in "Interview with Patterson Sims," in this volume, 9.

3   Wilmarth's first art museum survey would appear in 1979 at the Seattle Art Museum's Modern Art Pavilion on the 1964 World's Fair site. The former British Pavilion was improved and expanded by board member Virginia Bloedel Wright, whose mother, Virginia Merrill Bloedel, had underwritten its renovation. Mrs. Wright was also the daughter of R.D. Merrill, in whose gardens at Merrill House Wilmarth met Evans.

4   Dennis Evans, interview with author, July 29, 2021.

5   Evans, interview with Patterson Sims.

6   Charles B. Luce, interview with author, September 18, 2021.

7   Linda Farris Gallery press release for Whitney Biennial announcement, undated. Dennis Evans archive.

8   Evans, interview with author.

9   Evans, interview with author.

10   Evans, interview with author.

11   Evans, interview with author.

12   Evans, interview with author.

13   Evans, interview with author.

14   Washington State originally dedicated one-half percent. The One Per Cent for Art legislation of Seattle's King County predated that of the City of Seattle.

15   Regina Hackett, "Seattle Artists Picked for N.Y. Show," *Seattle Post-Intelligencer*, December 22, 1982: D6.

16   Kay Larson, "Uncommon Visions," *New York* 16, no. 20 (May 16, 1983): 60–61.

17   Regina Hackett, "Seattle Artists Come Home in N.Y. Show," *Seattle Post-Intelligencer*, October 19, 1983: C12.

18   Hackett, "Seattle Artists Come Home."

19   Ned Rifkin, *Outside New York: Seattle* (New York: New Museum, 1983), 16–17.

20   Rifkin, *Outside New York: Seattle*, 17.

21   Rifkin, *Outside New York: Seattle*, 19.

22   Rifkin, *Outside New York: Seattle*, 19.

23   William Shakespeare, *The Winter's Tale*, prepared and annotated by Neil Freeman (New York: Applause Books, 1998), 51.

Andrew Keating, *Palm de Terre*, 1978. Acrylic on paper, 22 x 30 in. Collection of the artist, New York

CHAPTER FIVE

Understanding Evans: Rise and Fall of the Art Critics

The one thing I'm pleased about is that now the reviewers seem to be paying more attention to those galleries that are really showing museum-quality work, contemporary work, very professional work. They are not giving as much exposure to the little shop. I think it was Tom Robbins on the panel I had on art criticism who said that … [what] the art critics were reviewing … was essentially why the papers weren't getting outraged. He said if a music critic insisted on reviewing barbershop quartets in Lynnwood instead of the Seattle Symphony, there'd be, you know, *harakiri* [all] around. But it was an interesting observation and I think reviewing has changed quite a bit in the past year since that observation was made.

—Linda Farris, interview with Sally Swenson, 1975[1]

Linda Farris's comments to Archives of Northwest Art interviewer Sally Swenson were both prescient and effective. The *Seattle Times* art critic Tom Robbins had long since left the position to pursue his passion, novel writing, in the village of La Conner, Washington, north of Seattle.[2] His replacement was John Voorhees (1925–2014), who, in turn, was succeeded by Deloris Tarzan (later Deloris Tarzan Ament), when Voorhees became the television critic. Things seemed to settle down after Tarzan's appointment; R.M. Campbell took the art critic's position at *Seattle Post-Intelligencer*, and there was a wave of younger, unaffiliated art critics (this author included) who freelanced for local and out-of-town publications, including a wide variety of art magazines. Before she joined the *Seattle Post-Intelligencer* as art critic, Regina Hackett freelanced and wrote for Group Health's magazine. As the art scene grew in the 1970s, editors of publications, daily and otherwise, became convinced that visual arts coverage was necessary.

Examining the critics' various responses to Evans over this period of time, including both high and low points of critical opinion about him, offers a better idea of how art critics and artists interacted and how, at the same time, they became oblivious of one another when familiarity bred contempt on both sides of the easel. Fortunately for Evans and all Seattle artists, employment of writers on the visual arts reached a new high point in the 1970s, bringing evaluation, analysis and greater credibility to the city's—and region's—cultural life. What had already occurred for classical music in the Seattle dailies happened for art in the late 1970s, thanks to intelligent, informed writing by Voorhees and Campbell. This lasted into the early twenty-first century, when it would all unravel in the shift to the Internet, art writing finding only much-diminished space or disappearing altogether. By the late 70s, Evans had received the most thorough range of commentaries on his art of perhaps any other artist in the area.

Evans grew, changed, matured and flourished.

Novelist and former *Seattle Times* art critic Tom Robbins at Traver Gallery, Seattle, c. 1986

Former art and classical music critic for the *Seattle Post-Intellligencer* R.M. Campbell

From the 1970s through the end of the twentieth century, the artist challenged critics to delve deep into his fascinating but complicated art. Such an art exceeded the interests of some—too learned, too spiritual, too conceptual—but, for others, it proved a meeting ground for intellectual issues surrounding much of the most interesting contemporary American art of the period. Evans had not moved to New York; instead, he quietly insisted that his art be taken seriously in Seattle. As his stature rose, effected by numerous gallery, art center and museum exhibitions, demand for his blend of objects and installations grew, so that, as with entertaining puzzles and conundrums, understanding Evans became a sport among critics and, occasionally, other artists. The original musical objects became sculptures, props in new settings that combined quasi-religious imagery, mathematical calculations, allusions to magic and Classical texts, among other things. Taken altogether, there was a lot for critics to discuss, analyze and, in some cases, attack as obscurantist and opaque or un-interpretable.

That Evans's works mystified many was widely acknowledged, both in the growing contemporary-art community and in the press corps. Andrew Keating, who also attended the University of Washington School of Art and maintained a studio in the Belltown neighborhood near Pike Place Market, painted *Palm de Terre* (1978), a cartoon of Evans and Charles B.

Luce, who exhibited together at Linda Farris Gallery and in the Seattle Art Museum exhibition *New Ideas #1* in 1978. Keating placed arcane hieroglyphics on the palm of each artist's hand, and flanked them with two faces to represent fans who enjoyed the esoteric dimensions of their work. At the time, Keating and other artists saw the pair continuing the work of Mark Tobey and the Northwest School, with their subject matters of spiritual transcendence and admiration for hermetic wisdom. The punning title places the pair in the tradition of West Coast humorists and punsters such as William T. Wiley (1937–2021) and Robert Arneson (1930–1992), and also draws attention to the relentless punning in Evans's titles.

Who else could see or say the most about Evans and his work? Who would dare to dissect or dispute the layers of textual and iconographic meaning which seemed to jam-pack his assemblages? Especially after his shows in New York, the 1978 *Harmonious Craft*, the 1979 Whitney Biennial and the 1983 *Outside New York: Seattle*, much was at stake for the critics. Their judgments would be compared to New York's, often supplanting or substituting the embarrassing let-down of the New York review with home-grown viewpoints. It is not too extravagant to suggest that writing about Evans pushed the nascent art-critical community to do its best, outdo one's rivals, and present intelligent commentary that could contribute to a national dialogue on art. Yet, only some of the region's critics and curators choose to dive into Evansiana, the dark dreamworld of culture, myth, science and language he fashioned in his magical cave of a studio.

A central challenge to art critics writing about Evans was the paradoxical nature of journalism, always veering between the twin gods—or demons—of

(left) *Kabbalistic* from the series *The Critique of Pure Writing*, 1992. Encaustic on canvas-covered wood panel, mixed media, 52 x 42 x 8 in. Collection of Stuart Silk

(below) *Addendum to the HERO'S MYTH, Notes for the Hero*, 1977. Ink on paper, 22 x 28 in. Collection of the artist

Matthew Kangas, Linda Farris and Rheta Deal at Linda Farris Gallery, Seattle, 1986

felt about it—I always feel that will probably bring in just as many people as a fine review. I really think we could use it here; it would help all of us."[4]

Bearing in mind the relative explosion of art writing, reviewing and criticism that occurred in Seattle in the 1980s and 1990s, Farris's comments went so far as to negatively single out the art criticism in New York's *Artforum* to make a point about the type of art writing she thought would best serve Seattle:

> A lot of the time, criticism gets a bit wordy, a bit un-understandable; the artists don't even like to read it. The types of criticism you read in *Artforum*. I still have trouble reading it myself and I figure if I have trouble reading it, that's really a problem! That kind of writing, I don't know that I . . . would necessarily want to see, but strong criticism or analysis, I think could really make a difference here, simply because over a period of time, it can get people to see things differently. You do at times need people to interpret art for you at different stages, especially when you're changing the whole value system for judging it.[5]

description and analysis. Over the years, writers became caught or ensnared in one camp or the other. Each had its assets and pitfalls: if one got bogged down in description or, worse, transcribing the artist's explanations, the review would end up without any criticism or judgment, just simple transmission of the artist's intentions. With the other approach, favored by those who had trained as English majors rather than journalism, the danger was to get weighted down in dizzying layers of explication, symbol-seeking, and a final recourse to ambiguity.

Linda Farris, in the 1975 interview with Swenson for the Archives of Northwest Art (several years before Farris began showing works by the UW MFA cadre), singled out R.M. Campbell and Deloris Tarzan for praise, another of her savvy moves: "Deloris Tarzan with the [*Seattle*] *Times* is certainly making every effort to give in-depth reviews of shows. In fact, so is Richard Campbell with the *P-I*—you don't any longer see just these little four-liners. She usually tries to give some sense of what the work is about. Both reviewers are trying to interview the artist when it is possible. . . so I think that's really changing. . . . I'm just much more pleased with the way the reviewing is going."[3]

Nevertheless, Farris took the opportunity to be prescriptive as to the kind of art criticism needed, as she lamented the uniformly positive tone of the new coverage: "And there's times when I wish they just would have torn my shows to pieces if that's what they

In her final comment, Farris could have been referring to the seismic shift occurring between schools of critical thought—formalism or modernism as articulated by the influential critic, Clement Greenberg (1909–1994), and postmodern criticism, which sought to revise or obliterate canons of masterpieces and correct the neglect and oppression of women and artists of color.

Evans would benefit from both trends, but also risked becoming a battered volleyball between competing camps. Greenberg made several visits to Seattle during these years; he was friends with Virginia and

Bagley Wright, whose New York School collection he informally monitored and tried to advise. Greenberg further clarified the issues that were discussed widely among Seattle reviewers who read his writings and heard him speak in public during these visits. These critics included David Berger, Laura Brunsman, Gary Reel, Jae Carlsson, the Canadian critic Russell Keziere (who watched Seattle closely as the editor of *Vanguard* in Vancouver, BC) and myself. Lyn Smallwood and I, both writing about art for *Seattle Weekly* (partly owned by Bagley and Virginia Wright at the time) were invited to the Wrights' home in The Highlands to dine with Greenberg on one occasion and engaged in a discussion about art past and present.

As to the reportorial wing of the critical axis—description vs. analysis—Evans was fortunate in Claire C. Kelly, who reviewed Lucy Lippard's exhibition at the Portland Center for the Visual Arts, *In Touch: Nature, Ritual and Sensuous Art from the Northwest*, including the work by Evans. The review appeared in *Artweek*, an Oakland, California, publication.[6] Kelly's account is valuable as description, both for its documentation of Evans's performance art and for the inclusion of her careful witnessing of the dreadful accident that occurred at opening. Kelly included Evans as one of the "few whose work I think is really impressive," listing the crafted objects and praising their technical expertise, and describing his opening-night performance of *Slaying the World Parents:*

> As Ubu shot his porcelain arrows, there were startling sounds of real impact and tearing destruction as the targets were really pierced, and the shocking discovery soon followed that the targets were stained with the artist's blood from the barbed skirrs of the Sun-Father. It was extraordinary how the ritual, momentarily, became real in an emotional, visceral

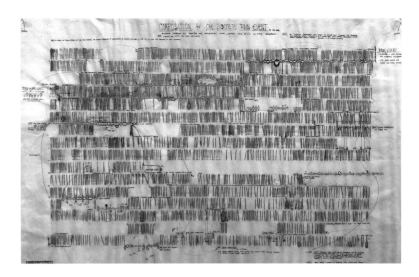

Score for *Composition for One Discrete Rain Event*, 1977. Ink on paper, 22 x 28 in. Collection of the artist

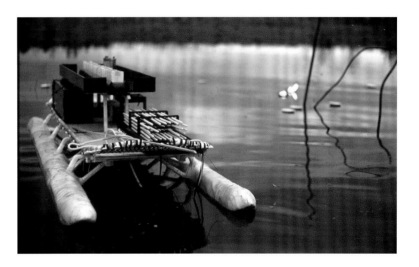

Transversal Vehicle with Instruments, 1977. Wood, Fiberglas, cloth, lacquer on wood boxes, porcelain. Collection of the artist

> sense, and the atmosphere of humorous, ironic distance from the theme of the activity was completely dissolved. Long ago (at least for those of us descending from European cultures), art used to touch these bases of spiritual shamanistic purpose, emotional intensity, and necessity in a cultural or tribal context. For a moment, for some, it did again.[7]

With her gruesome but elegant report, Kelly was the first out-of-town critic to hail Evans's peculiar persona and growing achievement. Along with Barbara

Taylor's observations later published in the spring 1980 Henry Art Gallery journal, *Insight*, her riveting eyewitness account remains the best commentary on Ubu's performances. It, in fact, goes beyond Taylor's report to leave the reader with more questions than answers, just where a Dennis Evans admirer should be.

Three exhibitions in 1978—*New Ideas #1* in March at SAM, a show at Farris's gallery in September, and one at Ruth Braunstein's Quay Gallery in San Francisco in October—filled out an important year for the artist, and occasioned the largest number of critical responses to date. The reviews shed light on approaches to the complicated but whimsical work and its creator. Of the four artists included in *New Ideas*, Evans shared more with Charles B. Luce than with the other artists in the show, Jeffrey Bishop and Keith Beckley. In this sense, mixing the austerity of Beckley and Bishop with the excess of Evans and Luce, Cowles's selection presented a stunning contrast: minimal versus overkill, evacuation of content versus masses of intellectual stuffing.

The first review of *New Ideas #1* to appear was mine in *Argus*, a conservative Seattle weekly, in which I struggled to place the four in some kind of contemporary art context, most of which I was largely ignorant of at the time. Of Evans, at least I could see, if not highly illuminate, that "[h]e emerges as the most original and ground-breaking of the artists there—and perhaps in the region. The recent acquisition by New York's Museum of Modern Art of his *Composition for 100 Discrete Rain Events . . .* underscores his gradually increasing stature and reinforces my own opinion that much significant art in this area appears in disorienting form."[8]

Campbell's extensive review in the *P-I* the following week was a milestone in that it also drew attention to Cowles's kind of curating—small thematic shows, rather than the huge juried annuals. (For many reasons, programmatic as well as financial, the annuals had become an albatross around the museum's neck,

and Cowles ended them as one of his first acts after being hired.) While beginning descriptively, praising the "beautiful and unusual objects" in the exhibition, Campbell qualified his praise, noting that: *Theurgic Imperatives,* with its suspended float, photographs and studies, reveals not only the complexity of Evans's ideas but the sometimes incoherent, or so it seems, originality of his mind."[9]

Commenting on the overriding conceptual nature of the art—new and different at this time—Campbell exposed his discomfort with the new, postmodern art when he concluded that "[t]he four artists share a certain verbal pretentiousness . . . the cognitive processes seem too apparent, the esthetic passion too absent."[10]

Deloris Tarzan's regrettably headlined review, "Art ain't what it used to be," did not disguise her open sense of bafflement. Taking pains to calm readers of the *Seattle Times*, she repeatedly cautioned that "confusion and frustration" are no surprise or that art might not any longer concern itself with beauty. Such an "impulse, if not dead, is being thoroughly throttled by artists with other concerns."[11] However, to her credit, by the end of the review, she had performed either a self-conversion to the postmodern or was driven to defend it by the power of the art she saw, voiced in her pleading conclusion: "The content of these pieces is not what is before the eye, but the thought processes they generate. Art continues to transform itself. We can only watch, if not always with comprehension, at least with an open mind."[12]

Seattle was busting out all over with emerging art critics in the late 1970s. For example, an unpublished review by another writer, David Berger, was shared with this author by Charles B. Luce, to whom Berger had sent a copy, product of a burgeoning writers' group, Seattle Arts Writing (SAW). As Berger recalled: "Publication was informal and way before blogs and such. You might call it samizdat. . . . These were typewritten, but then they were copied for distributing around. . . . I can't remember whether the story was given to Luce before or after its distribution, but presume after."[13]

Berger's essay is largely descriptive and details several works in the exhibition, including ones by Evans, but raises a number of points that are pertinent to our discussion here. For example, he was the first art critic to make the point that "urban Seattle, rather than some generalized Northwest, is the focal point for these new ideas. In hindsight this group show may be seen as a kind of landmark watershed for these reasons."[14]

Berger also introduced the idea that both Evans and Luce "combine narrative, visual and performance elements and are conceived within the context of an ongoing autobiographical 'book,' whose author is other than the artist."[15]

However, after discussing Luce's Navigator persona, Berger took a stab at understanding Evans's photographs, objects and sculptures, pointing out how the artworks on view fit into the artist's "pseudo-scientific visual and verbal vocabulary," and noting how the elements set upon the "transversal vehicle" (a floating sled) were "half-scientific and half-musical in nature." Unlike the other critics, Berger explicated his own summary judgment on Evans, drawing broader conclusions that suggest deeper meanings:

> The Maestro's showman-like activities, combining absurdity with lavish attention, aesthetic judgment and systematic rigor, make us newly sensitive to the world and orient us in a fully meaningful universe. Ritualistic in nature, his work differs from traditional ritual in being removed from a social context where all share the same beliefs. Or is he telling us that our reality is only a collective fiction? At any rate, balanced by psychic health, humor, irony and a complete lack of

imperialism, the works are seducing and a lot of fun.[16]

Evans's second Farris gallery show, in October 1978, reviewed by both Campbell and Tarzan, revealed nearly opposing examples of the ongoing art-criticism battle between formalism and postmodernism. Appearing one day apart, as was usual in the weekend entertainment supplements both dailies carried, Campbell's response suggests his growing warmth for Evans's art while retaining his gentle skepticism. Acknowledging that the artist focuses on documenting "activities and ceremonies which Evans (as Ubu Waugh) does at specific natural sites," Campbell granted that Evans' intentions are stated, but not always clearly, so that "everything links together—I'm sure it does in Evans' mind. . . . Evans has united . . . science and art . . . for Evans has mocked both with equal flair and directness."[17]

By contrast, although she was later to sympathize with the occult implications of Evans' art, Tarzan stuck to formalist analysis throughout her response, praising it as "richly theatrical, but more than that, the boxed arrangements have their own formal esthetics . . . elegantly ordered. . . . One is drawn to the clarity and vigor of the pieces—as crisp and clear as the written portions are obfuscated." All the same, perhaps covering her bases, midway through Tarzan somewhat relented on her strict formalist approach, admitting that "as pleasant as is their appearance, it is the geometry suggesting magic, ritual and the rejuvenation of life through the seasonal changes that gives the pieces resonance."[18]

Together, the reviews of Campbell and Tarzan combined to express high seriousness toward an artist who persisted with humor as a component in art of utmost contrasts.

The saga of the artist's San Francisco debut in October, 1978 at Quay Gallery reveals amusing rivalries among Bay Area critics as well as the close cooperation

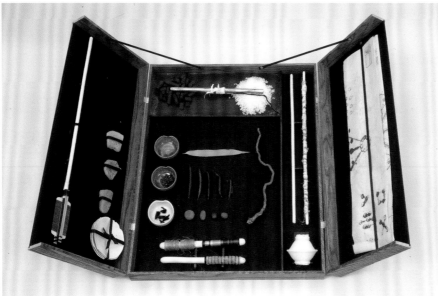

(top) Installation view of exhibition at Quay Gallery, San Francisco, 1978

(above) *Box for Instruments with Score*, 1978. Wood, porcelain, mixed media, variable size. Collection of the artist. This work was included in the Quay Gallery show.

between Farris and her San Francisco colleague Ruth Braunstein (1923–2016). The arrangements were set up with an August 5, 1978 letter from Braunstein's gallery to Farris: "We were delighted to hear that Dennis Evans will do a show here with us. . . . We are also delighted that you plan to attend the opening as we will be having a small party afterwards. . . . Our set up is that we work on a 50-50 split, with you getting 10% from our side. We hope that will be agreeable to you."[19]

Exhibiting new work and some of the pieces that were shown in Seattle, the show received only one review, but it was, perhaps, the most important of Evans's career. The *San Francisco Chronicle's* second-string art critic, Thomas Albright (1936–1984), was assigned Evans's show, rather than the newspaper's senior art and music critic, Alfred Frankenstein (1906–1981). A letter sent from Braunstein to Farris in late October read, "I'm glad Albright had a go at the exhibition as I think Frankenstein wouldn't have tried to understand what the exhibition is about."[20] Albright was the first art critic to successfully synthesize all the different aspects of the artist into a coherent whole, basing his analysis on the concept of shamanism, something featured in the headline (usually written by editors), "Invasion of the Shamen [*sic*]."[21] Could it be that Evans's art made more sense in the New Age atmosphere of the Bay Area than in Puget Sound? Beginning with comparisons to local shaman-persona artists William T. Wiley, Nathan Oliveira (1929–2010) and Stephanie Weber, whose exhibitions were also reviewed in the same column, Albright quickly noted that Evans was "the truly complete shaman. . . . Most of his show consists of portable closets filled with ceramic wands, bowls, funnels, dried beans, pods and all manner of other paraphernalia, like the medicine bundles in which the Plains Indians preserved their talismans."[22]

While remaining faithful to his descriptive/journalistic mission and describing the objects in detail,

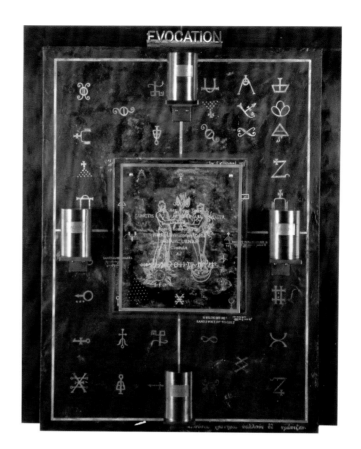

Station 7, The Fountain, Day Four from *The Philosopher's Wedding*, 1994. Encaustic on canvas-covered wood panel, mixed media, 51 x 42 in. Collection of Mary Alberg

Albright concluded by cautioning the artist about excessive irony, the veil of the "uncommitted," as Albright put it, adding that "[t]here are also diagrams in which Evans, a former chemist, provides his rituals with a conceptualist foundation, including symbols from chemistry, mathematics and so on—plus plenty of fine-print hints, and half-hints, that he may be putting us on. Thus, as so many artists of recent years, Evans finally takes refuge in irony, the great haven of the uncommitted; if one finds the work thin on a serious level, the artist can always counter that he was just pulling your leg."[23]

Less than two years later, with Evans's next Farris gallery show, Tarzan cooled down her judgments about his work, completing her arc of enthusiasm and praise with weary skepticism and disenchantment. Nevertheless, persisting in his gallery shows and

Page from the magazine *People Weekly*, part of a profile on Dennis Evans, July 16, 1979

supplementing them with numerous installations and public art projects, Evans continued to be a force to be reckoned with, not easily ignored. The cluster of critics who wrote about him early in his career was joined by a few others, some of whom, like Berger, reappeared. Berger seemed freshly minted, as if out of nowhere, a long while after his underground review of *New Ideas #1*. With the advent of the freelancers' careers, more out-of-town publication venues became available as well. Long after Lippard's travel diary of the Northwest appeared in *Art in America* in 1976, an Evans exhibition was also noticed by *ARTnews*, in a story filed by local stringer Lyn Smallwood.[24] Even more national coverage, in the form of a feature on the artist in *People Weekly*, appeared in 1979 and put Evans on a plane above all of his Seattle peers.[25] As one itinerant wag put it at the time, it was better to be on the front page

of anything, if only to get off the arts pages, which nobody read. Answering *People* reporter Nancy Faber with a straight face, the artist described his formation of the Institute for the Conservation of Ephemeral Events and was called "a giant put-on" by Faber. When pressed about meaning, Evans relented, saying "That is a real delicate place—somewhere between absurdity, irony and profundity. . . . At worst it's Groucho Marx; at best, it's too profound."[26]

The responses of Hackett and Tarzan to the artist's third solo show at Farris gallery in 1980 exposed cracks in the monument to Ubu Waugh they had both earlier helped construct. It was then that Hackett made her oft-quoted comment that Evans was "a bit of a magician and a bit of a fraud."[27] Perhaps cowed by the *People* article the year before, she quoted it only to refute it with her reservations: "I see the first quality [absurdity] but not the second [profundity]. Looking around the gallery, I was reminded of Thomas Hess's famous phrase, "black-tie dada," used to describe the wacky yet safe happenings of Jean Tinguely. I think Evans chooses materials for spiritual reasons but to date has ended up with work that is more aesthetically pleasing than profound."[28]

Remaining tied to—and ultimately disappointed by—the spiritual potential of Evans, Hackett was also distressed by his manipulation of language, comparing him to characters in Jonathan Swift's *Gulliver's Travels* (1726) who restrict words and grammar in spoken language in order to address one another more directly. Stretching the linguistic analogy, she noted how his "black harness sculpture boxes and his drawings could be artifacts of [that] society. They are so concrete, direct and substantial they seem complicated. (No one is so confusing as the person who gets right to the point.)"[29]

Tarzan, too, was having second thoughts. Tarzan's review appeared three days after Hackett's and began by echoing her own headline, "Has success spoiled

Tarot card "The Magician" from Le Tarot de Marseille deck

bright, young Dennis Evans?" with the tone of a condescending elder: "When an artist succeeds too fast, too young, it can be the unmaking of him. . . . Dennis Evans, one of Seattle's brightest young talents, may be falling into the success trap."[30]

After quoting Evans's comment to her about the unity of his dispersed and diverse objects, sculptures, drawings and photographs, Tarzan's retort was "it's a piece of hokum." As if listing evidence for the decline, she mentions the Museum of Modern Art and Smithsonian Institution connections, with a kiss: "strong in formal esthetics and geometry, as rich in mystery as in fun," before drop-kicking another exculpatory bomb: "It has all deteriorated into pressing nonsense."[31]

Although she did not attend that summer's performance of *A Passion Play*, the twelve-hour performance at the Montlake Landfill, Tarzan meticulously described one of the events, the most extended and detailed performance commentary since the review by Kelly. Tarzan ended her review, in which she acknowledged that she had not attended the performance, on a note different from her prior conciliatory, pro-postmodern views. Bordering on anti-intellectual prohibition of complex meanings, in what might have been the fiercest review of her career, she ended with: "If you're baffled by the significance of it all, peace. There is no significance. Nor would [there] need to be, if there were something more afoot than tongue-in-cheek doubletalk. . . . Admission is free. It's worth it."[32]

About a decade later, Tarzan (writing as Deloris Tarzan Ament) renewed her interest in the aspects of Evans's work that allude to magic, alchemy, cosmology and, crucially for Ament, the pack of fortune-telling Tarot cards, central to one of the artist's new sculptures at the Farris gallery. Evans's accomplishments in the intervening years made it possible for the *Times* critic to turn her earlier outrage to awe as she wondered about the unseen world Evans so slyly invoked with the works in this show: "Those who don't know or care anything about the Tarot can enjoy the florid beauty of Evans's arrangements of words and objects on a formal level. But anyone intrigued with decoding symbols can linger a long time at each station, working it all out."[33]

Ament then made several lengthy analyses of the Tarot stations the artist had created. Symbolism, gender and the Classical world were all implicated by Tarzan, as the prodigal convert returned to the fold of Evansiana. At the review's end, she evoked a compliment cum epithet: "a man who has based his career on the role of magician."

Chief among the freelancers in the Puget Sound area was Ron Glowen, trained as a painter at Washington State University, employed sporadically at Boeing Company, and living in the rural farming community of Arlington in Snohomish County. This perfectly positioned Glowen between Bellingham, Whatcom County; Everett, Snohomish County, where he wrote for *The Herald*; and Seattle, where he filed stories and reviews about Seattle and environs at *Artweek* and *Vanguard* (a Vancouver, British Columbia, art monthly). Addressing Evans's third Farris gallery show, in 1982, he realized it was the artist's "most ambitious exhibition to date," and rather than denigrate or doubt à la Hackett, over time Glowen wrote about Evans seriously, in depth and with close attention to philosophical and religious influences on the appearance and

Kathy Glowen and *Artweek* critic Ron Glowen at Bumbershoot
music and arts festival, Seattle Center, c. 1986

meaning of his art. Picking up on the slow transition
from spiritual or mystic to the scientific and cosmological strains in Evans, Glowen foresaw a "perplexing
blend of algebraic, alchemic and spiritual or mystical
symbolism that seems at home in the laboratory."[34] He
drew attention to Jungian archetypes in Evans's works
and, reserving the right to compare the new work to
earlier examples, as in "not up to his usual standards,"
he wrote: "The exchange of dialogue between artist
and viewer has become less eloquent. On the other
hand, Evans continues as perhaps Seattle's most daring
artist. . . . He has leapt ahead of his audience and the
passage through *The Chymical Nuptials of Soma and
Agni* [title of the 1982 Linda Farris Gallery exhibition
and the 1985 Klein-Niemi wedding ceremony] leaves
the viewer bewildered and bewitched by the betrothal
of alchemy and art."[35]

Seminary (1983) at the Whatcom Museum of
History and Art in Bellingham was the biggest (and
last) exhibition gathering of the *New Ideas #1* artists.[36]
Glowen wrote extensively on the exhibition, which
had been closely curated by Evans, for the Canadian
magazine *Vanguard.* It proved to be the definitive
comment on the milder minimalists, Keith Beckley
and Jeffrey Bishop, with whom Mee was included. It
took over the entire Whatcom Museum and director George Thomas gave full rein to Evans as de facto
curator. Glowen pointed out, Evans's way of installing
their work may have been jarring, amid the laying on
of his "cluttering madness." Seeing the artists fighting a
losing battle, he feared the partners' "collaborative contributions to *Seminary* are more equally shared visually
and structurally than by its indoctrinating demeanor
of a cabalistic fortress or alchemic laboratory, which is
uniquely Evans's."[37]

Visually among the most stunning works of this
new phase of Evans's art, and in collaboration with
others such as Nancy Mee, *The Seminary*'s central
structure (a pyramidal copper roof and floor covered
with rock crystals) was brilliantly detailed by Glowen.
His portrayal perhaps loses the battle of description vs.
analysis, but wins the war in terms of respecting the artist's insistence on complex meaning, trying to translate
it into terms the viewer will grasp, and setting the artist's work into the context of his prior grand projects.
Glowen concluded: "It seems excessive and yet offers
so much that it remains mysterious and compelling. In
another respect, *Seminary* is an ersatz theological fun-
house, bewildering and exhausting, but all the while
memorable."[38]

Seminary proved to be a testing ground for other
collaborations, such as full-scale, institutional-strength,
on-site museum installations. Contemporary art curators in Portland, Boise, Tacoma and Seattle hopped
aboard the tugboat to Evansiana, and where they
would stop, nobody knew. That is, until David Berger
resurfaced at the *Seattle Times* and reviewed Evans's
1985 return to the Seattle Art Museum, where his career
had begun in 1978, with the installation of *The Seven
Halls of AeDvAeM.* This time, modern-art curator
Bruce Guenther (who had replaced Charles Cowles)
organized *Documents Northwest: Dennis Evans* at the
Seattle Art Museum's annex at the old world's fair
site. Drawing attention to another Evans installation,
Sin Tax/Syntax, running concurrently at Linda Farris
Gallery in Pioneer Square, Berger's task was three-fold:

(top) Installation view of *The Seminary*, 1984, Whatcom
Museum of History and Art, Bellingham, WA

(above) Detail of *The Seminary*, 1984

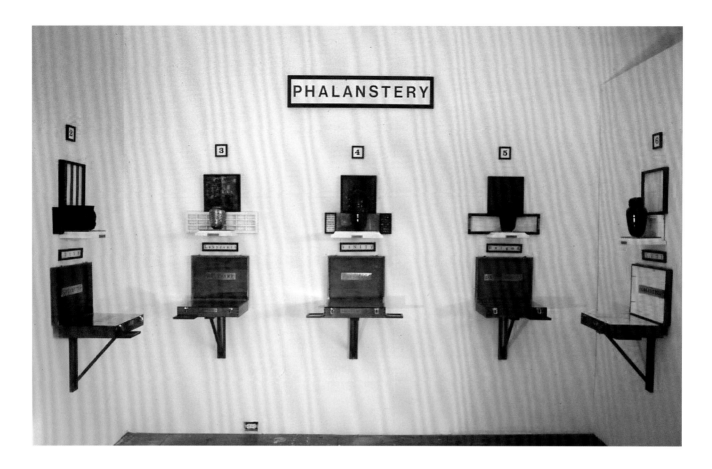

PHALANSTERY

Installation view of *Phalanstery* from *The Seven Halls of AeDvAeM,* 1985, Seattle Art Museum Seattle Center Pavilion

describe the installation, analyze its more complicated sides and don't frighten viewers away, the latter solved by falling back on the same idea he used in the unpublished 1978 review of *New Ideas #1*: "it's all fun and games." In what is still among the most thorough and clearest explanations of Evans's work, Berger's review takes us on a virtual walk-through of the rooms at Seattle Center, which included "large cabalistic maps of the rooms we are about to enter." Not at all avoiding an attempt at deciphering meaning, Berger allowed that "It's a remarkable illustration of the forms and structures of communication systems, the most generic of which is language. But the most 'de-constructed' system is the aesthetic system, because the installation itself is the presentation of objects."[39]

Siding with the postmodernists (note Berger's use of the term "de-constructed" above), close to the fashionable literary-criticism theory of deconstruction originated by the philosopher Jacques Derrida (1930–2004), Berger at least allowed for the possibility of aesthetic meaning of any kind, even if his assessment tilted

the interpretation of the exhibition toward a take-off or dismantling of a science or natural history museum. Derrida was another idol of Evans's at this time, no doubt attracted to the Frenchman's frustrating insistence on the impossibility of fixed texts or meanings in literary contexts. Needless to say, both favored a dense, nearly impenetrable approach to interpretation.[40]

Although here were several more shows of Evans's work at the Farris gallery through 1995, joined by more out-of-town exhibitions in Portland, San Francisco, Boise and New York, Evans's studio practices began to be divided between active gallery commitments, public art projects and on-site invitational museum installations. As for the critics, Sheila Farr succeeded Tarzan, who left the *Seattle Times* in 2000, and continued as staff art critic until 2009, and Berger and I continued for some time as *Times* freelance contributors, joined by Gayle Clemans, PhD,

Installation view of *tHE gaRden for remeMbered dEireS*, 1989,
Linda Farris Gallery, Seattle

a novelist living in Seattle with a graduate degree in art history. Of the group, she contributed infrequently to the *Times*, as its editorial policies and shrinking budgets, much reduced for arts and entertainment, no longer allowed for regular weekly, in-depth coverage, as in this era of the rising art critics.

In the coming decades, both Evans's gallery exhibitions and on-site installations outside the gallery context gave him more time to construct, design and install his increasingly elaborate and complex environments (with the help of assistants whom he began hiring around 1990). Sadly, as most of these projects were shown or installed in spaces other than art-exhibition venues, they were not seen by the art-critical community in Seattle. As a result, in lieu of readable or even available writing on them, the Seattle critics concentrated on the gallery shows.

A mounting number of younger contemporary art curators (the position itself was new in the Pacific Northwest) beyond Seattle began to develop interest in Evans's art, exhibiting or installing it in prestigious

group shows or offering invitations to create settings in a museum—not in the usual contemporary gallery but in the spaces that housed historical-period art, such as Renaissance painting or medieval metalwork. Increasingly, Evans's messages found homes in these institutional settings, in addition to commercial galleries. It was a combination of teams, the critics and the curators, which dove into Evansiana, the dark dreamworld of culture, myth, science and language he fashioned in his magical cave of a studio.

Two articles that appeared around the time Evans's exhibition *tHE garden foR remeMbered dEsireS* opened at the Linda Farris Gallery have a respectful, but valedictory tone. Hackett's January 1989 interview articulated a great disappointment in the Yakima altar boy who left belief and faith behind in favor of a mystical rationalism and indeterminate approach to the universe. And, published just before Hackett's

Seattle Post-Intelligencer art critic Regina Hackett and artist George Chacona at Linda Farris Gallery, Seattle, 1986

Post-Intelligencer article appeared, Tarzan Ament's *Seattle Times* commentary on the show was printed. Although both she and Hackett continued to write sporadically about Evans in the coming years, these reviews presented a stock-taking rarely exposed in daily newspapers. Tarzan Ament's quasi-devotional prayer came at a propitious moment in her own life, her marriage to Allen Ament in 1987 and subsequent conversion to Judaism. More attuned than ever to Evans's vast reservoir of knowledge about complex ancient thought, she reiterated her recognition of the role of the Tarot pack and added that it was a "fusion of the constructive symbolism of Freemasonry, mathematics, the traditions of the Kabbala and alchemy, whose practitioners encoded their learning into symbols taken from ancient metallurgy."[41] Summing up Evans's career, she generously introduced him in the context of the larger international contemporary art scene, wherein: "Symbols that appear . . . tend to be personal, and often cryptic even to the conscious mind of the artist who made them. They are like un-interpreted dreams."[42]

After the lengthiest description of the installation's Tarot elements that had yet appeared, Tarzan Ament gave a painstaking reading of the card symbolism according to her apparently extensive knowledge of the occult card pack. She ended by pleading for a museum, any museum, to keep one of the installations

intact, rather than subject to their being "cannibalized and broken, [so] they are lost," because Evans is "one of the Northwest's most original and gifted artists. . . . Yet his biggest and most important works—the installations—have vanished. . . . No doubt that disappearance is a symbol in itself; an apt one for a man who has based his career on the role of magician."[43]

Faced with the disappearance of overt Catholic symbolism in Evans's work of the late 1980s and 1990s, Hackett turned to a biographical profile, covering everything from the altar boy's childhood to his relegation to art museum installations that nobody saw or that people just didn't understand. The interview combines an attack on Vatican II with a kind of blood-and-soil nostalgia for his ancestral agricultural background that is hard to credit solely to the artist. She quoted him: "'We ate what the land offered, and followed Catholic dietary rules . . . . Lent meant giving up a lot, Christmas was a food festival," then wrote "As Evans sees it, both Catholicism and family farms have nearly disappeared. The Church has moved from Latin to English—from obscure, meditative services to matter-of-fact exchanges. The family farm has been largely subsumed into agribusiness."[44]

She also wrote that his family's "ingrained association between seasonal change, crop rotations, and religious ceremonies almost summons up visions of the British horror film *The Wicker Man* (1973) with 'crop rotation' all tied up with sacrifice and seasonal cycles of virginity and licentiousness." Hackett went further, putting words in his mouth: "Evans wants people late in the twentieth century to care about what he sees as the demise of an essentially medieval religion and the disappearance of the farmer, the man of nature."[45]

Concluding with another kiss and a kick, as would Ament, Hackett praised the Farris installation, "An exaggerated visual feast . . . its major themes are basic: the relation between male and female, the law and desire, the joker and the hermit. His work is lush, decadent and excessive." Sounding decisive, but wary of final critical judgment, she gave Evans the last word in a skirmish that had occurred over a twenty-five-year period, allowing him to turn the tables once more on the critic as audience: "I'm the magician and everybody is the fool . . . that's the missing card. The viewer fills it in."[46]

NOTES

1   Linda Farris, interview with Sally Swenson, February 26, 1975, Archives of Northwest Art, University of Washington Libraries.

2   See Tom Robbins, *Another Roadside Attraction* (Garden City, NY: Doubleday, 1971). This book was followed by seven other novels and an autobiography, *Tibetan Peach Pie: A True Account of an Imaginative Life* (2014). His reviews are collected in *Wild Ducks Flying Backwards: Shorter Writings of Tom Robbins* (New York: Bantam Books, 2005).

3   Farris, interview with Swenson.

4   Farris, interview with Swenson.

5   Farris, interview with Swenson.

6   Claire C. Kelly, "Sense and Sensuality in Northwest Art," *Artweek*, October 23, 1976: 1.

7   Kelly, "Sense and Sensuality."

8   Matthew Kangas, "Part of the Way Up From Verbosity-as-Art," *Argus*, March 10, 1978: 8.

9   R.M. Campbell, "Art Pavilion Show—Small is Beautiful," *Seattle Post-Intelligencer*, March 15, 1978: D13.

10   Campbell, "Art Pavilion Show."

11   Deloris Tarzan, "Four Artists Present 'New Ideas'/Art Ain't What it Used to Be," *Seattle Times*, March 10, 1978.

12   Tarzan, "Four Artists."

13   David Berger, interview with author, November 4, 2021.

14   David Berger, "New Ideas From Seattle," unpublished manuscript, review of *New Ideas #1*, 1978. Charles B. Luce archive, New York.

15   Berger, "New Ideas From Seattle."

16   Berger, "New Ideas From Seattle."

17   R.M. Campbell, "Evans: It's Not Your Standard Gallery Show," *Seattle Post-Intelligencer,* September 29, 1978: 18.

18   Deloris Tarzan, "Evans Explores Art as Apparatus," *Seattle Times*, October 1, 1978: M7.

19   [Quay Gallery], letter to Linda Farris, August 5, 1978. Dennis Evans archive, Seattle.

20   [Quay Gallery], letter to Farris.

21   Thomas Albright, "At the Galleries: Invasion of the Shamen," *San Francisco Chronicle*, October 28, 1978: 37.

22   Albright, "At the Galleries: Invasion of the Shamen."

23   Albright, "At the Galleries: Invasion of the Shamen."

24   Lyn Smallwood, "Seattle/DENNIS EVANS/Linda Farris," *ARTnews* (January 1985), 179.

25   Nancy Faber, "Arts," *People Weekly*, July 16, 1979, clipping, Dennis Evans archive, Seattle.

26   Faber, "Arts."

27   Regina Hackett, "She Strives For 'Pure' Responses in Her Work," *Seattle Post-Intelligencer*, May 11, 1980: G6.

28   Hackett, "She Strives For 'Pure' Responses."

29   Hackett, "She Strives For 'Pure' Responses."

30   Deloris Tarzan, "Has Success Spoiled Bright, Young Dennis Evans?," *Seattle Times*, May 14, 1980: D1.

31   Tarzan, "Has Success Spoiled Bright, Young Dennis Evans?"

32   Tarzan, "Has Success Spoiled Bright, Young Dennis Evans?"

33   Tarzan, "Has Success Spoiled Bright, Young Dennis Evans?"

34   Ron Glowen, "Altered States," *Artweek*, September 25, 1982: 16.

35   Glowen, "Altered States."

36   The exhibition lacked work by Luce but gained work by Nancy Mee, one of the MFA/Ritchie/Triangle Studios group.

37   Ron Glowen, "Seminary," *Vanguard* 13, no. 3 (April 1984): 46–47.

38   Glowen, "Seminary."

39   David Berger, "Museum Piece Plays Well on Several Levels," *Seattle Times*, May 17, 1985.

40   Dennis Evans, interview with author, January 25, 2022.

41   Deloris Tarzan Ament, "Dennis Evans: A Career Based in Magic," *Seattle Times*, January 11, 1989: C1.

42   Tarzan Ament, "Dennis Evans: A Career Based in Magic": C5.

43   Tarzan Ament, "Dennis Evans: A Career Based in Magic": C5.

44   Regina Hackett, "Artist Eulogizes Ritual He Knew As a Catholic Farmboy," *Seattle Post-Intelligencer*, January 14, 1989: C1.

45   Hackett, "Artist Eulogizes Ritual."

46   Hackett, "Artist Eulogizes Ritual."

Installation view of *The Philosopher's Wedding*, 1994, Bellevue Art Museum, Bellevue, WA

CHAPTER SIX

Installations: Environments of Uncertainty

Presenting a myriad of objects and associations, Dennis Evans raises questions about the relationship of mythology and the art of the past to contemporary culture. Together these elements are meshed in layers of allusion and association. Through this work, which remains open-ended and loosely metaphoric, Evans has created an environment of uncertainty.

—Sandy Harthorn, "Mnemosyne's Alphabet," 1994[1]

By the time Boise Art Museum curator Sandy Harthorn concluded comments in her essay on his large-scale exhibition, Dennis Evans had been creating installation projects for over a decade. Harthorn encapsulated the growth of his work up to that point in ways that no critic ever had room to develop. As we have seen, as early as 1982, Ron Glowen and Regina Hackett were addressing the different natures of connections between art object, in-house site-specificity and responsive viewer. To her credit, Deloris Tarzan Ament's defining stance was one of defending the confounding nature of contemporary art to a largely unknowing readership. Filling space alone was not Evans's foremost task in these years, but rather, the untangling of meaning within each installation component and in their relationships one to another as parts of a totalizing thought system, such as alchemy, the nature of sound, astrology and pre- and post-Hellenic Classical mythology. Evans crafted allusions to medieval Christianity so that the viewer perceived them as residual in the construction of analogous shrines or communal devotional sites, rather than as underlying content or spiritually redemptive

rituals of dogma or doctrine. The ghost of a Marian framework, literally a *matrix* or maternal container, led to the artist's innumerable reinterpretations of bodies of knowledge such as chemistry, astronomy, the blurring polarities of gender, the limits of cognitive perception and, eventually, the origins and structure of the Copernican solar system and foundations of an Einsteinian universe. By the early 2020s, Evans was detailing the construction of an expanding universe—in easy lessons when concentrated upon. Such works could borrow the title of a work by Marcel Duchamp, *To Be Looked at (from the Other Side of the Glass) with One Eye, Close to, for Almost an Hour* (1918), as a teasing viewer's guide for Evans's installations.[2] Scrutiny is repaid handsomely.

When she called them "environments of uncertainty," Harthorn may have been alluding to the Uncertainty Principle formulated by Albert Einstein (1879–1955) colleague and rival Werner Heisenberg (1901–1976), who posited that when something was observed, it changed; hence, the uncertainty of perception in an expanding universe. Upon observation or contemplation of Evans's works, one may get the impression of grasping the meaning, but then meaning shifts, like the world around us, transforming itself into another possible significance. Our uncertainty as viewers is not the same as that of Heisenberg or Einstein (who attempted to refute Heisenberg), but the uncertainty that is realized when one is faced with rigid, unyielding interpretations or, alternatively, maddening ambiguity. In Evans's rich multiplicity of objects and his manipulation of surrounding museum or gallery space, interpretations—searches for meaning amid all the chaos—become fluid and unstable, uncertain in the best sense. Once meaning is locked down, aesthetic experience is frozen, something that is never the case anywhere in Evans's art.

Cosmology is the study of the origins and development of the universe. Replacing alchemy as it emerged in early modern science, it offered an unending source of inspiration for Evans, who laid out allusions to it in rich, imaginative detail in the museum and gallery installations in Seattle (1985); Portland, Oregon (1989); Boise, Idaho (1993); Bellevue, Washington (1994); and New York (2003). The occult side, which had so enamored Tarzan Ament, subsided into a less pervasive, but no less pictorially implemented backdrop, veiling unfulfilled prophecies and revealing unexpected counterpoints to Christianity that led to science, the Enlightenment, the modern and postmodern eras, and the current Anthropocene Age. Rooted in the past, Evans's installations in the 1990s and early 2000s drove the participant temporarily outward into timeless, planetary space, toward orbiting signs and symbols that were faintly recognizable or deliberately undecipherable. This was especially true when they were dimly lit.

With these developments, language persisted as another underlying and sometimes perplexing subject. According to the artist, "the subject is nothing less than the evolution of writing and language from the caves at Lascaux up through all the orthographic forms of expression and symbols which, with cuneiform,

became a common theme in my work."[3] Affixed like ornaments or compositional elements in each work, the referential dimensions of Evans's language can be better ignored or skimmed over for fear of being trapped in a labyrinthine maze of words that may or may not be connected to the overall subject or topic in question. Taken up in a playful way by the viewer—take it or leave it—language merges onto an overall panoply of coexisting sculptural components, immeasurably enriched by their material presentation and display, all experienced simultaneously by mind and body.

The interpolation of words into each sculpture raises a two-pronged dilemma. As there are two types of language involved in the art of Dennis Evans, how do we deal with them? The first tangle is the words themselves, inserted, engraved, displayed, misspelled, encoded and layered into each work. Questions such as "What do they mean?" and "Why are they on this work?" are asked as part of the hermeneutical act, the search for interpreting signs and symbols. Secondly, taken collectively, the words constitute an important, overlooked facet: the complete body of Dennis Evans's writing outside, within and upon each artwork. No critic, curator or art historian has yet begun to investigate this body of writing as a whole, which could reveal additional insights into his achievement and the art of our times. It is not the expressed purpose of this chapter to encompass Evans's writings in their entirety and comment upon them. However, if translating the Paris newspaper headlines torn up and glued into Picasso's first collages merits scholarly articles and books 100 years later, why not explore the ceaseless verbiage and hypertexts of Evans at some not-so-distant point? This could constitute deep reading indeed.

The second aspect of such a fruitful dilemma is the *writing about the writing* and the art, i.e., the wealth of critical commentary on Evans, what German literary historians and critics refer to as reader-response criticism.[4] The reception history of four art-museum installations is the core subject of this chapter, partly

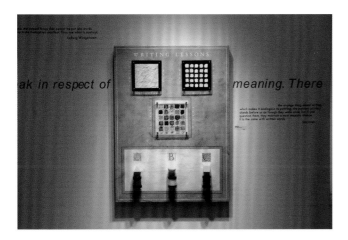

(top) *The Great Cycle*, 1984. Paint on paper, 18 x 60 in.

(above) Installation detail of *Writing Lessons/Reading Sessions*, 2002, Woodside/Braseth Gallery, Seattle

(right) *Writing Lessons*, 2002

because of the special nature of his art: much of the work has been dismantled, destroyed or recycled into other works in the studio. That is to say, the original works are now only known to us via their reception history, in reviews, essays, catalogues, magazine articles and other media. The privileged first readers are, in this case, the critics and the curators. In this chapter, we will examine four art-museum installations

and one private residential commission in Sun Valley, Idaho. Our only records of the museum installations are in photographs and commentaries. Both sets of voices, of curators and critics, heard through extensive quotations, give us a glimpse at how engaged viewers respond differently to the same work, as in the case of the artist's 1982 Linda Farris Gallery exhibition, reviewed by Ron Glowen, Regina Hackett and Sue

Ann Kendall. (Kendall was the first *Seattle Times* contributor with a PhD in art history from the University of Washington.) Compared to Glowen's *Artweek* analysis and description of the layout,[5] Kendall's review could be appreciated by readers as an attempt to make Evans more accessible to viewers rather than hermetic or totally obscure. She wrote:

> The whole concoction is a kind of Evansiology, derived from a host of world mythologies. Mysterious by design, it conjures up the kind of mental connections that poetry does through metaphor and allusion.
>
> This work is probably the most accessible the artist has created to date. Most of it is sensuous enough to attract the eye and most of the allusions are apparent enough to tickle rather than repel the brain. I think it could stand to be even more accessible, but for Evans, the

Installation view of *tHE gaRden for RemeMbered dEsireS,* 1989, Linda Farris Gallery, Seattle

piece already represents a big step in that direction.[6]

It took several out-of-town art-museum and art-center exhibitions of Evans's work (in Washington, Olympia, Bellingham, Tacoma, and Cheney; and in Oregon, Portland) to provide sufficient validation of his work and prompt an invitation to participate in the new Documents Northwest series at the Seattle Art Museum Seattle Center Pavilion. Like *New Ideas #1, Documents Northwest: Dennis Evans* was a career milestone of enduring significance. Thanks to modern art curator Bruce Guenther, the artist received carte blanche to transform the Seattle Center space. Guenther wrote the most comprehensive description and analysis of any of the installations up to that time. Whereas Kendall had carefully walked the reader through the entire installation in the latter half of her article, Guenther went further and wrote at greater length to describe the aerial view (which revealed a male figure), the various rooms and the overarching themes of "polarities, especially of male/female, personal cosmologies and the genesis of ideas from simple to complex."[7] In yet another example of the *Rashomon*-like responses to the performance, Guenther proffered his own account of the Portland Center for the Visual Arts affair: "An absorbing and strangely musical performance unfolded as Evans recited and, following an elaborate, scroll-like score, ritually shot elegant white porcelain arrows, 'skirrs,' against a target on the wall. The monologue fused in my memory with the image of the artist's bloody hands cut by the rough edges of the porcelain skirrs, and the sound of them shattering—an unforgettable performance with both humor and anxiety."[8] Guenther provided a brisk walkthrough, room-by-room, with a summation that takes into consideration all the artist's earlier work ("balanced between profundity and absurdity"), and brings the reader up-to-date by addressing both the "arcane, esoteric or occult," and how it fused with the rational or scientific in later years. In his conclusion, Guenther noted that "[t]his intellectual orientation implies the order in the complex, multileveled thought structures that for centuries informed the human intellect. Although today we view them as antithetical to rational and linear thoughts, these systems guided human endeavor far longer than has the scientific method. It is to the matrix of this patrimony—artifact, symbol, language, poetry, power—that Dennis Evans's work returns us."[9]

John Weber, contemporary art curator at Portland Art Museum, invited the artist in 1989 to create *tHE gaRden for remeMbered dEsireS* for the museum, based on a prior version at Linda Farris Gallery earlier that year. Weber's catalogue essay builds on Guenther's seriousness and plays down the whimsical or humorous, though granting it "playful ambiguity."[10] As the whole installation structure was based on Tarot cards, Weber claimed that "Evans has chosen the Tarot deck as his fundamental iconographic key, and familiarity with the tradition of the Tarot as a tool of fantasy

and divination greatly enhances an understanding of his piece."[11]

Providing a lengthy history of the Tarot and its role in medieval and Renaissance culture, Weber explained that experiencing *tHE garden* occurs in two ways: "learned, conventionalized meanings located in images, situations or ritual activities, yet art also requires the viewer's own highly subjective acts of perception and cognition."[12]

While walking through the various alcoves, cloisters and rooms of the installation, taking in the imagery and multiple layers of words, the sympathetic viewer could soak up the totality of the immersive experience, recalling, remembering and discarding allusions to sex, mythology and other elements of the Tarot pack, in order to process the complicated but beautiful constructions.

Following Guenther and Weber, her fellow regional contemporary art curators, Sandy Harthorn's challenge with her exhibition of Evans's *The Seven Halls of AeDvAeM* was somewhat familiar and perhaps even somewhat streamlined or reduced by earlier efforts to install it. She gave Evans control over the installation, who designed its dark-painted walls and organized the framed elements in two opposing rows of five, with various mute sculptural objects in between. This confrontational arrangement commented on both the make-up and content of the competing five-packs (examples of ancient forms of writing vs. early formulae of alchemy), and pointed out the aerial cruciform, surely an embrace of a cathedral floor plan.

(top) Former Seattle Art Museum curator of modern art Bruce Guenther, 1985

(above) Former Portland Art Museum contemporary art curator John Weber, c. 1989

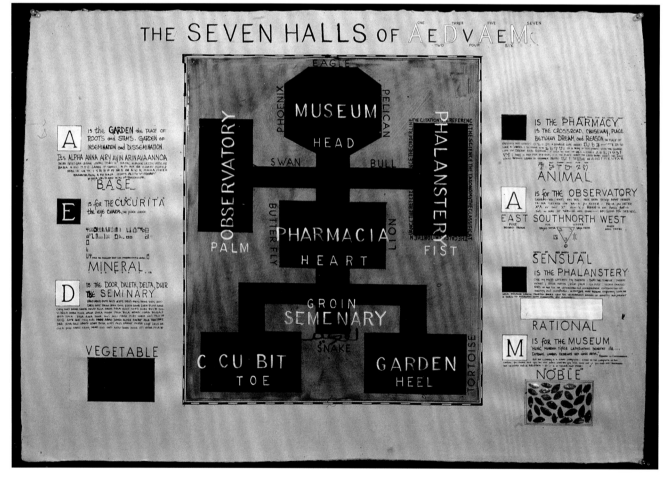

(top left) *Museum* from *The Seven Halls of AeDvAeM,* 1985.
Acrylic on canvas, 96 x 96 in.

(top right) Installation view of *Museum* from *The Seven Halls of
AeDvAeM,* 1985, *Documents Northwest: the PONCHO/Dennis
Evans,* Seattle Art Museum Seattle Center Pavilion

(above) Drawing for *Museum* from *Seven Halls of AeDvAeM,*
1985. Mixed media, 22 x 32 in.

(top) Installation view of *Phalanstery* from *The Seven Halls of AeDvAeM,* 1985, *Documents Northwest: The PONCHO/Dennis Evans,* Seattle Art Museum Seattle Center Pavilion

(middle) Installation view of *Seminary* from *The Seven Halls of AeDvAeM,* 1985, *Documents Northwest: The PONCHO Series/ Dennis Evans* at Seattle Art Museum Seattle Center Pavilion

(bottom) Installation view of the exhibition *Drawings and Sculptures of Joseph Beuys/Contemporary Inspirations,* Bellevue Art Museum, Bellevue, WA, 1994

Mnemosyne was the Greek goddess of memory. Each element in the Boise museum presentation of *The Seven Halls of AeDvAeM* appeared to be a fragment or mnemonic trigger represented by language, chemical formulae or other script. A wall with multi-plane mountings of objects faced one that largely featured language play, including a rebus, that toyed with links between language and alchemy. Piles of books in the middle of the gallery confronted a facsimile of an alchemic urn in which various metals were heated to extreme temperatures in the hope of making gold, or, as Evans put it, an "alchemically transforming of self."[13] The connection between language and alchemy is Evans's theory, not that of historians of science, necessarily, or of magicians. As he noted about this work, "The reflecting shadows in the room were allusions to Plato's Cave on one level and, on another, the journey from the primitive cave dweller to the refined semiotician, an alchemical transformation from an early primitive, raw self into a refined golden self, the 'Domus Aureum.'"[14]

It is due to Evans's great artistry that he juxtaposed them, strengthening our misty grasp of medieval history, the misnamed "Dark Ages," and stimulating recognition of mathematical calculations or symbols from the Periodic Table of Elements (seen in greater detail in Boise than in other installations). Harthorn wisely granted the viewer the ultimate say-so in her essay for *The Science of Secrets*, in which she counseled the reader to respond: "Whether this golden tablet is a metaphor for the mind, memory, the future or a pristine piece of paper, is left to the discretion of the viewer."[15]

In 1994, Evans was invited to participate in the exhibition *Drawings and Sculptures of Joseph Beuys/Contemporary Inspirations* at the Bellevue Art Museum, across Lake Washington from Seattle in the state's most affluent population center. The museum, at the time situated in the Bellevue Square shopping mall, offered a capacious program, including exhibitions of

(top) Installation view of *The Philosopher's Wedding*, 1994,
*Drawings and Sculptures of Joseph Beuys/Contemporary
Inspirations,* Bellevue Art Museum, Bellevue, WA, 1994

(above) Installation views of *Mnemosyne's Alphabet*, 1993, Boise
Art Museum, Boise, ID

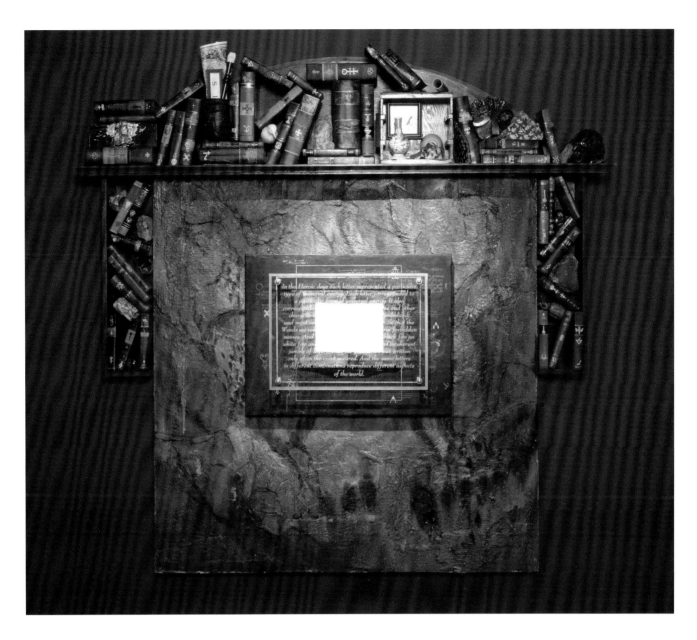

The Palace: Day Seven from *The Philosopher's Wedding*, 1994.
Encaustic, mixed media on canvas, 80 x 78 x 8 in. Collection of
Jonathan Loop

both discrete objects and installations, and was easily
accessible to the public. The artist accepted curator
Susan Sagawa's invitation enthusiastically and created
The Philosopher's Wedding, based on the writings of
another esoteric group dating from the late-nineteenth
century, the Rosicrucian Order.

"This way," the artist commented in a recent interview, "I was able to revisit the metaphysical theme of
the Union of Opposites, the Mysterium Conjunction,
which was an earlier motif in my *Chymical Nuptials
of Soma and Agni*."[16] Blending the mysterious and the
sacred, the Rosicrucian Order, which had a meeting
center in the Ballard neighborhood of Seattle and is
still active in Chicago, combines tropes of Christianity

with aspects of earlier thought and belief systems. *The
Philosopher's Wedding* was loosely based on a manifesto or myth of the order about "a young monk
who was invited to attend the wedding of a King and
Queen . . . and makes a seven-day journey to the palace," during which the reader grasps that the allegory
of the journey is the path to enlightenment and universal knowledge. Sagawa described the work in her
essay, adding that the Rosicrucian movement "has its
roots in the mystical traditions and philosophies of

ancient Egypt, Greece, China, India and Persia . . . [and] focuses on the enlightenment of humanity." Sagawa called Evans an "enchanter, creating a visionary mystical environment for our active participation in and experience of acquiring spiritual knowledge."[17] In these works, Evans explored his fascination with alternatives based on Christianity, such as Rosicrucianism. In this way, his systems and images imitate esoteric or heretical improvisations on Roman Catholicism or act as embroideries of its tenets.

With the floor plan and installation of components resembling those in Boise, ten large panels faced each other, representing stations of the path to enlightenment such as those the young monk might have encountered. Calling them "stations," as in Stations of the Cross, Sagawa noted a dividing trough of rock salt between them, punctuated at the end by *The Palace*, a metaphorical altar for the tale of the King and Queen, surrounded by toppled books and other objects.[18] Another component of the exhibition installation incorporated subjective, personal objects of the artist into the sculptures, much as the German artist Joseph Beuys used found objects and even live animals to support various anecdotes derived from his life experiences. Although we cannot disentangle which are which in Evans's work, the echoes of the arcane and unknowable recall Beuys.

Finally, Sagawa invoked another significant critic without whose insights our perspectives on Evans would be poorer. A leading art critic from the 1970s into the mid-1990s, Suzi Gablik, an art historian and art professor, wrote the books *Has Modernism Failed?* (1982) and *The Reenchantment of Art* (1992), which were widely influential in their proposals of non-formalist sources for innovation in contemporary art, such as religious systems and more obscure ideologies. Sagawa deferred to Gablik in the epigraph of her essay in *The Science of Secrets*, including a quote by her: "In the visionary mode, myths from all times and cultures

James McNeill Whistler, *Harmony in Blue and Gold: The Peacock Room*, 1877. Oil paint and gold leaf on canvas, leather, mosaic, tile, glass, wood, 166 x 241 x 404 in. overall. National Museum of Asian Art, Smithsonian Institution, F1904.61. Gift of Charles Lang Freer

(opposite page) Two views of *Contemplorium*, 2015. Mixed media. Collection of Thomas and Vicki Griffin.
This is a full room installation depicting history of the universe from the perspective of *Homo sapiens* as an author.

are available to us; we touch into a seemingly magical dimension from which emanates a sense of the mysterious and sacred; we have experiential access to the past or the future and the limitations of our cultural conditioning are transcended."[19]

While not exclusively, the term "visionary" is often applied to untutored, driven figures that are outside society's realm, hermetic, and unassociated with any established institution. The term is often used to indicate a variant of folk artist. None of this applies to Dennis Evans: highly educated, literate in several languages thanks to his Jesuit education, and participant in the contemporary art market and art museum system, he is, instead, commenting on visionary art—emulating or satirizing it, but not presenting it as a literal faith focus for devotees. It's all a metaphor, or a joke, or a yearning for the profundities of knowledge and existence. It is Evans's achievement that he summons up such analogies, but it is unlikely that such successive bodies of learning and explorations of existence, skewed as they often are, qualify as visionary in the customary sense of religious fanatic or

out-of-touch esoteric prophet. To illustrate this point: Morris Graves was called a "visionary," and with his lack of formal education and his wandering, lifelong attraction to occult religions, the term makes more sense. Graves's attraction to Eastern wisdom, for example, was hardly based on encyclopedic reading, but was more experiential, part of a youthful credulity that provided creative stimulus throughout his life. This is not the case with Evans; in comparison, he is a scholar, cold and detached.

Numerous other exhibitions were held in commercial galleries, few of which had the same all-enveloping, immersive character of the exhibitions discussed above. However, one totalizing environment for a private collector in Idaho shares the "environment of uncertainty" quality Sandy Harthorn claimed for Evans's work. *Contemplorium* was executed, not in an art museum, but in a private home, and combines the practical, the subjective and the metaphorical. A brief examination determines how a more intimately scaled environment could also underscore or stretch the notion of uncertainty.

Contemplorium was commissioned in 2018, created exclusively for a Seattle-area health care professional with a second home in Sun Valley, Idaho. Limited access turns the public character of Evans's aesthetic on its head, creating an individualistic environment for writing, reading and contemplation of the great works of Western philosophy, reflecting the wide scope of Evans's undertaking. As we shall see in Chapters 7 and 8, public-library settings inspired a large body of work meant to celebrate the democratic character of literacy and learning, especially those Evans created for the original Carnegie Library system in the Puget Sound area working with Nancy Mee. After his earlier undertakings, fraught as they were with stress, disagreements and compromise, the artist was given relative carte blanche to reengineer the interior of a room in the house.

The artist turned to three models from art history for this project: the private viewing chamber of Leonardo da Vinci (1452–1519); the private-collector viewing room of Isabella d'Este (1474–1539) in her castle at Mantua; and *Harmony in Blue and Gold: The Peacock Room* (1876–77) created by James Abbott McNeill Whistler (1834–1903) for Frederick Leyland (1831–1892), a British ship owner and art collector; this last epitomized Gilded Age ostentation with a display of priceless Asian blue-and-white porcelain. Purchased by Charles Langdon Freer (1854–1919) in 1904, and now housed in the National Museum of Asian Art, Smithsonian Institution (formerly the Freer Gallery of Art), *The Peacock Room* made the transition from highly private to highly public accessibility. D'Este's *studiolo* was a plush collector's hangout, while *The Peacock Room* was meant to show off to selected robber barons and fellow hyper-capitalists.

Evans was able to evade client interventions such as the one d'Este gave Giovanni Bellini (1430–1516): "some ancient fable with a beautiful meaning as subject." Bellini turned d'Este down—and she made a subsequent approach to Leonardo: "If we are gratified by you . . . you shall know that . . . we remain so obliged . . . we shall think of nothing else but to do you good service." Her *studiolo* was designed with several blank walls, all the better for the patron, who was then able to commission paintings from Pietro Perugino (1446–1526) and Titian (born Tiziano Vecelli; 1488–1576). The former's negotiations with Isabella carried on for over a decade.[20] The materiality and ostentation of d'Este's *studiolo* and *The Peacock Room* long outlived their commissioners, surviving in public collections to inspire Evans and many other artists and scholars.

Evans's *Contemplorium* is used as a writing room, summoning Sun Valley resident Ernest Hemingway's comment that "Writing, at its best, is a lonely life." As in d'Este's *studiolo*, the walls are lined with a series of custom-fitted, stretched canvases, alternating with glass-encased sections, some of which are engraved with passages of writing. Each part is an exploration of a different possibility for the origins and expansion of the universe, a theme that would be explored at greater length five years later in Evans's 2021 *The Cosmic Code: Ten Cantos*, a suite of ten sculptural paintings commissioned by Seattle University for its new Jim and Janet Sinegal Center for Science and Innovation (see Chapter 7). The existing quadripartite windows were exploited to accentuate the strong sunlight available in bright summers and snowy winters and allow the external world to surround, but not disturb the contemplator. A low band of changing stripes of color unites the wraparound series, setting off individual and collective celebrations of great thinkers, learners, teachers and philosophical masters in human history. Naming them with engraving and inscriptions, their books are stacked in nearby areas as protectors of the learning environment. A culmination in shorthand of the decade's work in public libraries, with all those trials and triumphs, was bolstered in Sun Valley.

Before examining his fruitful and mutually influential collaborations with Mee and others, it is necessary to preface Evans's contributions to a phenomenon pursued in Seattle in the late 1970s and early 1980s: the artist-design team.[21] Increasingly legislated across the nation, following the models of Philadelphia and Honolulu, the elevation of artists' status in the planning and decorating of publicly funded buildings, also known as "art in public places," transformed American civic architecture. The programs funded art with allocations from capital construction budgets, ranging from one-half percent (Washington State) to one-and-one-half percent (City of San Francisco) to be spent on art. Adept at juggling the performances, the installations and the gallery commitments, there was no reason for Evans not to take on the looming library commissions in the region, often in suburban buildings, and occasionally working with highly regarded local architectural firms. Evans would learn a lot from the library experiences, undertaken both with and without Mee. Most of the projects remain on view today, contributions to communities that express the artist's deep pedagogical urge to help young readers curious about the big questions that can be answered by entering a library: What is the nature of the world? How did the universe begin? What are the sources of human knowledge?

NOTES

1   Sandy Harthorn, "Mnemosyne's Alphabet," in *The Science of Secrets* (Seattle: artist's studio, 1994), n.p.
2   See Margaret Goldwater, "To be Looked at with one eye, close to, for almost an hour: Marcel Duchamp" (senior thesis, Reed College, 1971).
3   Evans, interview with author, October 25, 2021.
4   See Paul Hunter Rockhill, "Hans Robert Jauss's *History of Reception*" (master's thesis, Portland State University, 1996).
5   Ron Glowen, "Altered States," *Artweek*, September 25, 1982: 16.
6   Sue Ann Kendall, "Divergent Styles Mark Two Artists' New Shows," *Seattle Times*, September 18, 1982.
7   Bruce Guenther, *Documents Northwest: The PONCHO Series/Dennis Evans* (Seattle: Seattle Art Museum, 1985), n.p.
8   Guenther, *Documents Northwest: The PONCHO Series/Dennis Evans*.
9   Guenther, *Documents Northwest: The PONCHO Series/Dennis Evans*.
10   John Weber, *Northwest Viewpoints: Dennis Evans*. Portland, OR: Portland Art Museum, 1989, n.p.
11   Weber, *Northwest Viewpoints: Dennis Evans*.
12   Weber, *Northwest Viewpoints: Dennis Evans*.
13   Weber, *Northwest Viewpoints: Dennis Evans*.
14   Evans, interview with author.
15   Harthorn, "Mnemosyne's Alphabet."
16   Evans, interview with author.
17   Susan Sagawa, "The Philosopher's Wedding," in *The Science of Secrets* (Seattle: artist's studio, 1994), n.p.
18   Sagawa, "The Philosopher's Wedding."
19   Suzi Gablik, quoted in Sagawa, "The Philosopher's Wedding."
20   See my essay "The Hand that Feeds: The Artist and the Patron," in *Relocations: Selected Art Essays and Interviews*. New York: Midmarch Arts Press, 2008, 147–55.
21   For more about the design teams, see my essay "Artists on the Design Team: 3 Seattle Projects," in *epicenter: Essays on North American Art*. New York: Midmarch Arts Press, 2005, 57–80.

The Culture Bringer from *Imagine—After the Deluge*, 2008. Mixed media. Collection of Nancy Mee. This work was shown at Friesen Gallery, Ketchum, ID, and Woodside/Braseth Gallery, Seattle.

CHAPTER SEVEN

Dennis Evans and Libraries: Sites of Contested Knowledge

The origin of libraries, like the origins of speech and of writing, is not known. . . . A library is a collection of graphic materials arranged for relatively easy use, cared for by an individual or individuals familiar with that arrangement, and accessible to at least a limited number of persons.

—Michael H. Harris, *History of Libraries in the Western World*, 1995[1]

There shalt thou find the volumes that contain
All the ancient fathers who remain;
There all the Latin writers make their home
With those of glorious Greece transferred to Rome.

—Alcuin of York Cathedral, 778 AD[2]

PROLEGOMENON

At that time, it was also hoped that a clarification of humanity's basic mysteries—the origin of the Library and of time—might be found. It is verisimilar that these grave mysteries could be explained in words: if the language of philosophers is not sufficient, the multiform Library will have produced the unprecedented language required, with its vocabularies and grammars.

— Jorge Luis Borges, "The Library of Babel," tr. 1962[3]

In the short story of Jorge Luis Borges (1899–1986), the famed library in Babylon becomes a metaphor for a container of all the world's knowledge and he asks, "who has access to it?" So it is with the public art commissions in libraries by Dennis Evans, both on his own and together with Nancy Mee, as they constitute the artists' most important permanent installations. Building on his earlier installations in art museums and galleries, the library works use architectural space, but also draw on the contents of the buildings, that is, books. Simulated and constructed facsimile books, often made of glass, were used as modules in these public installations as well as subjects for installations that he did for galleries, in several cases, with Mee. While his sites are libraries, his constructed components within them represent the intellectual contents of the books. Evans's earlier installations dealing with the contents of books—ideas—now appear as trial or preparatory procedures in advance of the permanent installations in the library branches. For example, in the self-contained series exhibited in Seattle and

(above) Dennis Evans and Nancy Mee, *Prospero's Trivium*, 2016. Glass, porcelain and lead books, mild steel. Collection of Carl and Renee Behnke

(right, top) Installation view, *Writing Lessons/Reading Sessions*, 2002, Woodside/Braseth Gallery, Seattle. This work was also shown at Gerald Peters Gallery, New York, in 2003.

(right, bottom) Installation view, *Seven Libraries of Babylon*, 1997, Meyerson Nowinski Gallery, Seattle

New York in 2002 and 2003, *Writing Lessons/Reading Sessions*, words taken from books were inscribed on walls surrounding the sculptures.

Even earlier, Evans's *The Critique of Pure Writing* (1992) dealt with components of writing, calligraphy, inscription, cuneiforms and hieroglyphics that predated and predicted the written and printed word, i.e., books before the book. Similarly, his *The Seven Libraries of Babylon* (1997) and *Book of Hours* (1998) incorporate book imagery as well as texts related to their subjects placed above, below and upon their surfaces.

FLASHBACK INTERLUDE

Let me recite what history teaches. History teaches.

—Gertrude Stein, "If I Told Him, A Completed Portrait of Picasso," 1923[4]

Since much of Evans's art manages to shift us back and forth in time at an irregular and dizzying pace, let us briefly go back to the origins of his themes, the liberal arts—Grammar, Logic, Rhetoric, Music, Arithmetic, Geometry and Astronomy—but also the embryonic manifestations of libraries in the East, the Middle East and North Africa, chiefly Egypt. The evolution of libraries both private and public can be traced from Athens to Rome to Alexandria and northward. At

Laurentian Library Hall, Florence, Italy, 1523–71. Michelangelo, architect, with Il Tribolo, Giorgio Vasari and Bartolomeo Ammannati

Royal Library, Monastery of San Lorenzo de Escorial, Spain, 1584. Juan Bautista de Toledo and Juan de Herrera, architects

each stage of library development, the building and its contents threatened to become contested sites of civilization. After all, what is more crucial and empowering than the ownership of all knowledge? This was the main motive for Louis XIV's librarian and financial minister, Jean-Baptiste Colbert (1619–1683), whose expansion of the Royal Library in Paris to an enormous size corresponded with and underscored the king's power. And so on, for Juan de Castro (1510–1570), librarian of El Escorial, the monastic palace of Philip II of Spain, and, to the south, the Colombina Library of Seville, begun by Christopher Columbus's fourth son, Fernando (1488–1539).

These libraries were foundational, as were the noble-aristocratic collections of Florence, with Michelangelo's Laurentian Library perhaps the most famous there; Venice, with its incomparable hoard of Greek manuscripts; and Naples, which held preserved papyrus from Herculaneum after the eruption of Mt. Vesuvius. However, before the Age of Revolution, it took an English monarch, Henry VIII, to destroy the monastic libraries and Catholic-owned libraries of Britain. From the time of the theft of the library in Athens by the Persians, through the brutal censorship of Christian libraries by Romans and vice versa, and

the literary extinctions carried out in Moslem libraries of Spain under Isabella and Ferdinand of Castile, censorship and political jockeying for power have shown libraries to be important sites of contested knowledge.

The Age of Enlightenment brought the Age of Revolution; both spawned the intellectual confidence of the *Encyclopédie*, edited by Denis Diderot (1713–1784) and published 1751–72. It was an attempt at comprehensiveness in a single repository of knowledge, and reflected new ideas developed through science while subtly subverting religion. The concept of an object that would contain all knowledge was satirized by Borges in "The Library of Babel," in which his aging librarian-narrator proclaims to the reader: "It does not seem unlikely to me that there is a total book on some shelf of the universe. I pray to the unknown gods that a man, just one even though it were thousands of years ago!—may have examined and read it."[5]

The scale and immensity of the library presented in Borges's short story offer an allegory for a wealth of visual and conceptual material. In the case of Evans's personal library, he has at his disposal in his studio storehouse over 10,000 volumes, all to aid his

indefatigable scholarly research. The library, begun as a child in Yakima and expanded in 1975 in his Ravenna-Bryant-area home in Seattle, gradually grew to become the radioactive-live mental center of his studio practice.

Censorship is written between the lines in Evans—what to include, what to omit—as it was in and out of recorded human history before, during, and after the ascension of philosophical and political ideologies. The French Revolution degenerated into a thought-control dictatorship, but it was Napoleon who secularized all church-library holdings and centralized a bureaucracy of knowledge-locators for all French civilization that came to be known as the Bibliothèque nationale, or National Library of France.

Historical precedents for accessible libraries in the United States include carefully maintained monastic and regional history libraries in California during the Spanish Colonial period in North America, 1750–1850. Prior to the Spanish, the British in New England, chiefly the Puritans and Pilgrims, established private lending libraries beginning in 1643. We know that Miles Standish owned fifty books. The growth

View of original installation of *Themis' Alphabet*, 1996, Norm Maleng Regional Justice Center Law Library, Kent, WA

of adult male and female literacy in the United States in the late-eighteenth and nineteenth centuries gave rise to important lending facilities in Boston in 1745, Philadelphia in 1751, and the first children's lending library in Salisbury, Connecticut, in 1803. Federal and state-administered libraries flourished in the last half of the nineteenth century, accompanying the Industrial Revolution and the explosion of urban populations. University, vocational school and prison libraries also increased considerably.

Precedents and Innovations

Closer to the present, the construction of what came to be known as the Carnegie Free Libraries was funded by the industrialist Andrew Carnegie, beginning in Braddock and Homestead, Pennsylvania, in 1886 in an effort to provide an opportunity for self-education, an oblique way of trying to better the lives of workers, who toiled in the grim steel factories owned by Carnegie,

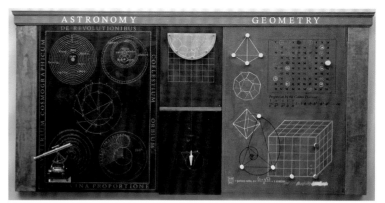

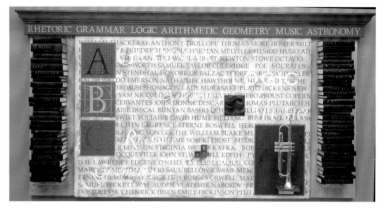

Installation view of *Grammar and Logic* from *The Seven Liberal Arts*, 2004, David R. Davis Reading Room, University Branch, Seattle Public Library, Seattle

(top) *Astronomy and Geometry* from *The Seven Liberal Arts*, 2004. Mixed media, 48 x 96 x 8 in.

(above) *Grammar and Logic* from *The Seven Liberal Arts*, 2004. Mixed media, 48 x 96 x 8 in.

and their families. The project expanded across the United States and continued until 1919, establishing 1,679 libraries across the country. Carnegie's literacy-focused philanthropy became his unimpeachable redemptive act.

Evans's Spokane Central Public Library installation (*Mnemosyne's Alphabet,* 1993), his first project in a library setting, was set in a Carnegie library. His other early public-art projects were not in Carnegie-funded buildings, but in post-World War II structures, such as Seattle University Law Library (*Eight Degrees of Separation*, 1994); the Norm Maleng Regional Justice Center Law Library in Kent, Washington (*Themis' Alphabet*, 1996); Port Angeles Library, Port Angeles, Washington (*Seven Pillars of Knowledge*, with Nancy Mee, 1998); and Auburn Public Library, Auburn, Washington (*Mnemosyne's Opus*, with Nancy Mee, 2000). Evans's later installations in Carnegie libraries (2004–5) engage in different ways the theme of

the seven liberal arts of the ancient world that were later revived during the Renaissance: Grammar, Logic, Rhetoric, Music, Arithmetic, Geometry and Astronomy.

Among the first library projects, *Themis' Alphabet* crystallizes the best aspects of Evans's increasingly important forays into art in public places. Not only is its subject site-related—an abecedarium of themes related to justice—but the assembly of its themes was the result of a decisive collaboration with a panel of attorneys, some of whom contributed accompanying texts to the glass-encased panels representing individual letters A to Z.[6]

The work's components were originally sited at the ends of long rows of bookshelves, with one letter affixed to each shelf-end, but the entire suite was relocated to a smaller space when the Law Library was

(top) Dennis Evans and Nancy Mee, *Mnemosyne's Opus*, encaustic and mixed media, 60 x 804 in. Commissioned by the Auburn Arts Commission and the King County Library System, 2000

(above) Detail of *Mnemosyne's Opus*

Details of the installation of *Mnemosyne's Alphabet I*, 1993, Spokane Public Library-Central, Spokane, WA

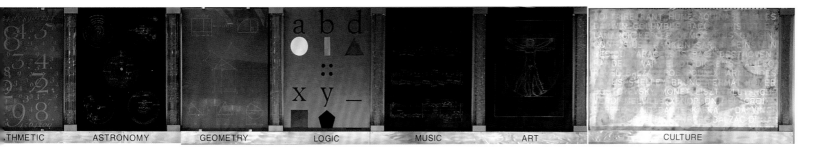

THMETIC · ASTRONOMY · GEOMETRY · LOGIC · MUSIC · ART · CULTURE

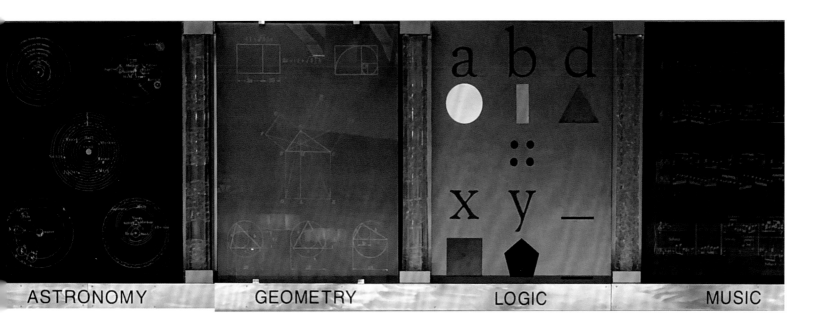

ASTRONOMY · GEOMETRY · LOGIC · MUSIC

(above) Installation view of *The Eight Degrees of Interpretation*, Seattle University Law Library, Seattle, 1994

(right) Detail of *The Eight Degrees*

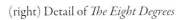

Dennis Evans and Nancy Mee, Maquette for *Seven Pillars of Wisdom*, 1998, for the Port Angeles Library, Port Angeles, WA. Photographs, sandblasted glass, fused and slumped glass, wood, steel. Collection of Seattle University, Seattle

relegated—thanks to digitization—to a smaller basement space in the same building. Remarkably, *Themis' Alphabet* can be read just as easily as before. Though, as a result of the move, some letters are isolated and others grouped, all are easily accessible, reinforcing the open-stack configuration of the parallel rows of bookshelves within the library. While commenting on another work by Evans, the artist Cameron Martin affirmed the relationship of Evans's insertions to the adjacent texts. According to Martin, the commentaries beneath each work in the Law Library "are not meant to explain the works but rather give the viewer a grounding to begin interpretation of this dense and expansive . . . work."[7]

CONTESTING THE LIBERAL ARTS

In their first important collaboration, Evans and Mee encountered not only a physically challenging space in a newly designed building in Port Angeles, Washington, a timber and fisheries center on Olympic Peninsula, but an engaged and surprisingly unhappy audience of library patrons and culture-warriors.[8] The entire process—hearings, threats, revisions, and compromises—attracted Internet attention and a pro bono offer from an Atlanta law firm, and risked becoming a poster child for the fourteen Christian

Port Angeles Fine Arts Center curator Jake Seniuk

Fundamentalist ministers in the small town who disapproved of the use of liberal-arts iconography derived from Greek mythology. Coming less than a decade after a horrific public-art showdown in the state's capitol, Olympia, when two artists, Alden Mason (1919–2013) and Michael Spafford (1935–2022), were forced to remove their previously approved murals, resulting in more unwanted national attention and glaring exposure of the increasingly degrading liberal/conservative divide within the state of Washington.[9] This was something Evans and Mee were determined to avoid at all costs. Fortunately, their defenders and articulate supporters were numerous, including in the media and on the library board, outweighing the objections of several pastors. Several who spoke on the topic at the meeting, including library board members, defended the use of Greek mythology; one held that the proposals are a "great symbol of a golden age." Another noted, "What we are seeing in the library is strictly mythology. . . . To say the muses are theological is stretching it." A self-described "strong Christian," Robert Coates insisted "they are part of our heritage. . . . I feel the muses are fit guardians for our library."[10]

Nevertheless, responsive to concerns, Evans and Mee shifted the emphasis from mythological figures to figures that connected to local indigenous traditions and bodies of knowledge. *Peninsula Daily News* reporter Brad Lincoln noted how, after the board approved the installation's nine panels over the vociferous objections voiced at the hearing, Evans and Mee did three things, proving that artists can be responsive to community issues by incorporating changes that reflect the interests of the community. They retained their basic subject of the continuity of human wisdom, they defended the contested site of a public library as an appropriate locale for commenting on the history of world culture, and they demonstrated the appropriateness of the liberal arts as a subject in a public setting dedicated to learning.[11]

The amended work was titled *Seven Pillars of Knowledge* and was dedicated in 1998. An exhibition honoring the two artists at Port Angeles Fine Arts Center, *Dennis Evans and Nancy Mee: Seven Pillars of Wisdom*, was curated by Jake Seniuk (1949–2016), who put the entire series of events into perspective with his essay on their art accomplishments and their integrity and ingenuity in their dealing with the library commission. Not only did he position their Port Angeles project in relation to their earlier achievements, his essay is possibly the best written about them by any museum curator: comprehensive, scholarly and insightful. Seniuk explained their decision to change the work despite the board's approval:

> Respectful of the Library Board's endorsement, yet greatly troubled by the cloudy atmosphere surrounding the project, Evans and Mee offered to further develop their proposal by unlinking their map of knowledge—which is the works' true content—from personifications such as the Muses. Choosing a more abstract metaphor, they called the new work the *Seven Pillars of Knowledge*. While similar in formal design, the reworked imagery presents the mission of the library with less ideological baggage, avoiding cultural associations grounded in any living

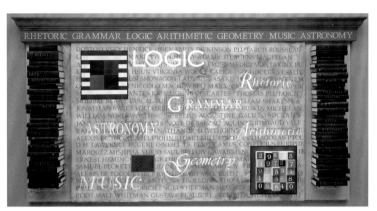

(top) *Grammar* from *The Seven Liberal Arts*, 2004. Mixed media, 48 x 96 x 8 in.

(above) *Logic* from *The Seven Liberal Arts*, 2004. Mixed media, 48 x 96 x 8 in.

religious heritage. The Library Board happily endorsed this revision in the fall in 1997, thus paving the way for the work's fabrication and installment.[12]

Comparing Mee and Evans, he appreciated how "Mee opens up space with delicate grace and formal simplicity, [while] Evans commands space with didactic structure and received lore."[13] Complimenting both artists on their solution to the library installation, Seniuk observed that with their *Seven Pillars of Wisdom*, "[t]he substitution of wisdom for knowledge also implies a less didactic mission and perhaps helps distinguish the public role of a library from that of an arts center.... Eager to expand the images and meanings of the Muses beyond the idiom of nubile maidens strumming harps, Evans

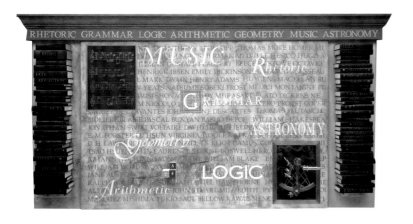

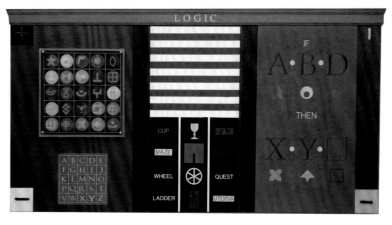

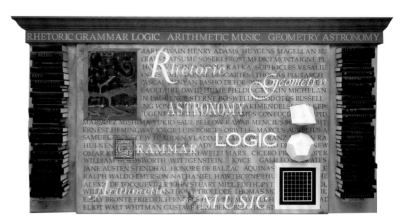

(top) *Music*; (bottom) *Rhetoric*, both 2004, from *The Seven Liberal Arts*. Mixed media, each 48 x 96 x 8 in,

(top) *Logic*; (bottom) *Astronomy*, both 2004, from *The Seven Liberal Arts*. Mixed media, each 48 x 96 x 8 in.

and Mee drew upon widely scattered world cultures for their interpretation of the theme."[14] The new elements included the Northwest Coast Kwakwaka'wakw Raven to replace Clio, the Greek muse of history and poetry, and Shiva, the Hindu god, who took the place of Terpsichore, the Greek muse of dance.

More than a decade later, in 2011, the installation of *Seven Pillars of Knowledge* was altered, this time materially. In its original state, seven glass squares representing Reason, Logic, Dance, Music, Ritual, Religion and Tradition were joined by ten etched rectangles representing Mathematics, Science, Linguistics, History, Information, Philosophy, Art, Humanities, Cosmology and Grammar. These comprised a wraparound frieze on the front and countertop of the curved reception desk. All of this was dismantled and placed in storage in 2011; the discrete elements remain

there with no plans for replacement. After good-faith actions on the part of the artists, it seems ironic that the removal of the works was the result of library administrators and architects' renovation plans, rather than religious zealots.

FROM ADVERSITY TO TRIUMPH

After the difficulties in Port Angeles, which were only abated by the shrewd professionalism of the artist-couple, their success at winning a competition from the Auburn Arts Commission and the King County Library System was gratifying. The solution for the new Auburn Library, *Mnemosyne's Opus* (2000) included a sixty-foot-wide expanse of plywood panels mounted with encaustic panels painted by Evans, each dealing with a different liberal art. Elevated above eight feet, these are separated by Mee's slumped, fused and etched glass columns that average sixty inches wide and six feet high. The columns provide transparent breathing spaces between the etched-glass panels, gleaming in the ample daylight that enters the main reading room. Almost unbelievably, when the structure was renovated in 2011–12, the mural was moved intact to an opposite wall where, if anything, it looks even better with additional daylight.

Library patrons are able to easily engage with the straightforward, didactic character of the individual components. For example, reading from left to right, there are sketches from the caves at Lascaux, France, the first cave drawings ever found in Europe, and signs of the zodiac, which conjure historical assumptions about the origins of the universe, a favorite topic of Evans. Hieroglyphs from Egypt fill the panel on Mythology. Panels for *Origin* and *Alphabet* present passages in classic calligraphic or italic lettering while the *Grammar* panel uses Roman capital letters. The *Arithmetic* section contains, of course, numbers. In the *Astronomy* panel, Evans and Mee have etched five early presentations of the Copernican solar system. *Geometry* combines overlapping Venn diagrams and equations from Euclid. In *Logic*, an imaginary problem uses the letters "A," "B," "D," "X" and "Y" to hint at a solution, while *Music* depicts a fragment of the musical score of a fugue by Johann Sebastian Bach. The final two panels, *Art* and *Culture*, are set on the far right of the wall. *Art* represents Western art with an image of *Vitruvian Man* (c. 1490) by Leonardo da Vinci, considered the ultimate symbol of the human-centered era known as the Renaissance. In *Culture*, phrases in various languages are depicted in Roman lettering as well as Chinese ideograms. Evans and Mee's most cohesive public artwork, *Mnemosyne's Opus* epitomizes the Greek muse of memory, Mnemosyne, in that each panel summons up memories of the history of humanity and its settlements on the planet, rich in allusions, appealingly colored, subtle and redolent of the learning that occurs daily within the library building. It constitutes the artists' greatest accomplishment in the public realm so far.

THE PHILANTHROPY OF LITERACY

There are forty-three Andrew Carnegie-funded public libraries in Washington State, with six still in operation in Seattle, King County. They were built in the early twentieth century, a period of progressive reform in the City of Seattle that also included bridge construction, highways and a park system, the 1903 plan for which was devised by the Olmstead Brothers, the son and stepson of the architect of Central Park in New York, Frederick Law Olmsted (1822–1903). With such foresight, the free public libraries funded by Carnegie were showcases of the city's expanding library system, offering a comfortable place for children and working people to read, learn and enjoy urban pleasures without interference or charge. This sensitivity to architectural preservation bore fruit in 2000 when famed Dutch architect Rem Koolhaas accepted the job of designing the City of Seattle's new (and third) Central Library. With the heritage of the Carnegie library architects W. Marbury Somervell (1872–1939) and Joseph S. Coté (1874–1957), Koolhaas and his firm OMA are already in welcome and distinguished company, including the precedents of Dennis Evans's artworks within five of the older buildings. Long-established One Per Cent for Art laws applied to the new Seattle Central Library, following a competition and garnering entrants and winners from all over the nation, including Ann Hamilton and Tony Oursler. Their work also sits in the context of Evans and Mee's prior breakthroughs with urban, suburban and regional libraries seeking to enrich the visual environments of library patrons.

Dennis Evans's proposal for public artworks for installation in multiple libraries during their 2004–05 renovation was approved partly because its nine panels were connected by the theme of the seven liberal arts; it was, in fact, titled *The Seven Liberal Arts* (2004).

(top) Exterior view; (bottom) interior view; both Fremont Branch, Seattle Public Library, Seattle

The Blethen family, owners of the *Seattle Times*, donated $500 toward the purchase of the land for the Queen Anne Branch Library.[15] The original architects, W. Marbury Somervell and Joseph Coté, provided a "Late Tudor" building for the system, later enhanced with a suite of five stained-glass windows (*Quintet*, 1975) by Richard Spaulding and Evans's paired paintings, *Grammar* and *Logic* (both 2004). Surrounding a gridded Roman alphabet are stacks consisting of a sphere, a cone and a cube on the one side and the letters "A," "B" and "C" on the other. *Grammar* is embodied visually: the jumbled surround suggests the disorder of language before the ordering of grammar. The geometric solids on the left recall the statement of artist Paul Cézanne (1839–1906) that all nature is reducible to the shapes of "the cylinder, the cone and the sphere."[16] The word "logic" is set in larger type, floating in white

above an array of words representing liberal arts and sciences and sheltered by stacks of books on either side. At its base is another grid, like a Rubik's cube or a colored numerical rebus.

Several blocks west of the University of Washington campus, the University Branch Library on Roosevelt Way Northeast features a diptych based on astronomy and rhetoric, two subjects taught at higher levels on the nearby campus.[17] Another stacked pile of the letters "A," "B," and "C" flanks the left-hand side of *Rhetoric*, with a real trumpet shelved on the lower right-hand side. Beneath the letters "A," "B" and "C," numerous names of famous writers appear as ghostly impressions on a white background. Authors who are represented in the contents of the library are thusly honored. *Astronomy* shows five models of the Copernican solar system, protected by an actual brass sextant and images of other star-gazing equipment. On the right-hand side are schematics of various geometric models, all of which are useful for calculating light years to distant stars.

Five miles northwest of the University Branch Library, the Green Lake branch faces the most picturesque of lakes within the city limits, in a residential neighborhood with a community swimming pool, tennis courts and boat rentals across the street.[18] There, *Rhetoric* has a bright red background, embellished by gold-framed ovals filled with inscribed mirrors. On the far left, the expansion of rhetoric is shown in a list of various styles of writing and speech: symbol, allegory, fable, poetic. Names inscribed on the red background are a mix of names, some drawn from mythology, others those of important cultural persons like Sigmund Freud. Seemingly disparate, the connections among them are left up to the viewer.

The West Seattle branch, also designed by Somervell and Coté in 1910, is the third of Evans's library renovation projects that feature series of sculptural paintings related to the contents of libraries.[19]

Installation view of Dennis Evans and Nancy Mee, *Sultan's Library*, 2011. Friesen Gallery, Ketchum, ID

Logic (2004) is radiantly colorful, visually pointing out how logic may be applied to numbers and words, shapes and categories; logic is the basis of all mathematics and analytical philosophy. A five-by-five-component grid of obscure signs and symbols hovers above a grid with the Roman alphabet stacked in rows. Over a blue background on the right-hand side, selected symbols and letters are reduced to an imaginary equation, similar to one that might become a logic problem ripe for solving.

The last Carnegie-funded library to be built in Seattle, the Fremont branch (1921),[20] was a replacement for the city's first branch library from 1903, and was designed by architect Daniel R. Huntington (1871–1962).[21] Seattleites are attached to their libraries and have consistently voted "yes" on funding initiatives. This enthusiasm is anecdotally explained by the city's reputation as one of book lovers and readers,

possibly due to the long rainy winters. The installation by Evans inside the Fremont library was commissioned at the time of the 2005 renovation by Hoshide Williams Architects. The work consists of two panels, *Arithmetic* and *Music*, with *Music* the more intriguing: it has a real violin attached in the lower right corner, floating beneath a black background with white musical notations reproduced from a score. Above that, on a dark-blue background, traditional musical-score fragments are accompanied by excerpts from avant-garde twentieth-century musical compositions, with accordingly different musical notations. To the left, in the companion panel, arithmetic reigns supreme, with related words and objects, including an abacus and a counting grid with Arabic numbers. Together,

Installation view of Dennis Evans and Nancy Mee, *Sultan's Library*, 2011. Friesen Gallery, Ketchum, ID

Installation views of Dennis Evans and Nancy Mee, *Sultan's Library*, 2011. Friesen Gallery, Ketchum, ID

they remind us how many musicians are also mathematically gifted, counting, calculating and memorizing countless formulae and musical notes. With them, Evans suggests the interrelatedness of all the liberal arts, no matter their diversity of approach or material substance.

CELEBRATING BIBLIOMANIA

The collaborations between Evans and Mee began before and continued after all the library jobs. However, the theme of the library—indicated with images of books, bookshelves, book-bindings, etc.— remained crucial for both, working separately and especially together on other series, nonpermanent installations, and two-person shows often related to imaginary libraries. For example, in their first collaboration, *Imagine—After the Deluge: Works from the 15 Masters of a New Utopia* (2009), for an exhibition at Woodside/Braseth Gallery in Seattle, the artists agreed on a theme, "who would be the essential characters to rebuild a utopia?, and created his and hers objects."[22] Each artist responded to a shared theme but made individual works that were displayed separately from one another. A year later, the couple repeated

the approach for Friesen Gallery in Ketchum, Idaho, with *Sultan's Library* (2011). There, they fastened on another capacious conceit, the delivery of books and objects to a fabulously wealthy ruler, and documented the project with another artist publication, part of a series the artist began in lieu of gallery- or museum-subsidized documents.[23] Dividing up the possible treasures ordered by the sultan, each artist created their own works of extraordinary beauty, and for the first time fully collaborated on a few works, such as *The Ouroboros* and *Double-Headed Serpent*, wherein the boxes are by Evans and the glassworks are by Mee.

Prospero's Library (2015–16) is the first of the artists' non-library collaborations to achieve a palpable balance of the artists' strengths and individuality, and a union of complementarities: smooth surfaces vs. rough, transparency vs. opacity, magic and science. The work presents the perfect analogy for the figure of the artist, and for Evans in particular, Shakespeare's legendary magician and scholar, Prospero. The hero of *The*

Installation view of *Prospero's Books*, 2016, Woodside/Braseth Gallery, Seattle

Tempest (1610) is marooned on an island, armed with only his knowledge of magical tricks—and the books in his beloved library. Cast-glass books were piled up, as if in the marooned magician's cave. *Mnemosyne's Opus* is widest of all in depicting a breadth of human learning, from panel to panel, interspersed with glass columns by Mee. If Auburn Library is the couple's most successful public-art collaboration, *Prospero's Books* (2015 as the installation was titled when shown in Idaho) and *Prospero's Library* (shown in 2016 at Woodside/Braseth Gallery), are their best nonlibrary collaborations. Both are documented in the *Prospero's Library*, a substantial publication, albeit one without a critical essay.[24] By this time, Evans seemed to be making up for diminishing reviews by writing his own explanatory commentaries in his publications.

Evans and Mee created a number of works with this theme, which now reside in collectors' homes

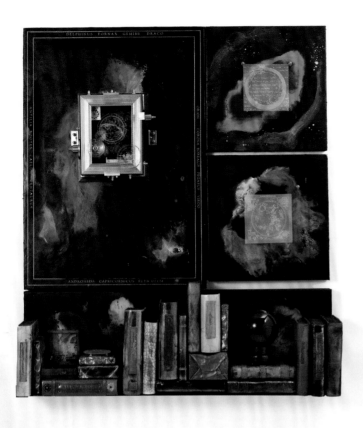

A Large Station for Constellations from *Prospero's Library,* 2016. Mixed media, 46 x 40 x 9 in. Private collection

from Ketchum to Seattle; the subject afforded them a successful, seamless fusion of their shared talents. After each exhibition, individual works were sold or dismantled to be returned to the studio. For example, in A *Large Station for Constellations* (2016), glass,

etched glass and porcelain book facsimiles by Mee share space effortlessly with Evans's paintings of the cosmos and framing enclosures. More stripped down and Mee-ish is *Bibliothèque des mythologies* (2015), which encloses her signature Classical-Venus head in a frame surrounded by eight frosted-glass books of varying sizes, complete with titles on their spines. *Prospero's Boat* is a see-through canoe, filled with pale white glass books and perched atop a metal stand. Here, we can see clearly both the division of labor and the fusion of concepts between the two. These projects took tremendous effort: there are a large number of works in the series, and the virtuosic handling of material in each sculpture or assemblage is impressive, as is the scale of some. A giant reading room, or shimmering antique bookstore, *Prospero's Library* affirms the words given to Miranda, the wizard's daughter, by Shakespeare: "O brave new world that has such wonders in't."[25] Mee and Evans's collaborations evolved as they created images of knowledge that allude to the past but also point toward a future—one that will not forsake the printed word or bound book. Library historian Michael H. Harris has characterized this moment, presenting a view in sympathy with that of Mee and Evans: "The problem is how to understand what is happening right now, as we all try to remain standing against the tidal

NOTES

1   Michael H. Harris, *History of Libraries of the Western World,* 4th ed. (Metuchen, NJ: The Scarecrow Press, 1995), 1.
2   Alcuin, quoted in Harris, *History of Libraries*, 102.
3   Jorge Luis Borges, "The Library of Babel," in *Labyrinths: Selected Stories & Other Writings of Jorge Luis Borges*, edited by Donald A. Yates and James E. Irby (New York: New Directions, 1962), 55.
4   Gertrude Stein, "If I Told Him, A Completed Portrait of Picasso," *Portraits and Prayers* (New York: Random House, 1934), 21–25.
5   Borges, "The Library of Babel," 56–57.
6   The topics that were selected with the panel of attorneys included Authority, Bigotry Divorce, Emancipation, First Amendment, Heresy, Insanity, Karmic Law, Liberty, Sedition, Verdict, Witness, Xenophobia and Zealot, among others.
7   Cameron Martin, in *Critique of Pure Writing* (Seattle: artist's studio, 1992), n.p.
8   Brad Lincoln, "Library's Art Fuels Debate," *Peninsula Daily News*, May 30, 1997: A1.

9   See my essay in the exhibition catalogue *Creating the New Northwest: Selections from the Herb and Lucy Pruzan Collection* (Tacoma, WA: Tacoma Art Museum, 2013), 17–31.
10   Lincoln, "Library's Art Fuels Debate": A2.
11   Lincoln, "Library's Art Fuels Debate."
12   Jake Seniuk, "Evans and Mee—Pillars of Wisdom—1988," *Strait Art: An Anthology of Exhibitions from the Upper Left-hand Corner* (La Conner, WA: Marrowstone Press and Museum of Northwest Art, 2019), 84–88.
13   Seniuk, "Evans and Mee," 88
14   Seniuk, "Evans and Mee," 86.
15   Queen Anne branch, 1910. 400 West Garfield Street. W. Marbury Somervell and Joseph Coté, architects. Listed on the National Registry of Historic Places and by the City of Seattle Landmarks Preservation Board.
16   Paul Cézanne, letter to Émile Bernard, April 15, 1904, in Herschel B. Chipp, ed. *Theories of Modern Art: A Source Book for Artists and Critics*. Berkeley: University of California Press, 1968, 18–19.

waves of traditional books and new media that are breaking over us. One vital point, and an easy one to miss, is that the Internet will not in fact bring us a universal library—much less an encyclopedic record of all human experience."[26]

Dennis Evans and Nancy Mee, *Bibliothèque des Mythologies* from *Prospero's Library*, 2016. Mixed media, 58 x 16 x 12 in.

17   University branch, Seattle Public Library, 1910, 5009 Roosevelt Way NE. W. Marbury Somervell and Joseph Coté, architects. Renovation in 2007 by Hoshide Williams Architects. Listed on the National Registry of Historic Places and by the City of Seattle Landmarks Preservation Board.
18   Green Lake branch, Seattle Public Library, 1910, 7364 East Green Lake Drive North. W. Marbury Somervell and Joseph Coté, architects. Renovation in 2004 by Snyder Hartung Kane Strauss Architects. Listed on the National Registry of Historic Places and by the City of Seattle Landmarks Preservation Board.
19   West Seattle branch, Seattle Public Library, 1910, 2306 42nd Avenue SW. W. Marbury Somervell and Joseph Coté, architects. Renovation in 2004 by Snyder Hartung Kane Strauss Architects. Listed on the National Registry of Historic Places and by the City of Seattle Landmark Preservation Board.
20   Fremont branch, Seattle Public Library, 1921, 735 North 35th St.

Daniel R. Huntington, architect. Renovation in 2005 by Hoshide Williams Architects. Listed on the National Registry of Historic Place and by the City of Seattle Landmark Preservation Board.
21   It is also the library where the author's mother received her first lending card, in 1932, not far from her home at the foot of Queen Anne Hill, just a walk across the Fremont Bridge and half-way up the hill to the new Spanish-style building.
22   Dennis Evans and Nancy Mee, *Imagine— After the Deluge* (Seattle: artist's studio, 2009), n.p.
23   Dennis Evans and Nancy Mee, *Sultan's Library* (Seattle: artist's studio, 2010), n.p.
24   Dennis Evans and Nancy Mee, *Prospero's Library* (Seattle: artist's studio, 2016), n.p.
25   William Shakespeare, *The Tempest*. Oxford, UK: Oxford University Press, 1996, 302. The quote is taken from Act 5, Scene 9.
26   Harris, *History of Libraries*, 292.

Garden of Souls, front entrance

CHAPTER EIGHT Utopian Heights: The Garden of Souls

As we trace the development of the art of Dennis Evans, much of our exploration involves probing beneath the surface of his images, many of which recur to reveal unexpected networks of meaning that aid in our appreciation. It is paramount to recall that enjoyment is an aesthetic goal. As such, all pursuits to decode, unravel and interpret what often appear as complex and inexplicable compositions can lead to enjoyment, partly in the satisfaction of arriving at a "solution," and partly to marvel at the often multiple attenuations of meaning the artist constructs.

After the public library projects, Evans and Mee were able to turn to one literally in their own backyard, a series of gardens and shrines inspired by a 1999 trip to Japan with close friend John Fairman, a widely respected Asian antiquities dealer. A classmate of Evans when both studied traditional Japanese-inspired pottery under Robert Sperry at the University of Washington, Fairman went on to open a Seattle branch of his parents' Hong Kong antique shop, Honeychurch Antiques. The store offered visibility and availability of fine traditional pottery and other *mingei* or everyday Japanese arts and became a constant site of visitation and homage for Seattle artists and collectors so inclined. Evans and Mee, whose Asian art collection expanded considerably in these years, responded

enthusiastically to the objects and, after their trip to Japan, their understanding of the original domestic settings of these objects grew. The Japan tour, taken together with Fairman, his wife Laurie, and collectors Christopher and Alida Latham, brought full circle the artists' years of visiting and studying Japanese and Chinese gardens on the West Coast, including many in British Columbia, Oregon and California. The experience of Zen gardens in Kyoto, for example, the fabled Ryōan-ji temple garden, proved critical upon their return, when Evans transformed the narrow lawn in front of their corner-lot house in the Ravenna-Bryant neighborhood of Seattle. Fenced in with a ceremonial gate and paved with flat stepping-stone paths, the couple's first garden balanced evergreen and seasonally blooming plants with areas that displayed appropriate garden objects, quietly climaxing with one of Mee's cast-glass and bronze sculptures.

It wasn't until the catastrophic events of September 11, 2001 that their horticultural impulses took on greater scope, involving community outreach as a response to the New York tragedy and a proffered gesture of healing. On the corner lot across the street to the south of their home, Evans and Mee acquired a small house with a backyard, which they turned into a meditation garden of sorts; they called it the Garden of Souls. The remaking of the backyard, complete

(top) Shrine in front of Utopian Heights Studios

(above) *Seasonal Sun Dial* in *Garden of Souls*

with rented bulldozer, had already been planned, but took on greater urgency after 9/11. Both artists felt the neighborhood's need for a quiet setting or repository of collective grief. Besides, Mee needed more outdoor exhibition space for her artworks that remained in storage or from her personal collection. After two months' work, the Garden of Souls was dedicated.

Mee's sculpture *The Lament* (1997) appeals for mercy and compassion with its upward-swinging "arms."

With the park open to the public and dedicated to the memory of the 9/11 victims, visitors were invited to write and deposit notes of sympathy or grief. Six months later, Evans, donning ambiguously priestlike attire, led a ceremony for everyone attending. A fire was lit to burn all 500 of the paper missives at once, thus pursuing another Asian custom: sending messages to the gods via conflagrations of inscribed notes.

While teaching part-time at Helen Bush School for fifteen years, Evans also worked as a helper to the school's head gardener Ed Simpson to make extra money. A decade later, Evans applied those skills to what became known as Utopian Heights, the place name an explicit nod to Queens, New York, artist Joseph Cornell (1903–1972), whose home was on Utopia Parkway.[1] Cornell is another previously unnoted influence on Evans,[2] both in their shared "shadow box" motifs of glass-encased display cases and in their frequent evocation of nighttime or dream-like states, a quality the French Surrealists particularly appreciated in Cornell's work when they discovered him while they were exiles in New York during World War II.

Utopian Heights has another, more local precedent, the turn-of-the-century plethora of socialist-anarchist communities that popped up in the Territory of Washington and later Washington State. Arising in towns named Home, Burley, Equality and Freeland, the communities became destinations for adventurers and losers before and after the failed promises of the Alaska Gold Rush of 1896–99. In addition, long before Alaska became a post-Gold Rush destination for those whose lives were flummoxed or ruined in the lower forty-eight states, Washington was the last word, with Seattle literally the end of the line of the Northern Pacific Railroad. It was appealing not only to those seeking to "get out of Dodge City," but those who also sought to fulfill a communitarian vision and

Garden of Souls, back garden with sculptures by Nancy Mee

spread good will through organized living systems or by forming a cult with little or no state interference. One by one, the early anarchist communities petered out, but their legacy inspired leftist communes as late as the 1960s and 1970s. Individuals sought instances of people coming together for healing, either therapeutic (hot springs) or spiritual (church camps). Evans, who became a de facto leader or self-appointed "mayor" of Utopian Heights, falls into this category. With the neighborhood's warm embrace of Mee and Evans's welcoming site of grief and healing, the artists also arranged small exhibitions in the corner house, which they had converted into a small private art gallery, both to display their own art under optimum lighting conditions but also to show the art of others who, in their opinion, had fallen through the cracks of the art market. These artists are Keith Beckley, Richie Kehl, and John L'Esperance.

The horticultural and spiritual rejuvenation project of Utopian Heights is a long-term venture. Several years were devoted by Evans to further replenishing the micro-neighborhood's green belt, before it became the subject of a widely read blog by Finnish horticultural columnist Liisa Wihman, *The Intercontinental Gardener*.[3] Evans made the extraordinary gesture of renovating a parking strip in 2002, planting a one-and-one-half-block-long sequence of dozens of non-fruit-bearing, flowering plum trees, *Prunus cerasifera* "Thundercloud." Supplementing the pink-blooming trees with smaller shrubs and North Dakota limestone garden stones, Evans set trees on both sides of the street, creating a dramatic spring canopy. Continuing one-half block south of the intersection at Northeast 62nd Street and 37th Avenue Northeast, the trees appear to form an endless procession when looking north or south during spring blooming season.

As for gaining permission for the city-owned parking strips to be altered, Evans's amelioration (given free to the city) was readily approved by the residents

Shrine in *Garden of Souls*

Garden of Souls in autumn

and the Parks Department, although it was followed up by two separate City of Seattle inspectors, whom the artist swiftly dispatched by explaining his purpose. They never returned. Homeowners were offered three years of free maintenance. With planting and watering guaranteed, the artist also inserted benches for contemplation and a number of bronze plaques set into the ground, cast with proverbs from nomadic Berbers of Morocco, such as "A permanent state of transition is man's most noble condition" and "The wise man changes his mind, the fool never."

It is worth noting another historical precedent for the double rows of plum trees, the gift of one thousand Japanese cherry trees to the City of Seattle by the Prime Minister of Japan in 1976 at the time of the US Bicentennial. Planted at the entry to Seward Park and along Lake Washington Boulevard South, the city's eastern perimeter road and five miles south of Utopian

Heights, the Boulevard was originally designed by Olmsted and Sons, heirs to the architect of Central Park in New York, Frederick Law Olmsted.[4] The Utopian Heights parade of pink blooming trees is not as long as the two-mile stretch on Lake Washington Boulevard, but it has a correspondingly civic purpose and celebratory impact when the trees are in bloom each April and May. They add a grace note to the city's annual Cherry Blossom Festival, albeit one visited by few but increasingly of international note.

Complementing the first shrine built in front of the house that contains their respective studios and living quarters and *The Lament*, the curved V-shaped shrine Mee created for the Garden of Souls across the street, Evans added an unusual variant of a sundial to the Garden in 2001. The demarcations of solstice and equinox are overlapped on the dial by eight "stations" of calendar events, rather than clock time. After the

Installation in progress at Auburn Library, with André Gene Samson, Dennis Evans, Nancy Mee, and Stephanie Schulz

inaugural ceremony for 9/11 victims in 2002 (with 200 people attending), periodic wish-burning ceremonies began to be held on cross-quarter days that take place around February 1, May 1, August 1 and November 1, each about midway between the solstices and equinoxes.

All this is complemented by cast-bronze and engraved-stone sayings. The sundial is another culminating piece for the artist, collecting recurrent themes of time, weather, the origins of the universe and planetary passages within the cosmos. Completed with the help of studio assistant André Gene Samson, the sundial soon became another popular quiet destination for neighborhood strollers. It also bookended the multipart project of Utopian Heights—landscape,

sculpture, real estate—that added to the broader visual vocabulary of the mini- or pocket-park program of the city. Unlike Evans's immersive art installations, one may experience the park subliminally, walking through or looking at it, without even knowing you are a part of a planned artwork, or *Gesamtkunstwerk*. A culmination of the collaboration of Evans and Mee, coupled with a growing interest in a kind of sustainable Earth Art, the geographically fragmented site of Utopian Heights perpetuates a shared vision of the future—sustained green growth—on an elegantly intimate, yet publicly accessible note. The world changes; seasonal passages recur. Art can reflect this verity, too, as Utopian Heights demonstrates.

THE STUDIO

Evans and Mee have separate studios within their home but share welding facilities and glass and ceramic kilns. Each became technically proficient at their craft as their art developed accordingly, building on skills learned since childhood as well as in undergraduate and graduate school. They refine material techniques in order to realize their respective ideas. With the help of a succession of studio assistants—part-time, full-time, and contracted as needed—Evans and Mee are able to undertake logistically complicated public-art commissions, alternating collaborations with individual commissions.

For example, Mee, who studied at Atelier 17, the fabled Paris printmaking studio of Stanley William Hayter, C.B.E. (1901–1988) in 1972, easily imagined how photographic images could be etched onto glass, a hallmark of her early work. The impulse to do so, however, grew out of her and Evans's shared interest in Classical Greek mythology, especially female deities like Aphrodite, goddess of beauty, which appears frequently in Mee's work in the form of *Venus de Milo* (150–100 BCE); the *Venus* is now considered to have

View of the studio with André Gene Samson with welding gear

been made by Alexandros of Antioch. Mee uses the *Venus* image to form a critique of traditional Western notions of female beauty; as she explained: "Classical Greek art was the Western idealized beauty, but I [in general] . . . take a notion, take it apart, and put it back together."[5]

Referring to their collaborative projects, such as the Auburn Public Library and the Port Angeles Library projects, Mee explained the breakdown of labor before the hiring of help: "If we applied together, it was because we thought our work would work together. . . . It would become a joint concept [in which] we would balance each other out. He would engineer things sometimes and we would build the models together."[6]

André Gene Samson, their longest-term studio assistant, came to them as a referral from Helen Bush School. First a student at Trenton State College in New Jersey, where he studied industrial arts and physics, Samson also taught at Bush School but, when he was suggested to Evans by a colleague, Meta O'Crotty, he joined the studio at an apprentice level, and learned as they went along. The three learned together, as the

artists' careers evolved at Linda Farris Gallery and then far beyond into public art. Samson reminisced: "I was able to join them permanently—half-time in 1990— eventually learning welding and doing all the metal fabrication for the substructures of Dennis's work and all the armatures and bases for Nancy's work. This was endlessly changing and refining because each job we would brainstorm. We know how to work together and talk things out."[7]

Expressing to Evans a desire to continue his own art as well, Samson was mentored by Evans, helping him assemble his portfolio at the rate of one project per week until Samson felt confident enough to apply to The Cornish School, Seattle's oldest art school. Founded by Nellie Cornish (1876–1956) in 1914 as an innovative, multidisciplinary school, it was originally called The Cornish School for Drama, Music, Dance. Martha Graham (1894–1991), John Cage and Mark Tobey all taught there. Samson received his Bachelor of Fine Arts in 1986. Samson was attracted to the ways in which Evans developed his art and aesthetics, offering this in an interview: "I was always interested in how creative Dennis is and how he took on a variety of interests in science, religion, philosophy, psychiatry, metaphysics and then used them all as a springboard for his visual vocabulary."[8]

On a more pragmatic level, Samson talked about working as a builder and facilitator to artists, saying "My philosophy of creating is you try to do the best with the tools at hand. How do we use what we have about?"[9]

Meditating on the considerable array of artistic projects the three had worked on together, both Samson and Mee shared their private responses to the controversy surrounding the Port Angeles Library project, thoughts they had withheld from the media at the time of the project and then again later, when half the library assembly was dismantled and removed. Samson commented on the couple's response to the

André Gene Samson

Nancy Mee

initial criticism and decision to redesign and construct a different piece, rather than risk a costly legal battle or, worse, a far-right hate campaign against them. Something similar had befallen Alden Mason and Michael Spafford in Olympia, when murals they installed in the State Capitol were taken down after state legislators complained they were inappropriate. In the case of the Evans and Mee's Port Angeles project, finding compromise with the community was the right thing for the growing studio to do at the time. Samson pointed out, "[t]hey were maturing as artists and we were maturing as a studio."[10] Samson also lamented that "It was so disheartening to me that people were so bitter and could have a lack of gratitude."[11]

Similarly, Mee applied some hindsight to the narrow theological framework of many of the library patrons, so unwilling to provide breathing space for historical representations of older belief systems other than Christianity: "At one point, they finally admitted their real agenda—they wanted Christ. . . . I wasn't going to quit. Dennis and I shared that, so we came up with something else."[12] The staff had strongly encouraged the artists to fight for their original plan. "They wanted to use us as an example on fighting censorship," Mee explained.[13] About the later, unpublicized removal of the etched-glass reception-desk plaques, Mee said that neither she nor Evans was ever informed of this act, which added insult to injury: "We did not know. I was shocked. What a cowardly act! Had they forgotten all the hassles we—and they—had gone through?"[14] There are no plans to restore the remainder of *Pillars of Knowledge*; the glass plates remain in storage in the building—in the basement, out of sight.

Another long-term, trusted studio assistant, Stephanie Schulz, was hired by the couple after they visited the undergraduate art studios at the University of Washington School of Art while Mee was teaching there temporarily. Describing herself as a "Jill of all trades," Schulz's work-time was divided between the projects of both artists, mornings with Mee, afternoons with Evans. Schulz worked on most of the public-library projects, including helping to install the library project in Port Angeles, and built canvas supports for Evans as well as cut metal for insertions over the painted canvas sections. Reflecting on the years she spent working with the couple, Schulz recalled: "The studio theme was familial, so alive. There was music, people passing through, cats, food. He's so kind and a natural teacher, a true art mentor. The whole environment was inspired. With Dennis, it was part minimal, part maximal. Their creativity and energy—it was so amazing to be a part of that."[15]

THERAPEUTIC STRATEGIES

The common fate of many public art projects is a much prolonged process, often taking place over a span of several years. In 1986, Evans was rewarded with one that, at first, might have seemed indeterminate and unending. Instead, it has proved to be the perfect match of artist and client, which has led to a large group of assemblage-paintings and continued well into the twenty-first century.

Formed by Dr. Howard Maron, MD² is a respected and successful purveyor of "direct primary care medicine," also known as concierge medicine. Evans was contacted in 1996 by the founders to devise and execute paintings for their first offices in Seattle. To be approached and offered such a commission was one of the most gratifying events of the artist's career. He instantly knew what he wanted to do, to create a suite of paintings called *The Structuration of the Anthropos*. Twenty-some years on, the suite has grown in size to nearly forty paintings, spread across installations at the firm's twenty offices. Already familiar with medical terminology and human biology thanks to his pre-med studies at University of Washington in 1966–69, Evans proceeded to create individual paintings for shared public spaces in the new MD² offices, which eventually opened in states as far-flung as Washington, California,

Illinois, Oregon, Wisconsin, Texas and New Jersey. Envisioning a multipart project united by the theme of the human condition, Evans seized the opportunity to make a deep exploration of different aspects of what he deemed the "mind-body-spirit" construct, drawing on historical sources of anatomical and medical illustration. Each is an encounter with an episode in the history of ideas about the human body, transformed into a tableau at once visually appealing and intellectually challenging, like a rebus puzzle or symbolic pattern. With this project, Evans has been able to reiterate his belief that the "function of a real artist is to touch people's lives."[16] In the MD² paintings, a panoply of fascinating biophysical formulae are wedded to representations of ancient and antiquated medical tools, cast into high relief by the state-of-the-art technology used in the firm's concierge clinics. Evans's structures of humanity stretched the limits of his imagination, offering him the task of an extended examination of the widely held Western view of the links—and the splits—between consciousness and body. The idea of the body's duality is closely associated with French philosopher René Descartes (1596–1650), whose dictum, "Cogito, ergo sum" (I think, therefore I am), was reinforced for centuries by European scientific convictions. With the artist intent on allowing the widest possible spectrum of expression, he introduced a controversial, non-Cartesian element, "the spirit." Unseen, undocumentable and therefore unknown, Evans posits that the term "spirit" (not soul) could cover areas of human experience that we are still unable to fully explain, refuting psychological explanations of deep trauma or undetectable neurological phenomena. This leaves the paintings open-ended—for patients, doctors and viewers. As usual, Evans has presented the viewer with more than he or she could possibly take in at one viewing, hence the significance of the permanent sittings at MD² treatment sites. Patients who return will guess anew at each exposure to the artwork. While

the paintings focus on humanity, medicine is the *locus solus* for the entire suite, with all its own uncertainties, despite the breakthroughs in treatment of chronic diseases, for example. To improvise and ornament medicine's long history, dating back to prehistoric injuries and remedies, Evans demonstrated his greatest command over multiple subjects, embracing contradictions as well as celestial harmonies.

Neo Vatikan Press

The poet and educator Carmine "Chick" Chickadel met Dennis Evans while both were teaching at Helen Bush School. They agreed in 1990 to collaborate on a series of artists' books that matched art with poetry and prose. These would be published by their new firm, Neo Vatikan Press, the title a take-off on the Holy See's policy of conferring *imprimatur*: approving, monitoring and, in some cases, banning or forbidding works of literature. Turning the concept on its head, the pair

(top) View of painting installation at MD², Dallas

(above) View of painting installation at MD², San Francisco

(top) Dennis Evans and Carmine "Chick" Chickadel

(above) Dennis Evans and Carmine Chickadel, *Dark Matter*, 2015. Limited edition artist book

describe the press as "Specializing in Topics of Arcane Interest," thus tapping into the artist's lifelong theme of off-beat versions of the divine and the poet's great curiosity about the unseen world.

Both shared sterling Roman Catholic primary and secondary educations. Chickadel, who was rapidly developing his poetry and publishing it in important magazines like *Paris Review*,[17] *Signs of Life, Prosodia* and *Philadelphia Poets*, saw the partnership as mutually beneficial. Educated at the University of Delaware, where he majored in English, and at the University of Montana, where his graduate degree was in interdisciplinary studies, Chickadel published a collection of his

poetry, *Houdini Right Where I Want Him*, in 2016.[18]

From the beginning, Neo Vatikan Press did not conform to conventional expectations of artists' books, i.e., handmade, hand-bound, and hand-set type, but played off aesthetes' notions of fine illustrated books. Working with commercial printer David Bethlamy of Atomic Press and Sheila Coppola of Sidereal Fine Art Press, the books, boxes and pamphlets combined poetry, prose and images relating to Evans's art. Computer software was employed for layouts, typesetting and graphic design, and the results were smooth and slick, rather than homemade or rustic. The closest art-historical precedents for Neo Vatikan Press's productions are the boxes and books by Fluxus artists such as George Brecht (1926–2008), George Maciunas (1931–1978) and others. In Neo Vatikan Press's *Thaumaturgy* (1999), for example, four containers and one folder encourage the reader to "take the ingredients before you and perform your own marvelous wonders by assembling the poems and images."[19]

Founded, according to the artist and the poet, "to produce unique and collectable [*sic*] collaborative work in limited numbers," Neo Vatikan Press has thus far produced five major publications, beginning with *The Seven Deadly Sins* (1990), a "fresh view of old evils." A companion volume, meant to be boxed together, *The Seven Cardinal Virtues* (1991), challenged readers to create their own order or sequence of virtues: "The order in which these words are to be read is always different and is signified by the numbers at the bottom of each page."[20]

Thus, the primary purpose of a book—to be read—is subverted into an audience-response activity—not just reading, but actually controlling or playing with word order and hence able to perpetually determine shifts in meaning.

Following *Thaumaturgy, The Canticle of Hours* (2000) was inspired by the exhibition catalogue *The Book of Hours*, published by the artist the previous year. *The Canticle* is a limited-edition folio of prints and poems that pays homage to illuminated manuscripts that chronicled daily court life and activities in medieval France. In *The Canticle*, Roman Catholic-prayer occasions are blended with images inspired by Buddhist devotional practice and the astrological zodiac, turning the "eight divisions of the day for prayer" into a vehicle for combining other religious stimuli with meditation and prayer. It is another example of Evans's growing attraction to world mythologies, an umbrellalike metaphor that welcomes all forms of divine worship.

With *Dark Matter* (2015), the series reached a culmination, both in its elegant design—loose pages in a somber gray mild steel folder—and in its hint at the current direction of the artist's practice: uncovering and examining the origins of the universe; in this case, black holes, the possible end of one world and the beginning of another. As the promotional brochure for *Dark Matter* explains: "Dennis and Chick broaden the concept to include not only the science but also its convergence with the complexity of humanity. . . . The images, poems and fundamental words placed on the page develop layers that make meaning. All matter dark and visible entices us to question what matters."[21]

CINTAMANI AND *THE COSMIC CODE*

Nature that framed us of Four Elements,
Warring within our breasts for regiment,
Doth teach us all to have aspiring minds.
Our souls, whose faculties can comprehend
The wondrous architecture of the world,
And measure every wandering planet's course,
Still climbing after knowledge infinite,
And always moving as the restless spheres . . .

—Christopher Marlowe, *Tamburlaine the Great,
Part the First*, 1590[22]

This excerpt of Marlowe's poem was quoted as a back-cover inscription for the booklet *Cintamani: Dennis Evans, Works from 2010 to 2018* (2018). It synthesizes beautifully the type of imagination that runs throughout two bodies of work dealing with origins of the universe depicted in religion and science, which are visually reconceived by the artist. As the Renaissance poet pointed out, God gave us minds to understand the world and added the new science of astronomy to assist in such searches. The publication chronicles a commission the artist executed for University of Washington Medicine's Karalis Johnson Retina Center, at the South Lake Union campus in Seattle. It proved to be a fully realized preparatory study for another work at an institution of higher learning, Seattle University's Jim and Janet Sinegal Center for Science and Innovation, *The Cosmic Code: Ten Cantos* (2021).

In *Cintamani*, dark matter celebrated in the Neo Vatikan Press publication of the same title is further explored. The wall-mounted objects present a close-up juxtaposition of painterly elements, sculptural additions and allusions to outer space in all its permutations. At the same time, references to global cosmologies are summoned to portray the multiplicity of explanations for how the world began—and how it might end. For example, though the publication lacks a critical essay or any publication data whatsoever, an unsigned foreword written by Evans clarifies his ecumenical viewpoint somewhat: "Cintamani is a wish-fulfilling jewel within both Hindu and Buddhist traditions, said by some to be the equivalent of the Philosopher's Stone in Western alchemy. In Tibetan Buddhist tradition, the Cintamani is sometimes depicted as a luminous pearl, or perhaps the object of man's continuing quest to understand the World."[23]

The twenty assemblage-paintings, five of which are at the Karalis Johnson Retina Center, are literally the artist's darkest compositions to date, integrating imaginary inventories of space rocks and mineral

Dark Matter, 2019. Encaustic, mixed media, raku-fired porcelain objects, 60 x 60 x 8 in. Collection of the artist

samples and documents dealing with how the world began, another extension of the artist's love of books and libraries as repositories of contested human knowledge. Richly textured backgrounds of black, gray, blue and green paint comprise the infinite latitudes of space, windows onto a perilous and uncertain outer world. Various explanatory approaches are honored, such as in *Alchemy: The Philosopher's Stone, Hebrew Mysticism: The Tree of Life* and *Literature: The Western*

Canon. The Western canon or so-called "Great Books," under increasing assault by social and cultural critics, contains centuries of utopian and dystopian chronicles as well the roots and evolution of science fiction and fantasy literature.[24] Using an institutional, academic literary canon as an origin source lifts the products of imaginative narrative onto another evolving, constantly shifting and unstable plane, far from the certainties of fixed literary-canon proponents, such as those espoused by Yale University professor and critic Harold Bloom.[25] Taken together, they set the stage for a larger, longer, more ambitious examination of such questions as "How did the world begin?" and "How will it end?"

The expression of these questions and some proposals for their fulfillment in Evans's *The Cosmic Code: Ten Cantos* attains a fusion of creative and theoretical brilliance. It is situated perfectly in the setting of the Seattle University building, where students not only experiment with materials and ideas, but engage in deep learning and explore underlying questions of science and to understand how seeking answers can support technological and scientific breakthroughs. The modest disclaimer of Sir Isaac Newton (1642–1727), "If I have seen further it is by standing on the shoulders of giants," easily applies to *The Cosmic Code: Ten Cantos*, a suite of sculptural paintings. The giants referred to are the founders of physics, astronomy, alchemy, cosmology, philosophy and art, several of whom are the dedicatees of the *Cantos*, the texts of which are available via a QR code accompanying each painting. Cantos are sections of long poems or epic narratives; a three-line rhyming-verse form was popularized by Dante Alighieri (1265–1321) in *The Divine Comedy* (1308–20). Evans's *Cantos* texts are celebrations, explanations, pedagogical tracts and lists of related events and names that offer a parallel to the material presence of the *Cantos* paintings with their paint, porcelain, minerals, precious metals, wood, cloth and even a highly visible live electrical charge that continuously simulates miniature lightning bolts in *Canto II*.

Arriving as an undergraduate student at SU in 1965, Evans benefited from a continuation of his

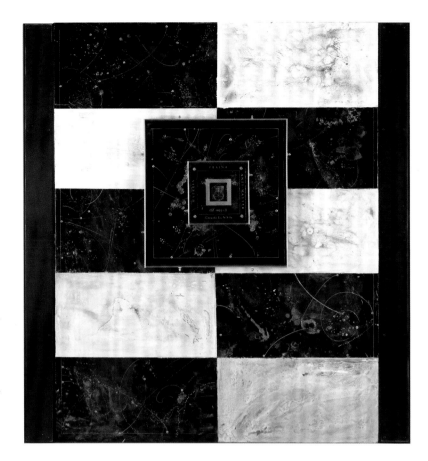

LHC, from Collider Series, 2020. Encaustic, mixed media, 60 x 60 x 8 in. Collection of MD², Seattle

education by Jesuits. With strong grounding in Latin and French, he was able to read the classics, although he determined early on to major in chemistry. In a similar way, the artist blends styles and genres and images and objects, activating his wide knowledge of the birth of European science and art. Science and art are intertwined in *The Cosmic Code* to create a summation of all his earlier work—from ritual performances to room-size installations to multipart objects—and bring full circle the studies begun on campus to culminate in structures that reflect scientific research, experimentation, and innovative applications.

No less than the origins of the universe are depicted by the artist in the ten glass-fronted boxes that emulate both Renaissance curio cabinets and Victorian funerary and treasure display cases. Symmetrically placed objects, such as mineral samples, may stand for fragments of the origins of planets, recalling the

Kunstkammer and *studiolo* as well as the curio cabinet. At each picture's base, a timeline is marked with the names of those whose theories and discoveries pushed human knowledge forward. The *Cantos* trace scientific inquiries and the imaginaries they inspired up to present-day awareness of "black holes," even suggesting the possibility of cosmic activity after the inexorable drive to the end of our own solar system.

While profound ideas and questions come to mind—What did the universe look like at the beginning?—an equally pleasurable experience can occur optically, just by looking closely. Surrounded by golden reader boards with pertinent words and names, the imagery of each painting is rendered in the color of a world that is forming before our eyes (for example, midnight blue in *Canto III*). "Samples" are mounted on shadow-box shelves, echoing the apparatus and atmosphere of the first scientific laboratories and specimen collections of flora and fauna. Appropriately, in *Canto V*, Charles Darwin (1809–1882) is quoted in the accompanying QR code text. The dawn of humanity and other events in human history from *Australopithecus* ("Lucy") to *Homo sapiens* are referenced on the side frames of the *Canto V* painting and Evans's title, "Reflective Consciousness," is at its base. To underscore and extend the idea of humanism, at the center of *Canto V* is a drawing engraved on glass of Leonardo's *Vitruvian Man*, considered the ultimate symbol of the Italian Renaissance, representing the centrality of humankind in the world.

Before its applications, there was just theory. *Canto VI*, which Evans titled "Theory Epoch," references a long period in time—14,000 years ago to the present—during which significant theories of cosmic origins, communication, philosophy and biological evolution arose. Exquisite charred and glazed porcelain books that represent the works of great thinkers—Nicolaus Copernicus (1473–1543), Galileo Galilei (1564–1542), Newton, Einstein)—are mounted over

Setting out on a Journey, illustration from *Splendor Solis,* German manuscript, 1582. British Library. Reproduced in Joseph L. Henderson and Dyane N. Sherwood, *Transformation of the Psyche: The Symbolic Alchemy of the Splendor Solis* (Hove, England: Brunner-Routledge, 2003).

a marbleized background. Enrico Fermi (1901–1954), Heisenberg, Ernest Rutherford (1871–1937), and Max Planck (1858–1947)—all Nobel medalists—are duly enshrined in inscriptions at the base of *Canto VI*.

As Evans metaphorically circumnavigated the planet, investigating how the sky and earth would look from high above to inform his representations, he continued constructing his pantheon of hunches, flops, and breakthroughs that have constituted much of twentieth-century physics. Thanks to the breakthroughs of the early professors listed above, humankind could better contemplate visiting and returning from above the earth's atmosphere; these investigators are the Discoverers of *Canto VII*. Beyond the moon, the Hubble Telescope extended a grasp into the formerly

Garden of Souls with sculpture by Nancy Mee

unknowable or un-seeable. The question posed by *Canto X*, the most haunting and magical of all these intimate visions, is the one that confronts the gigantic, unfathomable scope of the universe and the challenges of how to understand, encompass and depict it. Feeding an interest first piqued by his awareness of the confirmation of the existence of the Higgs boson particle, the subatomic-wave particle that completed the Standard Model of particle physics, Evans posited a view of the future of the universe with a shimmering mineral-encrusted panel of unknown fragments that flickers with life. He asks the question: will the universe continue to expand infinitely or will it compact into nothingness? From *Canto I* to *Canto X*, *The Cosmic Code* opens the viewer's world to discussion, contemplation and the aesthetic pleasure of sculpture and its expansive capacity to materialize deep meaning.

EPILOGUE

A word about the title of this book, *Apocrypha: The Art of Dennis Evans*. The word is from ancient Greek and is used to refer to books of the Bible that were rejected by Catholic Church councils and, more importantly, Anglican and Lutheran Churches of the Protestant Reformation in 1647.[26] The growth of Protestantism and its use of the Bible without the apocryphal books had widespread influence. The relevance of it as an analogy to the career of Dennis Evans rests on the history of its debate and its correspondence with Evans's acceptance, curiosity about and dismissal of the canons of art history and art criticism. While Church fathers did not question the sincerity of the writers of the various apocrypha, their theological opinions led to sidelining of well-known texts and stories. A useful term for this volume's exploration of Evans's art, "apocrypha" might also be applied to the vacillating acceptance and rejection embedded in critical observations of and opinions about the artist and his work, as we have seen in Chapter Five on the rise and fall of his critics. And, just as the Apocrypha challenged theologians, Evans undermined and subverted traditional expectations of performance as art and the definitions of sculpture and assemblages.

It is worth revisiting briefly a few cardinal moments and stages of development in Evans's oeuvre, partly in summation and partly in an attempt to encourage further discourse and analysis of his art.

Evans undermined and subverted traditional expectations of sculpture and assemblages. His insistence upon layers of content emerged out of his studies at the University of Washington School of Art, where he received not only a Marxian indoctrination, but a Marckian one, too. It was his follow-up to Jan van der Marck's seminars on Alfred Jarry that led Evans to the world of postwar and contemporary European art, extending far beyond familiar American innovations such as Abstract Expressionism into practices closer to theater. Over the course of a decade, Evans's sculptures and musical instruments evolved into theatrical props for peculiar, fascinating live events involving a wide range of influences, from Japanese folk art to medieval alchemy. The events, some up to twelve hours in length, resembled a distorted recapturing of childhood experiences as an altar boy, repeatedly pointed out by both his earliest critics and champions.

Gradually, the performances and concerts were superseded by more elaborate sculptures and assemblages, as if they were the remnants of the Passion plays and other outdoor theatrical forms, with Evans and performers wearing the sculptures and acting upon their functional properties. Separate from the live events, the sculptures attained an autonomy of their own. Later, Evans incorporated them into elaborate gallery and museum installations, combining them

with other objects fashioned from porcelain, wood, metals and minerals. With this body of work, the artist attained the devoted attention of several contemporary art curators on the West Coast and elsewhere.

After the considerable successes in New York, including the 1979 Whitney Biennial exhibition, Evans weighed moving to New York to continue on a substantial but risky path. He decided to remain in Seattle and sustain New York's interest in his work from a distance; that early interest eventually waned. Taken up by other art dealers, collectors and museum curators, the artist and his wife, Nancy Mee, decided to explore collaborating on art projects in public places, especially public libraries. These proved to be a highly respected and appreciated series of installations comprising paintings and etched glass panels in libraries across Washington State. Thanks to the artists' determination and persistence against the odds when confronted with bigotry and anti-intellectualism, the overall undertaking enjoyed enduring success. The library projects were perfectly matched, as it turned out, to both artists' dedication and commitment to the basic achievements of Western civilization, an underlying theme in this body of work.

With the accomplishments and trials by fire of the public-library commissions, Evans was well equipped to proceed with other projects, both for-profit and non-profit, and often accompanied by community-outreach activities. The remarkable contribution of Utopian Heights, a cumulative construction of residence, landscape, studios, exhibition area, shrine and outdoor meditation areas, is grounded in a belief in the therapeutic properties of gardens, the earth and seasonal passages. Its benefits to neighbors and visitors bring the artists' persistent efforts to understand the world in all its manifest operations full circle. The artists' deep interest in humanity, its history, its belief systems and its exploratory investigations have been evident in every phase: from the artists' close-knit

community in graduate school and the early Linda Farris Gallery years to the present moment. Inside the studios at Utopian Heights, Dennis Evans and the other artists quietly explore the mysteries of the universe, pursuing new insights not as latter-day Galileos, but as individuals who are convinced that representing

Dennis Evans with sled and instruments at twilight, 1977

such visions in the materials of the artwork and its environs is the way forward.

NOTES

1   See Deborah Solomon, *Utopia Parkway: The Life and Work of Joseph Cornell* (New York: Other Press, 2015).

2   Dennis Evans, interview with author, November 9, 2021.

3   Liisa Wihman, "The Garden of Souls in the Utopian Heights Neighborhood," *The Intercontinental Gardener*, May 3, 2011. http://www.intercontinentalgardener.com/search?q=utopian+heights.

4   Olmstead developed the Central Park project in partnership with Calvert Vaux (1828–1895).

5   Nancy Mee, interview with author, November 9, 2021.

6   Mee, interview.

7   André Gene Samson, interview with author, November 9, 2021.

8   Samson, interview.

9   Samson, interview.

10   Samson, interview.

11   Samson, interview.

12   Mee, interview.

13   Mee, interview.

14   Mee, interview.

15   Stephanie Schulz, interview with author, December 12, 2021.

16   Dennis Evans, interview with author, November 30, 2021.

17   Carmine Chickadel, "Tangles," *Paris Review* 101 (Winter 1986).

18   Carmine Chickadel, *Houdini Right Where I Want Him* (Seattle: Stapler Place Press, 2016).

19   Neo Vatikan Press promotional catalogue.

20   Neo Vatikan Press promotional catalogue.

21   Neo Vatikan Press promotional catalogue.

22   Christopher Marlowe, *The Plays of Christopher Marlowe* (London: Dent, 1912), 83.

23   Dennis Evans, *Cintamani: Dennis Evans, Works from 2010 to 2018* (Seattle: artist's studio, 2018), n.p.

24   A curriculum was developed by John Erskine at Columbia University in 1921 to encourage reading and discussion of the "great works of Western civilization" as the basis for a liberal education, later picked up by professors at the University of Chicago and other institutions.

25   Harold Bloom, *The Western Canon: The Books and School of the Ages* (New York: Harcourt Brace & Co., 1994).

26   Elaine Pagels, *The Gnostic Gospels* (New York: Random House, 2012), 16–22.

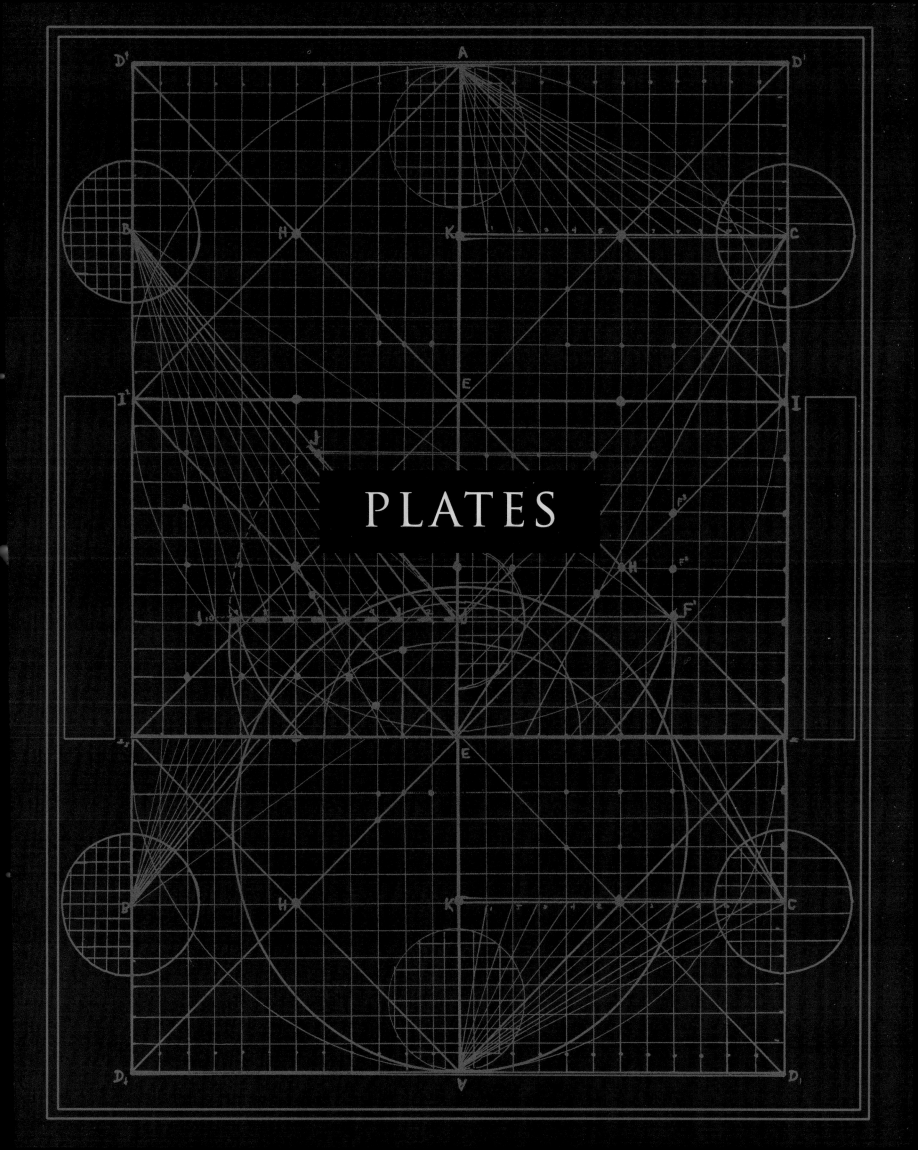

PLATES

№1 PERFORMANCES

NATURE STUDIES

SOUND STUDIES

A PASSION PLAY

FIELD US(E)AGES

MUSEUMS

First performance by Evans: Dennis Evans aka Ubu Waugh performing
Moon Bowl with Bow and Bar, Evergreen College, 1976

NATURE STUDIES

In 1975, Evans, performing as Ubu Waugh, began a series of outdoor performances ranging geographically from Seattle to Central Mexico. Incorporating natural elements such as water, fire, ashes and various assortments of seeds and fresh foliage, he created myth-inspired actions, on the isolated beaches of Mexico and open fields of urban Seattle. To facilitate his performances, he created beautifully crafted lacquered boxes and floating sleds to contain and transport his instruments and various paraphernalia to the beaches, ponds and marshes he frequented.

Dennis Evans in performance at University of Washington Center for Urban Horticulture, Seattle, 1976

Dennis Evans in performance on Los Muertos Beach,
Sayulita, Mexico, 1977

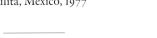

Dennis Evans in performance at University of Washington Center for Urban Horticulture, Seattle, 1976

SOUND STUDIES

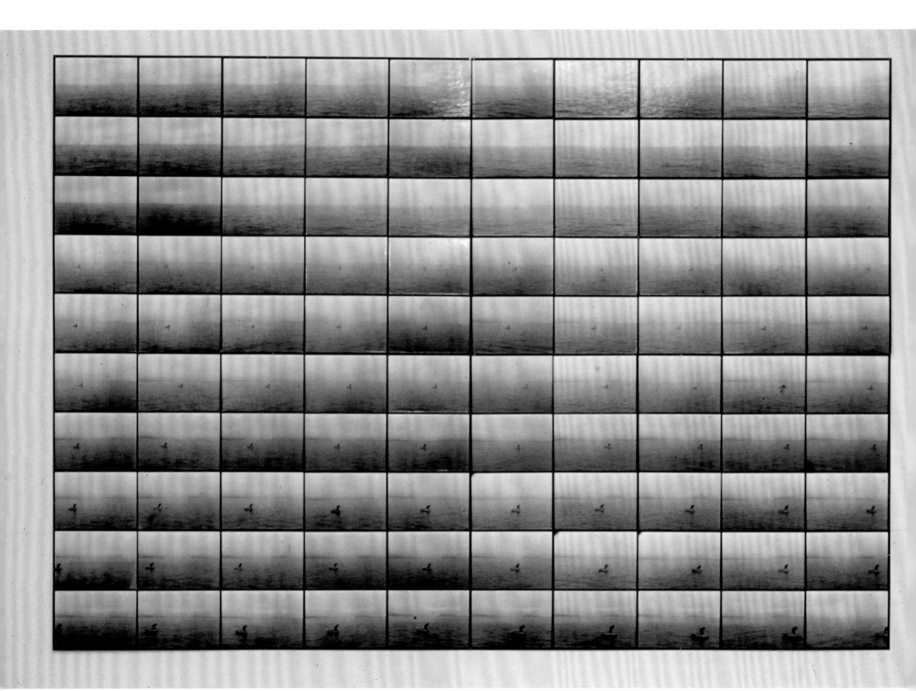

100 Discrete Tuned Sounding Stones for Puget Sound, 1978. 100 gelatin silver prints. Collection of the artist

(opposite page) Installation and detail views of *100 Discrete Tuned Sounding Stones for Puget Sound*, 1978. 100 gelatin silver prints,
tuned river stones, mixed media. Collection of the artist

Performance of *100 Discrete Tuned Sounding Stones for Puget Sound*, 1978

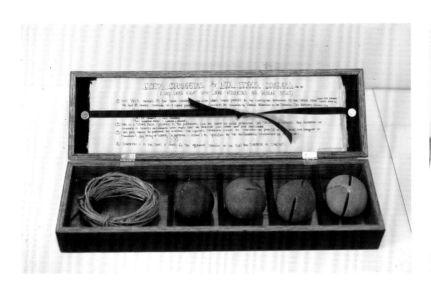

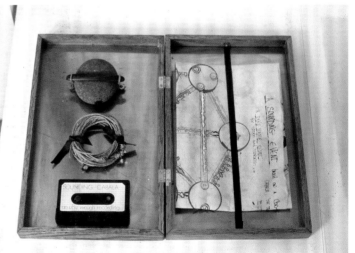

(top) Various scenes from *Sounding* and *Zero Entropic Driftola* events

(center) Recording of *Zig Zag, A Sounding Multiple*, 1978. Mixed media. Collection of the artist

(bottom, left) *Box for Four Discrete Sounding Studies*. Mixed media. Collection of the artist

(bottom right) *Box for a Sounding Event*, based on a configuration from the Kabbalah. Mixed media. Collection of the artist

A PASSION PLAY

In 1980, Evans undertook one of his most ambitious endeavors. *A Passion Play*, a twelve-hour event, was comprised of short, ten-to-fifteen-minute activities every hour, starting at 6 a.m. and ending at 6 p.m. In some of the performances, he would be joined by a female performer (Mary Anne Peters). The resulting documentation and display of the "Body Boxes" was shown first at the Whatcom Museum of History and Art and then the Henry Art Gallery on the University of Washington campus. It remains for Evans one of the most original and significant works of his career.

Twelve Field Us(e)ages/A Passion Play, 1980. Twelve-hour performance on the grounds of the University of Washington Center for Urban Horticulture, Seattle

Installation views of instruments used in *Twelve Field Us(e)ages/A Passion Play*, 1980, Henry Art Gallery. *Twelve Field Us(e)ages* was a twelve-hour performance on the grounds of the University of Washington Center for Urban Horticulture, Seattle.

FIELD US(E)AGES

After the performance of *A Passion Play* in 1980, Evans began a series of activities using his "Body Boxes," again engaging with a female participant. These activities, referred to as *Field Us(e)ages*, were sited outdoors, sometimes with an invited audience and sometimes with casual passers-by, joggers and walkers.

The structures of these performances were often organized around days of the week and times of day. Every performance was accompanied by drawings and/or choreographically inspired paintings.

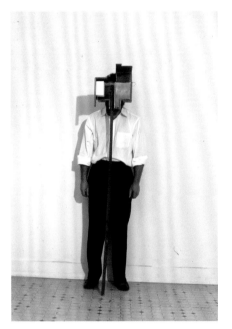   

(top) *Hymen Head* from the performance *Seven Garments and Seven Lies for the Passing of Days,* 1981. Mixed media
(above and right) Mary Ann Peters and Dennis Evans performing *Between Two Desires* from the performance *Seven Garments and Seven Lies for the Passing of Days,* 1981
(opposite page, far right, top to bottom) Catherine Mee and Dennis Evans performing *Between Two Desires* from the performance *Seven Garments and Seven Lies for the Passing of Days,* 1981

MUSEUMS

In 1975, Evans was invited to perform his new music at a New Music festival at Evergreen College in Olympia, Washington. This was Evans's first performance. Using his unique instruments and original scores, Evans donned a Goodwill-purchased tuxedo and appeared as Ubu Waugh, to the delight of the audience.

Throughout the rest of the late seventies, when not in a pond or wild landscape, Evans found himself in museum settings performing his ritual-inspired activities, in front of what he referred to as "civilized and acculturated audiences."

(opposite page) Dennis Evans performing at Eastern Washington University, 1978
(above) Dennis Evans, Mary Ann Peters and Andy Bateman in performance at Merrill House, Seattle

№ 2 INSTALLATIONS

Installation view of *The Fool's Journey* in the group exhibition
Dreams and Shields, Salt Lake City Arts Center, 1992

THE CHYMICAL NUPTIALS OF SOMA AND AGNI

This was Evans's first installation. It was installed at the Linda Farris Gallery in 1982 and encompassed five rooms that were interconnected. The viewer had to navigate through rooms and corridors, lending a ritualistic, processional quality to the installation. For Evans, this work began a long and deep enthusiasm for ideas found in Western alchemy. It also initiated his imposition of a sequential way of viewing his subject matter as a strategy to control his audiences' experiences.

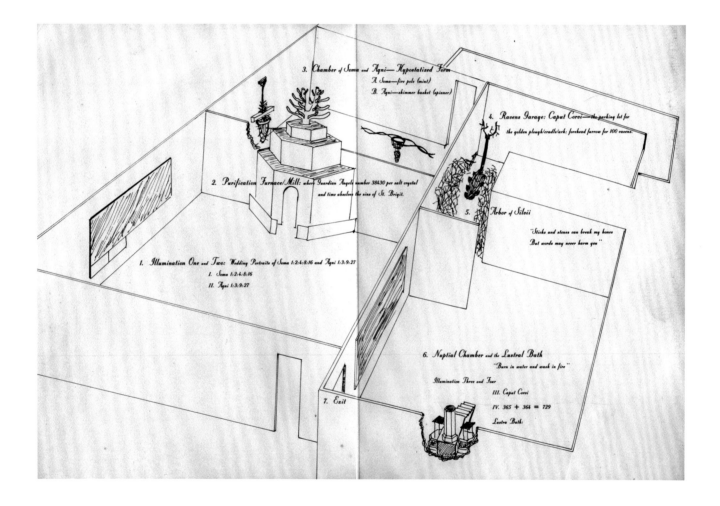

(above) *Diagram for Installation*, 1981. Ink on paper, 8 x 11 in. Collection of the artist
(opposite page, left) *Purification Furnace Mill*, 1981. Copper, mixed media, 120 x 120 x 144 in. No longer extant.
(opposite page, right) Views of *Caput Corvi*, 1981. Mixed media, dimensions variable. No longer extant.

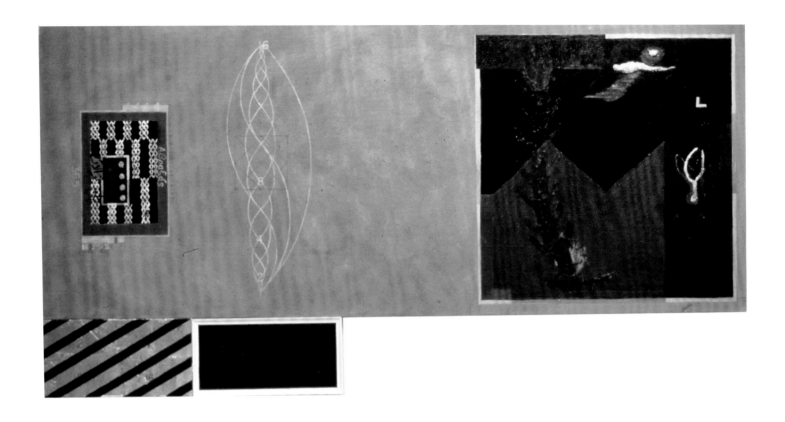

(top) *Wedding Portrait, Soma*, 1981. Mixed media on canvas, 48 x 84 in. Collection of the artist
Wedding Portrait, Agni, 1981. Mixed media on canvas, 48 x 96 in. Collection of the artist

(top) *365 + 364*, 1981. Mixed media on canvas, 48 x 120 in. Collection of the artist
Caput Corvi, The Lustral Bath, 1981. Mixed media on canvas, 48 x 120 in. Collection of the artist

THE SEVEN HALLS OF AeDvAeM

Note: The inter-text spells Adam and Eve.

In 1985, the Seattle Art Museum invited Evans to create an installation inside a large room at the Modern Art Pavilion (later known as their Seattle Center Pavilion) on the grounds of Seattle Center. Evans and his team constructed a complex environment. The architectural plan for this piece was a diagram of a man lying on his back with outstretched arms. There was an inscription above each doorway: "man is the measure of all things." Entry was made through a door at either foot and an exit lead out through the left ear. Some of the room's walls were heavily embellished with various examples of early written alphabets, such as Egyptian hieroglyphs, Phoenician, Aramaic and proto Greek alphabets. Each room had a specific theme and subject matter.

(above) Banner at entrance to *The Seven Halls of AeDvAeM,* 1985. Collection of the artist
(opposite page) Installation views of *The Seven Halls of AeDvAeM,* 1985. Objects and components now dispersed.

THE SEMINARY

The Whatcom Museum of History and Art in 1985 commissioned an installation entitled *The Seminary*.

Artists Jeffrey Bishop, Keith Beckley and Evans's wife Nancy Mee collaborated on this project, which continued the thread of Evans's investigations into questions about language and its origins.

By deconstructing the word "seminary," Evans's *Seminary* became a place of insemination, dissemination, a breeding ground, a place where roots were planted . . . a seed plot for seminal languages. Evans's *The Seminary* was a Garden of Languages.

Installation details of *The Seminary*, 1989. Mixed media. Objects and components now dispersed.

(above and opposite) Installation details of *The Seminary*, 1989. Mixed media. Objects and components now dispersed.

THE PHARMACY

In 1986, Ned Rifkin, a curator from the New Museum in New York, invited eight artists from Seattle to exhibit work. Evans created an installation entitled *The Pharmacy*.

The installation was based on ideas Evans had gleaned from reading the work of Jacques Derrida, specifically the philosophical essay titled "Plato's Pharmacy." Evans at that time was also reading and synthesizing works by Joseph Campbell and Carl Jung, focusing on the ideas of Western alchemy.

This piece was a synthesis of these influences.

It later traveled back to Seattle and was shown at the Seattle Art Museum.

(above and opposite) Installation views of *Pharmacy* in *Outside New York: Seattle*, New Museum of Contemporary Art, New York, 1984. Mixed media, variable dimensions. Collection of the artist

tHE gaRden for remeMbered dEsireS

Note: The inter-text spells HERMES.

This installation was created for a show at the Linda Farris Gallery and then exhibited at the Portland Art Museum in 1989. The central principle of this work was based in Hermeneutics, the branch of knowledge that deals with the art of interpretation.

For this piece, Evans chose the Tarot deck as his fundamental iconographic key.

Each individual station corresponded to one of the major arcana.

Installation views of *tHE gaRden for remeMbered dEsireS*, 1989.
Objects and components now dispersed.

NOTES FROM THE ARTIST:

The ancient philosophers were admirable for their ability to cover over so dexterously the secrets of their inquiries with pleasant poetic fables. This set of works is dedicated to the world of occult sciences and mysteries and the artful sleuthing of those willing seekers of nature's secrets.

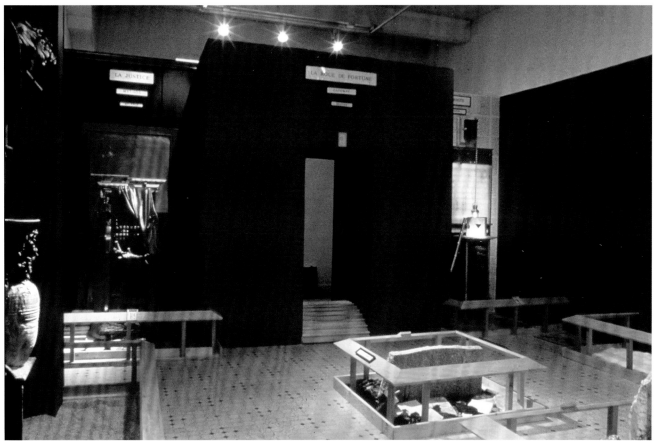

(top) *Le Empereur,* 1989. Encaustic, mixed media on canvas, 96 x 96 x 4 in. Location unknown.
(bottom) *Le Bateleur,* 1989. Encaustic, mixed media on canvas, variable size. No longer extant.

(left) *La Justice,* 1989. Encaustic, mixed media on canvas, 96 x 56 x 20 in. No longer extant.
(right) *L'Ermite,* 1989. Encaustic, mixed media on canvas, 96 x 56 x 15 in. No longer extant.

MNEMOSYNE'S ALPHABET

This chapel-like installation was shown first in Seattle at the Security Pacific Gallery and then at the Boise Art Museum and the Spokane Central Public Library in 1993.

In this work, Evans continued his interest in constructing pieces that explore the function of language and examine the multiple mechanisms of meaning. This piece referenced Plato's Cave and the idea that knowledge comes from what we see and hear in the world, i.e. empirical knowledge, and that words are only "husks" of true meaning.

Views of *Mnemosyne's Alphabet,* 1993. Mixed media. Objects and components now dispersed.

THE PHILOSOPHER'S WEDDING

This piece was shown at the Bellevue Art Museum in 2006, in a small group show in conjunction with works by Joseph Beuys and Edward Kienholtz.

Evans did a short performance for the opening of the exhibition and also created an installation loosely derived from ideas found in *The Chemical Wedding of* *Christian Rosenkreuntz*, a manifesto of the Rosicrucian Order. This piece continued Evans's fascination with "the Mysterium Conjunction or Union of Opposites," which was a major theme of Western alchemy outlined by Carl Jung and Joseph Campbell.

Installation views of *The Philosopher's Wedding*, 1994. Encaustic, mixed media on canvas.
Objects and components now dispersed.

(opposite page, top left) *The Philosophy of Rhetoric*, 1994. Encaustic, mixed media on canvas, 48 x 36 x 4 in. Location unknown.
(opposite page, top right) *The Philosopher's Dilemma*, 1994. Encaustic, mixed media on canvas, 48 x 36 in. Location unknown.
(opposite page, bottom left) *The Ambiguity of Negation*, 1994. Encaustic, mixed media on canvas, 48 x 36 x 4 in. Collection of Zymogenetics
(opposite page, bottom right) *Revelation*, 1994. Encaustic, mixed media on canvas, 48 x 36 in. Collection of Tom and Cherie Hanses

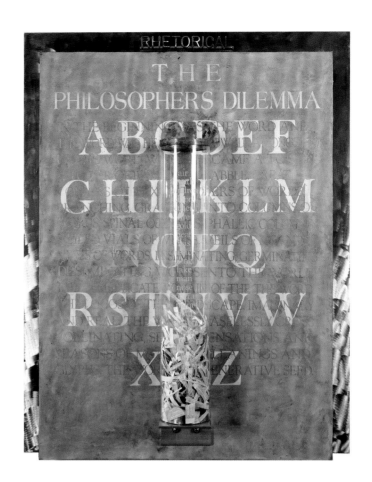

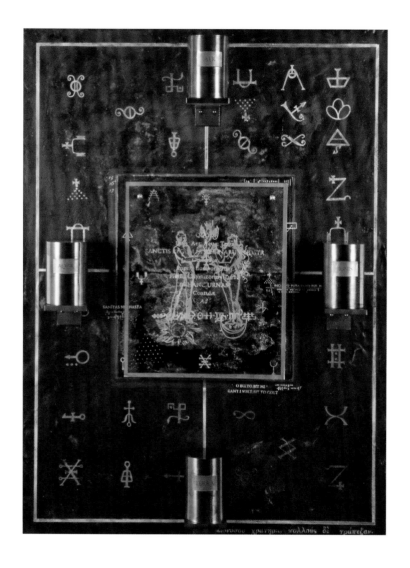

THE MECHANISM OF MEANING

The practice of dialectical disputation Was based on the notion of a definite disputation. And tHis idea of disputAtion was base simply but definiTely on a meaning for every term. Simply Yes of Thus certain woŕds are regarded aS reciprocal and some words a regarded as equivocal. Meaning is then an inTrinsic property; a unique unanalysable Relation to other things the otHer Words annExed to a Word in the Dictionary; the connotation of a Wor A; An activity projected onto an Object, an Event, inter a Volition; The place of anything in a SysteM: The practical con of a thing in our future Experience; The Theoretical consequen involved in or implied by a Statement. Emotion arouse by anytH ThAt which is actually related to a sigN by a chosen relation; The Mnemic effects of a StImulus. AssociationS acquired. Some other occurence to which the Mnemic Effects OF any occurrenc are Appropriate. That which is Sign interpreted as being of. What anything suggests. ThAt to which the user of a SyMbol o to bE referrING ThAt to which the user of a symbol believ himself to be referring. That to which INterpreter of a Sym Refers; BelIeve himself to be referriNg Believes the User to be referrinG.

The Fountain, 1994. Encaustic, mixed media on canvas, 48 x 36 x 4 in. Collection of Mary Alberg

(right) *The Mechanism of Meaning*, Encaustic, mixed media on canvas, 48 x 36 x 4 in. Collection of the artist

The Bedchamber, 1994. Encaustic, mixed media on canvas, 48 x 36 in. Collection of Lou and Joni Pritchard

№ 3   COLLECTIONS

THE 72 (   ) OF GOD

THE SEVEN LIBRARIES OF BABYLON

BOOK OF HOURS

THE SORCERERS OF THE RIVER

CARNEGIE LIBRARIES

Time-lapse photograph of Dennis Evans with a candle in his studio, 2014

THE 72 (   ) OF GOD

In November 1990, Evans completed the first section of the suite *The 72 ( ) of God*. Comprised of seventy-two framed works on paper, the set was divided into eight groups of nine works. Each group related to one of the seven days of creation as depicted in the book of Genesis. The eighth group was created by dividing the fifth day into two groups, one for Adam and one for Eve. It was a homage of sorts to Joseph Campbell's *Hero with a Thousand Faces*.

Installation views of *The 72 ( ) of God,* 1990, Linda Farris Gallery, Seattle. Framed drawings, mixed media on paper.
Now in the collection of Museum of Northwest Art, La Conner, WA.

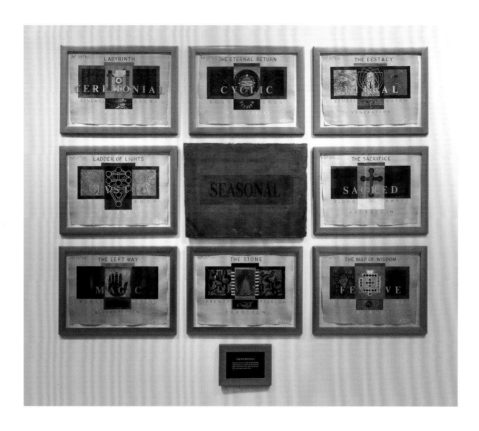

(top) *Seasonal* from *The 72 ( ) of God*, 1990. Framed drawings, mixed media on paper. Museum of Northwest Art, La Conner, WA
(bottom) *Creatures* from *The 72 ( ) of God*, 1990. Framed drawings, mixed media on paper.
Museum of Northwest Art, La Conner, WA

THE SEVEN LIBRARIES OF BABYLON

This exhibition was shown at the then-new Meyerson Nowinski Gallery in Seattle in 1998. It was comprised of seven very large paintings organized around imaginary fragments found in the Seven Libraries of Babylon, a fictional construct imagined by Evans.

(this page and following pages) Installation views of *The Seven Libraries of Babylon*, Meyerson Nowinski Gallery, Seattle, 1997

NOTES FROM THE CATALOGUE *NANCY MEE/ DENNIS EVANS: IMAGINE—AFTER THE DELUGE*

After the Great Flood, mortal men and women began building their great cities and founding great civilizations. The city of Babylon was built in an attempt to forge some link with the sacred. Here, great ziggurats were constructed in order for the mortals to be closer to their gods.

It was also here in Babylon, the city of great egotism and pride, that the people attempted to build a culture that would give them an immortality of sorts. They constructed not only a tower where they could approach divinity but also a library where they could store and access all knowledge both revealed and concealed. That Great Library of Babel came to be known as The Seven Libraries of Babylon. It was their desire that in these seven great libraries all knowledge could be compiled and stored.

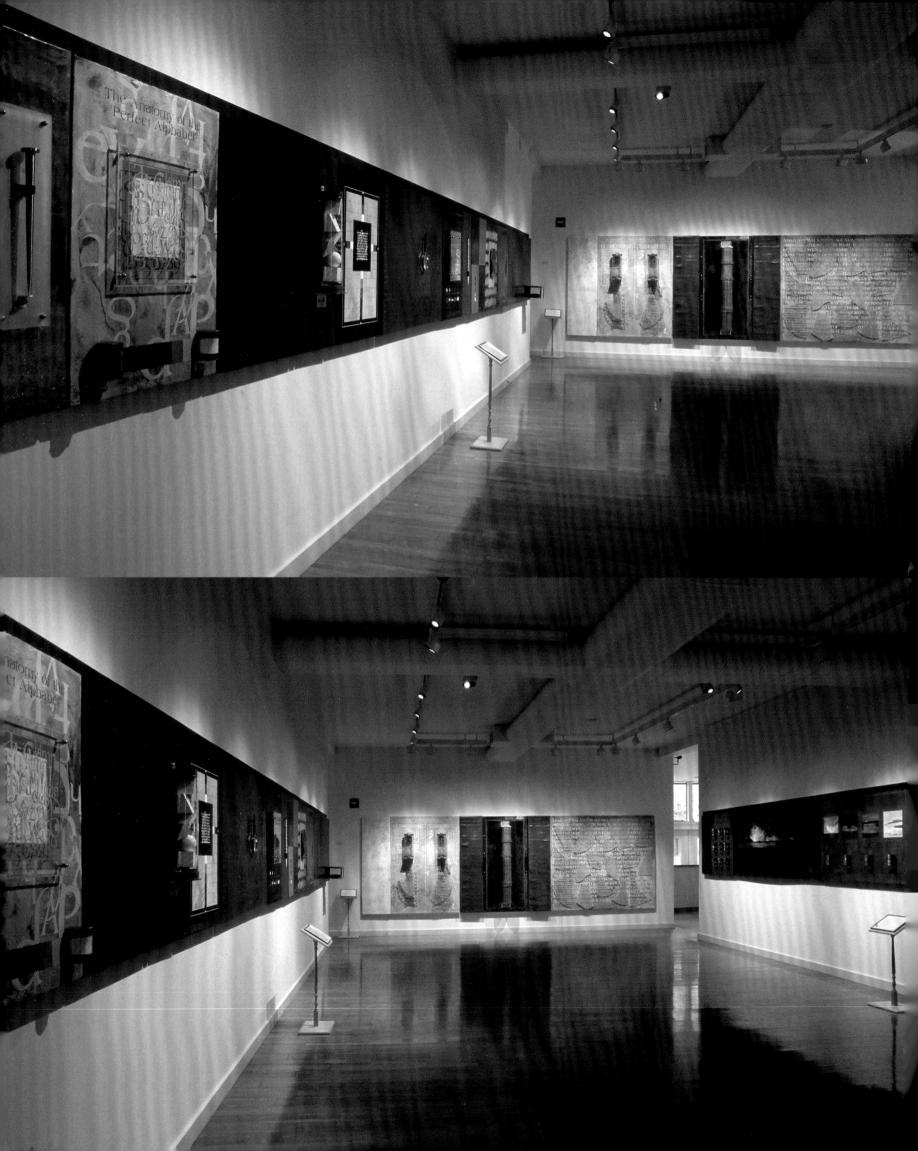

BOOK OF HOURS

Evans's love for illuminated manuscripts was the inspiration for this collection of eight paintings, which were made specifically for an exhibition at Erickson & Elins Gallery in San Francisco.

These diptych paintings can be thought of as large illuminated manuscripts.

The Ephemeris of Frost, 1998. Encaustic, mixed media on panel, 48 x 72 x 4 in. Private collection

During the Middle Ages, a Book of Hours was a compendium of different devotional texts that a person could read in private. They were small and very beautifully made. They were meant to be very intimate objects that one could hold in one's hand and admire. The core of the manuscript was The Divine Office, which was a series of eight prayers to be recited at three-hour increments, eight times a day. These are Matins, Lauds, Prime, Terce, Sext, None, Vespers and Compline, which became titles for the paintings in this collection.

The Book of Contemplation, 1998. Encaustic, mixed media on panel, 48 x 72 x 8 in. Private collection

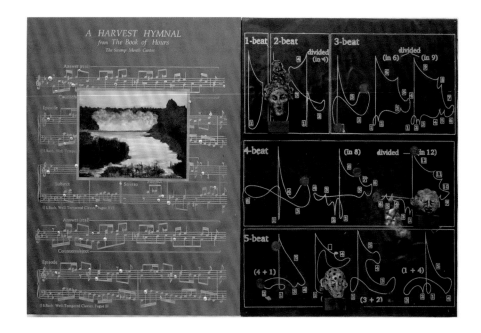

(top) *The Harvest Hymnal*, 1998. Encaustic, mixed media on panel, 48 x 72 x 5 in. Private collection

The Salting Anelets, 1998. Encaustic, mixed media on panel, 48 x 72 x 8 in. Private collection

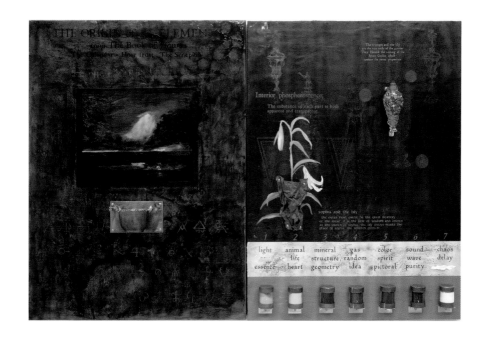

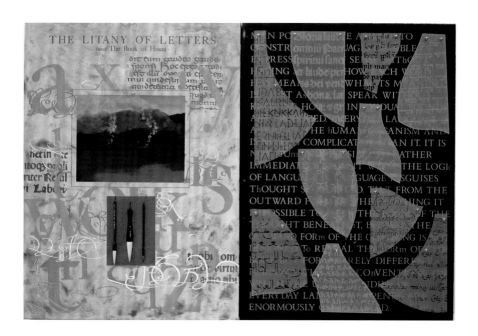

(top) *The Origin of the Elements*, 1998. Encaustic, mixed media on panel, 48 x 72 x 8 in. Private collection

The Litany of Letters, 1998. Encaustic, mixed media on panel, 48 x 72 x 6 in. Private collection

The Primer of Small Ruins, 1998. Encaustic, mixed media on panel, 48 x 72 x 5 in. Private collection

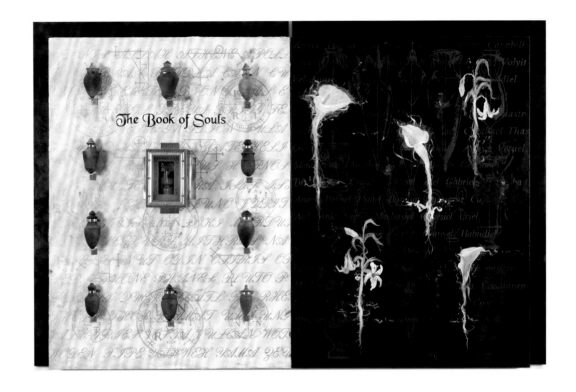

The Book of Souls, 1998. Encaustic, mixed media on panel, 48 x 72 x 8 in. Collection of Chap and Eve Alvord

THE SORCERERS OF THE RIVER

These large paintings belong to a series entitled *The Sorcerers of the River* and are multimedia works that draw their iconography from different aspects of the sacred. They were created after Evans returned from a mind-altering trip visiting many of the sacred sites in Turkey and Greece. Each work represents an abstract rendition of specific deities from the Levant.

Installation view of *The Sorcerers of the River*, 2010. Woodside/Braseth Gallery, Seattle

Sapientia XXII, 2010. Mixed media, encaustic on canvas, 57 x 40 x 8 in. Collection of the artist

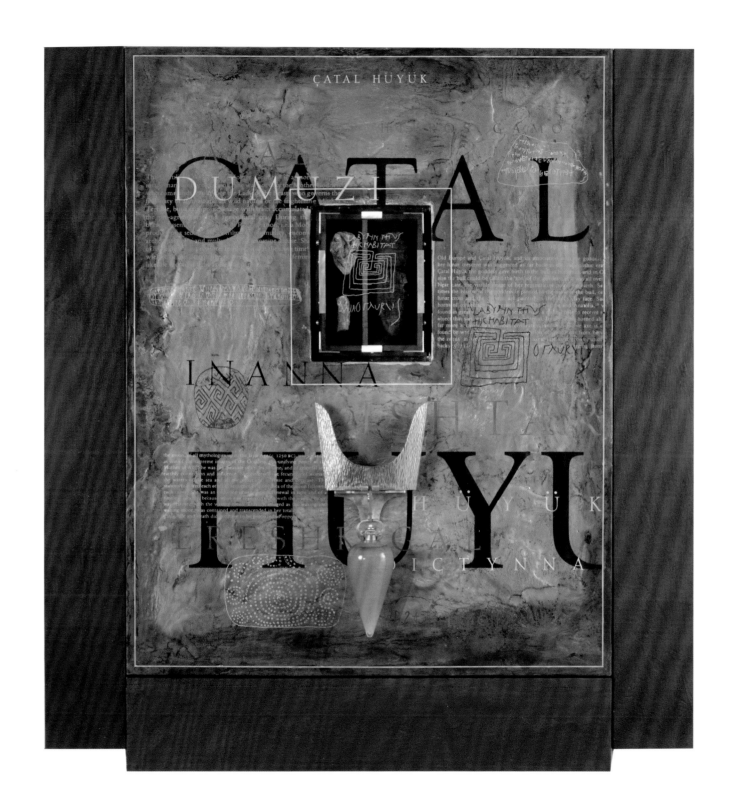

Catal Huyuk, 2010. Mixed media, encaustic on canvas, 67 x 60 x 10 in. Private collection

CARNEGIE LIBRARIES

Evans always loved libraries as places for housing great ideas. For him, a library was a palace containing knowledge and a place of fabulous discovery.

In 1996, the Seattle Library System commissioned Evans to do a series of ten paintings based on the theme of the Seven Liberal Arts. The ten paintings were distributed, two each for five of the Carnegie Libraries in the Seattle Library System.

Rhetoric Astronomy, 2004. Encaustic, mixed media on canvas, 48 x 96 x 9 in. Seattle Public Library System

In the medieval times, a proper education was based on the Seven Liberal Arts, which were grammar, rhetoric and logic (the trivium) and geometry, arithmetic, music and astronomy (the quadrivium).

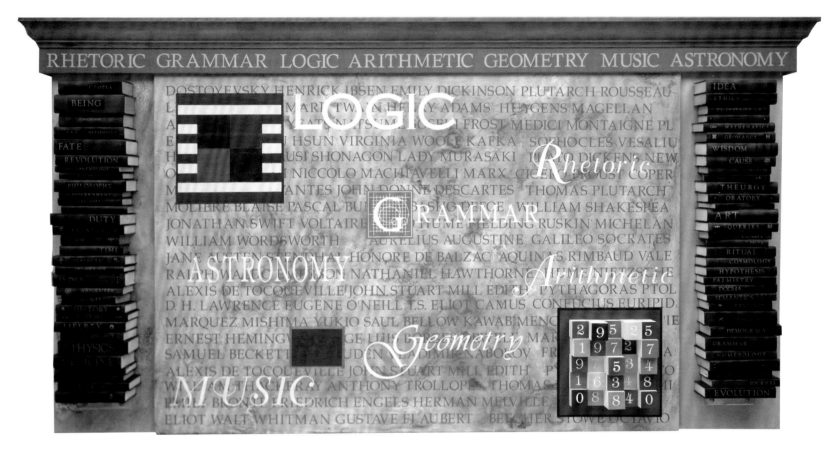

Logic Arithmetic, 2004. Encaustic, mixed media on canvas, 48 x 96 x 4 in. Seattle Public Library System

(top) *Grammar Music*, 2004. Encaustic, mixed media on canvas, 48 x 96 x 4 in. Seattle Public Library System

Rhetoric, 2004. Encaustic, mixed media on canvas, 48 x 96 x 9 in. Seattle Public Library System

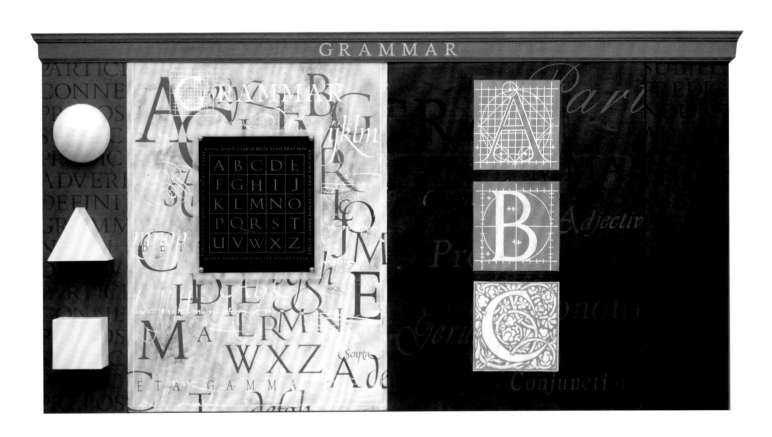

(top) *Music*, 2004. Encaustic, mixed media on canvas, 48 x 96 x 6 in. Seattle Public Library System

Grammar, 2004. Encaustic, mixed media on canvas, 48 x 96 x 10 in. Seattle Public Library System

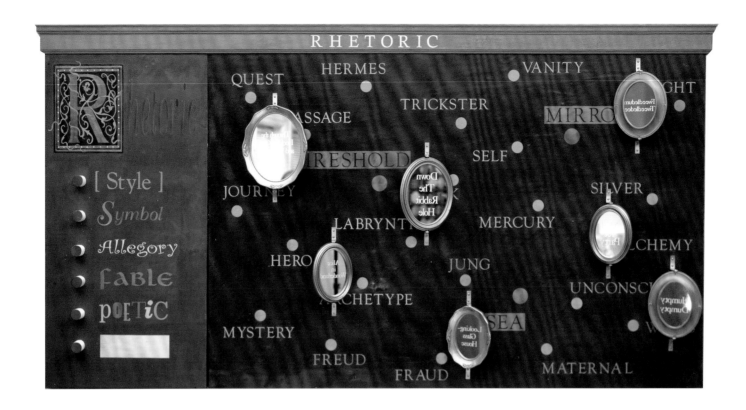

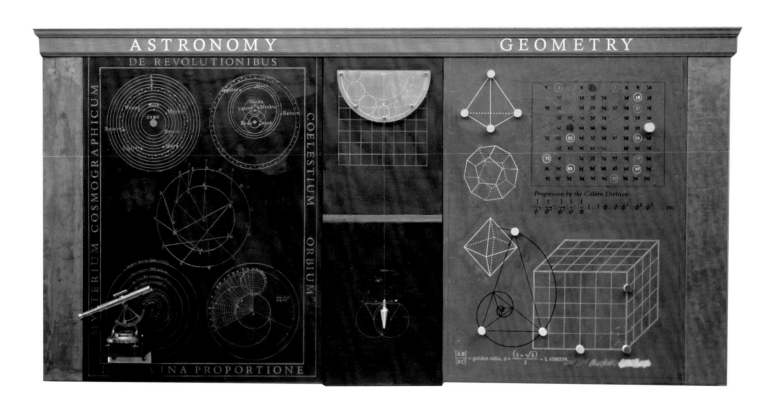

(top) *Astronomy Rhetoric*, 2004. Encaustic, mixed media on canvas, 48 x 96 x 9 in. Seattle Public Library System
(bottom) *Astronomy Geometry*, 2004. Encaustic, mixed media on canvas, 48 x 96 x 6 in. Seattle Public Library System

(top) *Arithmetic Music*, 2004. Encaustic, mixed media on canvas, 48 x 96 x 9 in. Seattle Public Library System
(bottom) *Logic*, 2004. Encaustic, mixed media on canvas, 48 x 96 x 4 in. Seattle Public Library System

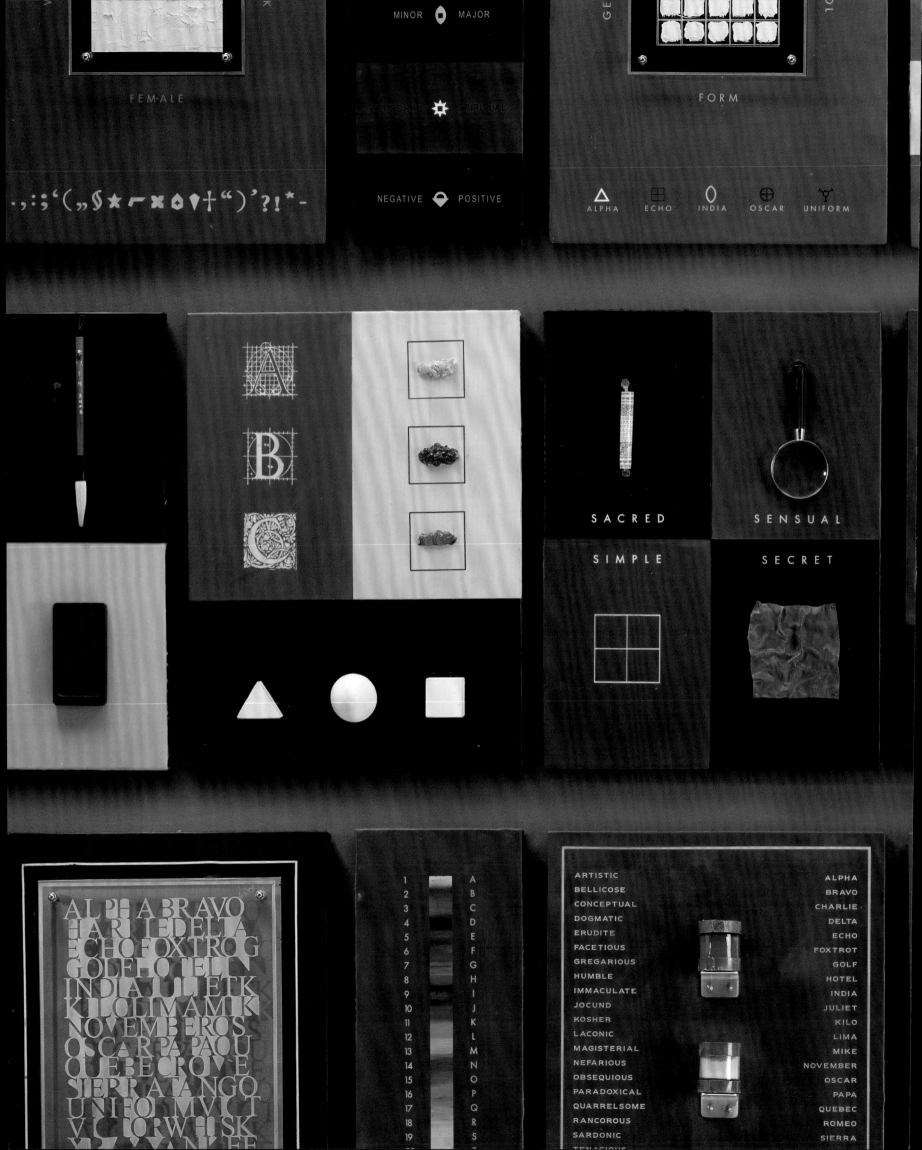

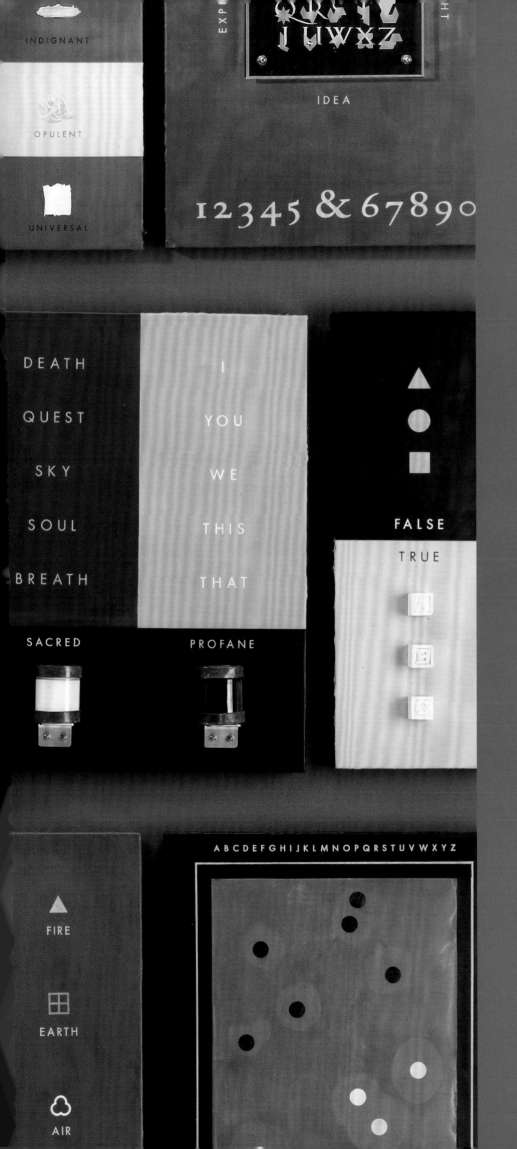

INDIGNANT

OPULENT

UNIVERSAL

IDEA

12345 & 67890

DEATH

QUEST

SKY

SOUL

BREATH

I

YOU

WE

THIS

THAT

FALSE

TRUE

SACRED

PROFANE

ABCDEFGHIJKLMNOPQRSTUVWXYZ

FIRE

EARTH

AIR

№ 4 LANGUAGE STUDIES

THE ANATOMY OF THE PERFECT LANGUAGE

THE CRITIQUE OF PURE WRITING

WRITING LESSONS/ READING SESSIONS

Detail of *Writing Lessons/Reading Sessions*, 2015. Encaustic, mixed-media on multiple panels. Tacoma Art Museum

THE ANATOMY OF THE PERFECT LANGUAGE

GRAMMARS OF EDEN

During the 1980s, Evans became interested in the idea of a Utopian Perfect Language.

    Several large bodies of work resulted from this enquiry.

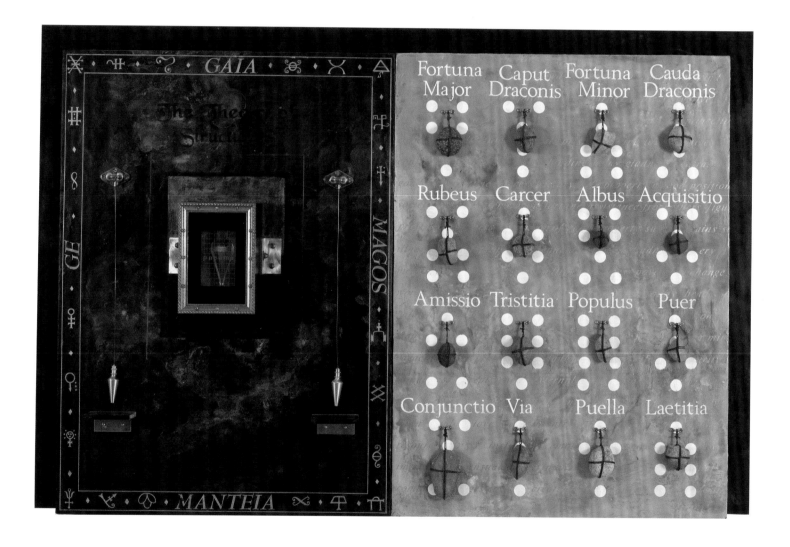

(above) *The Theory of Structures*, 2000. Encaustic, mixed media on canvas, 48 x 72 x 6 in. Collection of Faiza el Sohl
(opposite page) *The Nature of Reality*, 2000. Encaustic, mixed media on canvas, 41 x 52 x 6 in. Private collection

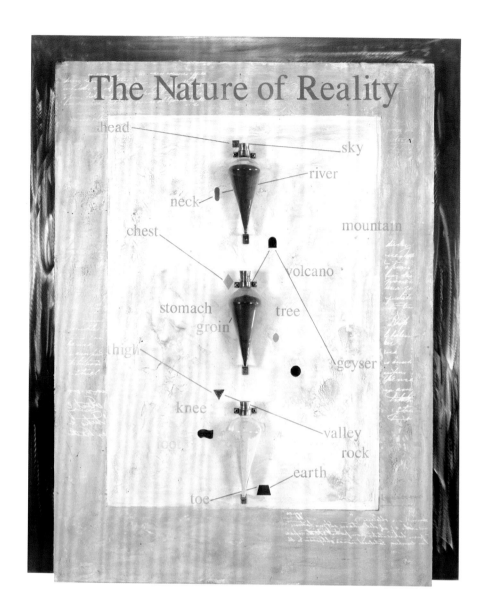

NOTES FROM THE CATALOGUE
THE ANATOMY OF THE PERFECT LANGUAGE

There is a notion that there once existed a universal language, which could be used by all the peoples of the world and which could communicate all things to all people. This language preceded the confusion of tongues and since then it has been a grail sought after to be redeemed from obscurity.

We are told that God [existed] before all things and with his word all things came into being. Thus, Creation arose through an act of Speech. "In the Beginning was the Word and the Word was with God and word was God." We are also told that the world was created by means of the twenty-two letters of the Hebrew alphabet.

And that under the newly created firmament and above the great abyss, God spoke to Adam and told him of this duty to Name all things. Thus, Adam became the Name Giver—The Creator of Language—The Nomothete.

As the story continues, it tells that, after the great flood, men in their vanity attempted to erect a tower that would reach to the heavens. But God punished them for their pride. He confounded their speech so that they could not understand each other, thus the confusion linguarium. So, once there was one language and then there were many.

What followed was a passionate quest to redeem the loss of the perfect language.

These paintings tell this story.

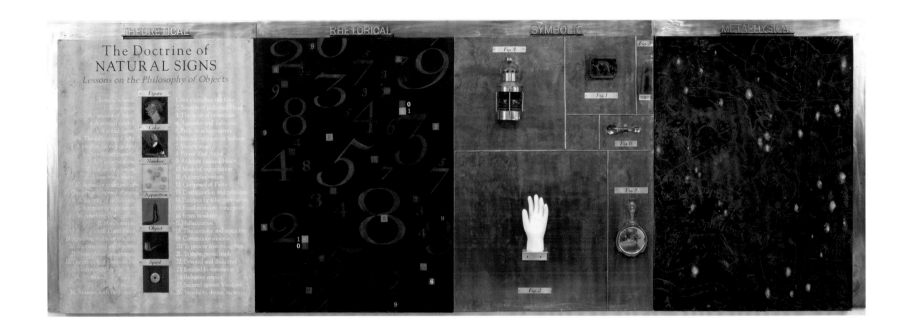

(top) *The Doctrine of Natural Signs*, 2001. Encaustic, mixed media on canvas, 48 x 144 x 8 in. Collection of Bristol-Myers Squibb
(bottom) *The Nature of Man*, 2001. Encaustic, mixed media on canvas, 48 x 84 x 8 in. Private collection

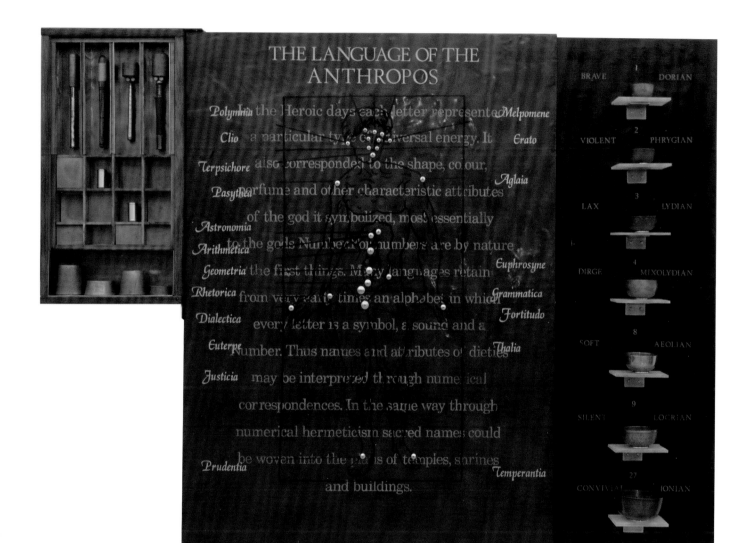

THE LANGUAGE OF THE ANTHROPOS

Polymnia the Heroic days each letter represents Melpomene Clio a particular type of universal energy. It Erato Terpsichore also corresponded to the shape, colour, Pasythea perfume and other characteristic attributes Aglaia of the god it symbolized, most essentially Astronomia Arithmetica to the gods Number. For numbers are by nature Geometria the first things. Many languages retain Euphrosyne Rhetorica from very early times an alphabet in which Grammatica Dialectica every letter is a symbol, a sound and a Fortitudo Euterpe Number. Thus names and attributes of dieties Thalia Justicia may be interpreted through numerical correspondences. In the same way through numerical hermeticism sacred names could Prudentia be woven into the parts of temples, shrines Temperantia and buildings.

BRAVE — 1 — DORIAN
VIOLENT — 2 — PHRYGIAN
LAX — 3 — LYDIAN
DIRGE — 4 — MIXOLYDIAN
SOFT — 8 — AEOLIAN
SILENT — 9 — LOCRIAN
CONVIVIAL — 27 — IONIAN

The Language of the Anthropos, 2001. Encaustic, mixed media on canvas, 48 x 72 x 8 in. Private collection

The Four Degrees of Fire, 2001. Encaustic, mixed media on canvas, 4 panels, each 30 x 18 x 10 in. Collection of the artist

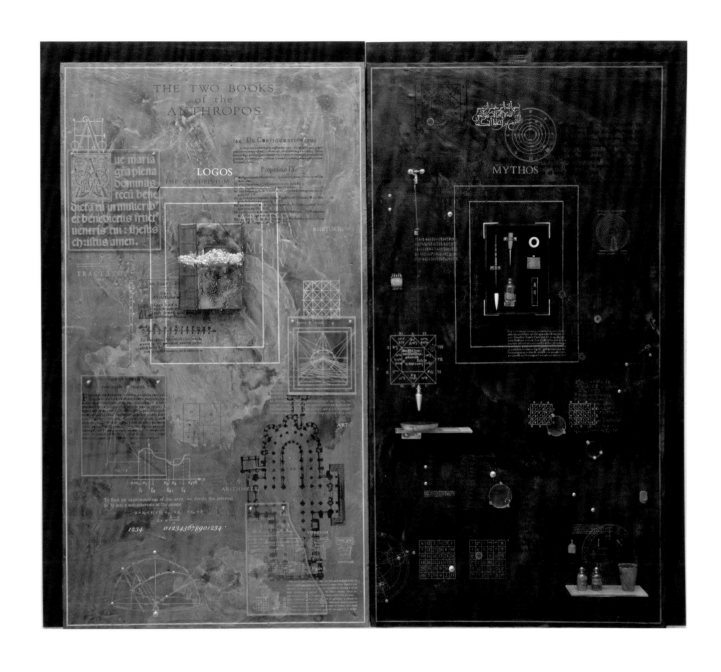

The Two Books of the Anthropos, 2003. Encaustic, mixed media on canvas, 2 panels, each 96 x 48 x 8 in.
Collection of Steve and Sharon Huling

THE CRITIQUE OF PURE WRITING

The Critique of Pure Writing was the second completed
section of the Language Studies suite.

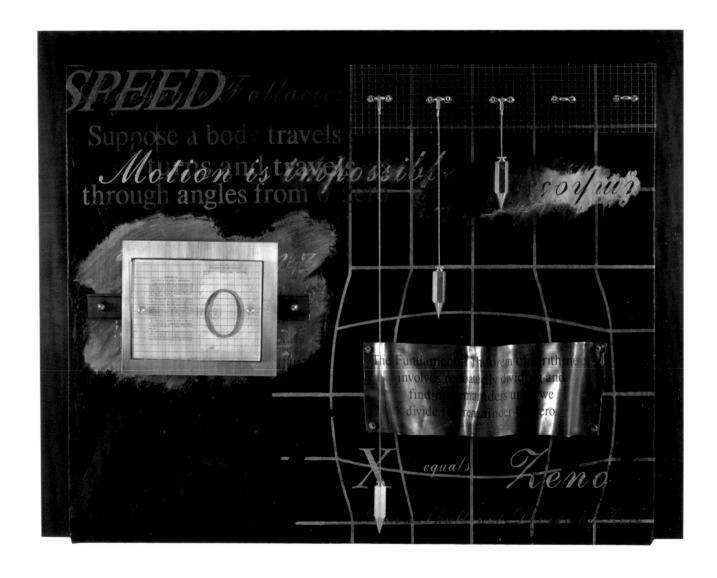

(above) *Speed*, 1992. Encaustic, mixed media on canvas, 32 x 48 x 6 in. Private collection
(opposite page) *Illumination*, 1992. Encaustic, mixed media on canvas, 32 x 60 x 6 in. Collection of the artist

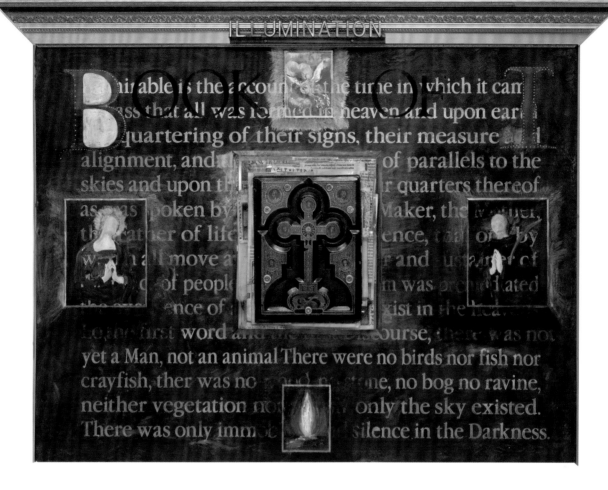

FROM THE CATALOGUE *DENNIS EVANS, THE CRITIQUE OF PURE WRITING*

There were a total of twenty-six works in this set, one for every letter of the alphabet. Each letter begins a word, the word in turn becoming the topic for the piece it labels. More than any of his previous bodies of work, this group cogently covers Evans's broad range of perennial topics: comparative religion, the sciences, philosophy and his love of the written word. The project deliberately emphasizes the use of text as a semiological tool of communication and depictions of meaning. Each piece contains an actual book, which operates as a foundation for the dialogue that occurs between the richly painted images and texts that cover the encaustic panels.

Q is for Query, 1992. Encaustic, mixed media on canvas, three panels, overall 60 x 96 x 6 in. Private collection

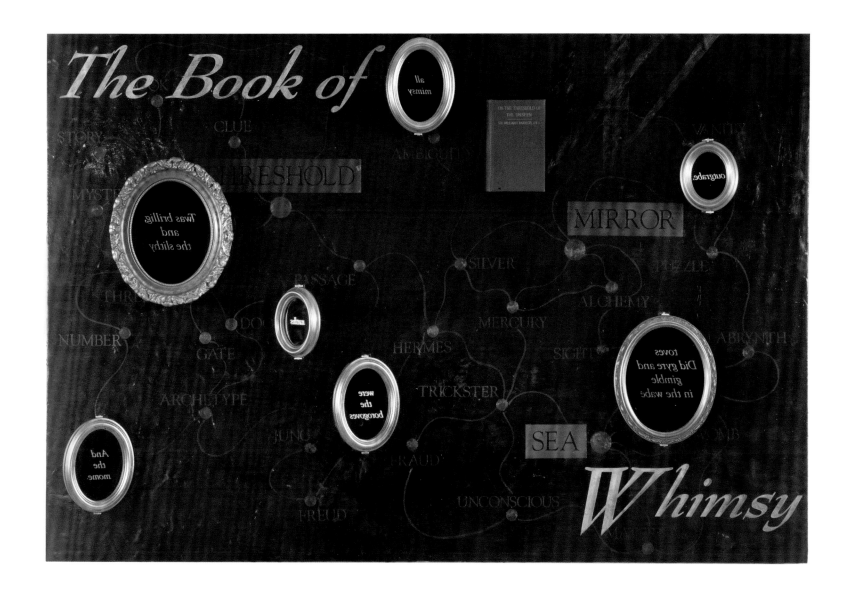

W is for Whimsical, 1992. Encaustic, mixed media on canvas, 48 x 72 x 6 in. Collection of the artist

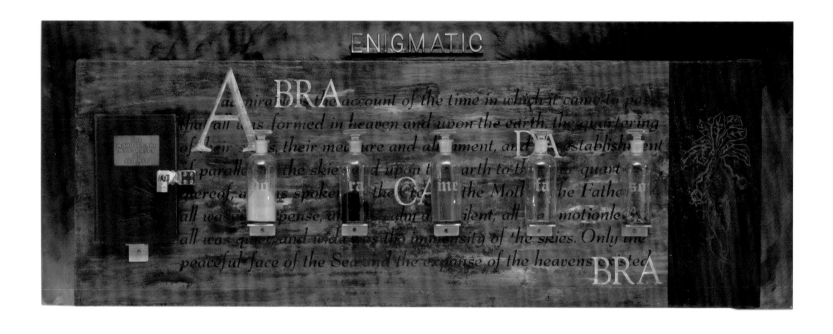

E is for Enigmatic, 1992. Encaustic, mixed media on canvas, 21 x 58 x 6 in. Private collection

Y is for Yin Yang, 1992. Encaustic, mixed media on canvas, 64 x 72 x 6 in. Boise Art Museum

P is for Phenomenologic. Encaustic, mixed media on canvas, 27 x 36 x 5 in. Location unknown.

S is for Symbolic, 1992. Encaustic, mixed media on canvas, 35 x 62 x 8 in. Collection of the artist

WRITING LESSONS/READING SESSIONS

Writing Lessons/Reading Sessions was first shown at the Gerald Peters Gallery in New York in January, 2003. One year later, it was exhibited at the Woodside/ Braseth Gallery in Seattle, Washington. The majority of the work's components now belongs to the Special Collections Department of the Suzzallo Library at the University of Washington.

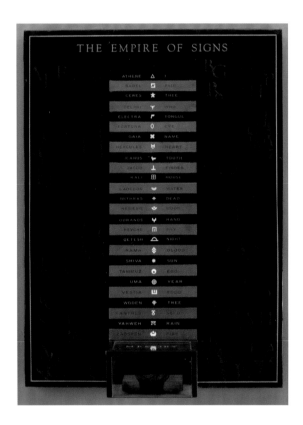

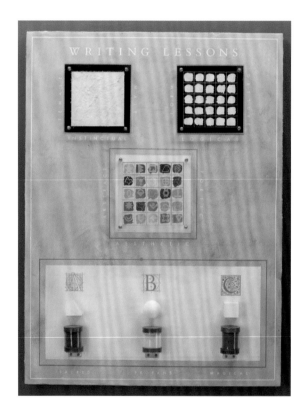

(left) *The Empire of Signs*, 2002. Encaustic, mixed media on canvas, 48 x 36 x 8 in. Collection of the artist
(right) *Writing Lessons*, 2002. Encaustic, mixed media on canvas, 48 x 36 x 8 in. Collection of the artist
(opposite page, top) *The Three Levels of Interpretation*, 2002. Encaustic, mixed media on canvas, 30 x 120 x 6 in. Swedish Hospital.
(opposite page, bottom) *Writing Lessons, The Poetic*, 2002. Encaustic, mixed media on canvas, 24 x 54 x 4 in. Collection of the artist

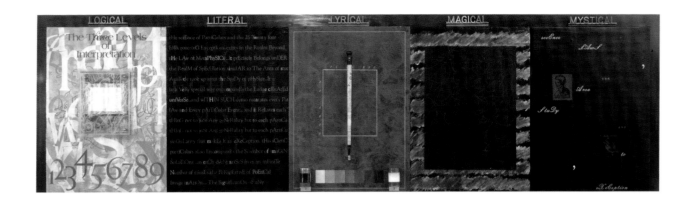

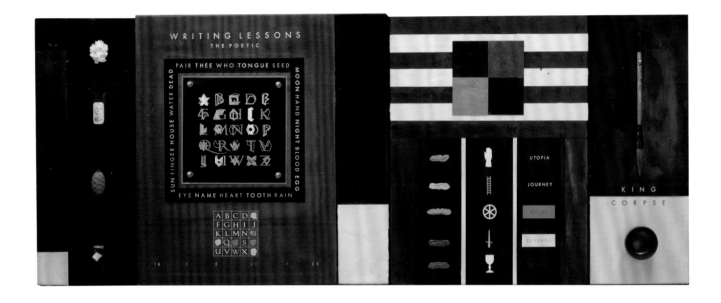

NOTES FROM THE CATALOGUE
*DENNIS EVANS, WRITING LESSONS/
READING SESSIONS*

From the invention of letters the machinations of the human heart began to operate; falsity and error daily increased; litigation and prisons had their beginnings, as also specious and artful language, which causes so much confusion in the world. It was on these accounts that the shades of the departed wept at night. But, on the other hand, from the invention of letters all polite intercourse and music proceeded and reason and justice were made manifest; the relations of life were defined, and the laws were fixed; governors had a lasting rule to

refer to; scholars had authorities to venerate; the historian, the mathematician, the astronomer can do nothing without letters. Were there not letters to give proof to passing events, the shades might weep at noonday as well as night and the heavens rain down blood, for tradition might affirm what she pleased, so that the letters have done much more good than evil; and as a token of the good, heaven rained down ripe grain the day they were first invented.

Henry Noel Humphreys
*The Origin and Progress of the Art of
Writing*, 1853

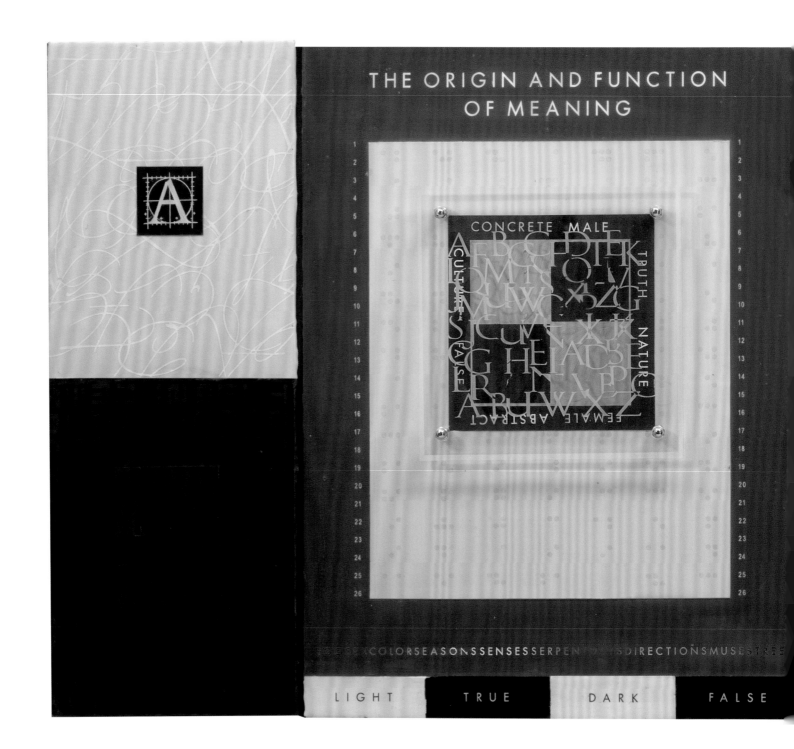

The Origin and Function of Meaning, 2002. Encaustic, mixed media on canvas, 54 x 24 x 4 in.
University of Washington Libraries, Special Collections

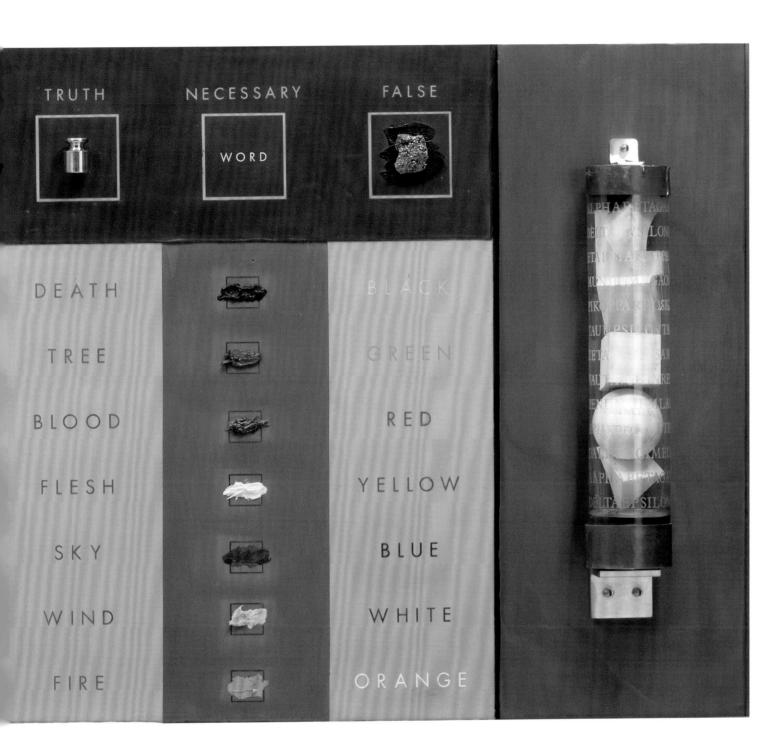

Proof of an External World, 2002. Encaustic, mixed media on canvas, 24 x 54 x 4 in.
University of Washington Libraries, Special Collections

The Anatomy of Writing, 2002. Encaustic, mixed media on canvas, 24 x 54 x 4 in.
University of Washington Libraries, Special Collections

№ 5 COLLABORATIONS WITH NANCY MEE

IMAGINE—AFTER THE DELUGE

SULTAN'S LIBRARY

PROSPERO'S BOOKS/PROSPERO'S LIBRARY

Installation view of *Prospero's Library*, Woodside/Braseth Gallery, 2019

IMAGINE—AFTER THE DELUGE...

WORKS FROM THE 15 MASTERS OF A NEW UTOPIA

In the early 2000s, Evans began a series of collaborations with his wife and studio-mate, Nancy Mee. For this exhibition, the two artists loosely worked together on a single idea, with the result that each artist produced a work representative of that idea executed in their own style.

The first collaboration was based on the fictional idea of a need to reconstruct a new Utopian Society after some imagined apocalypse. Who would be the essential characters to rebuild society? The artists imagined such a list and attempted to give life to each of them.

A physician, a master builder and architect, a geometer, a mapmaker, a keeper of the calendar...?

Installation views of *Imagine—After the Deluge*, Friesen Gallery, Ketchum, ID, 2008

The Calendar Keeper, 2008. Encaustic, mixed media on canvas, 57 x 60 x 9 in.

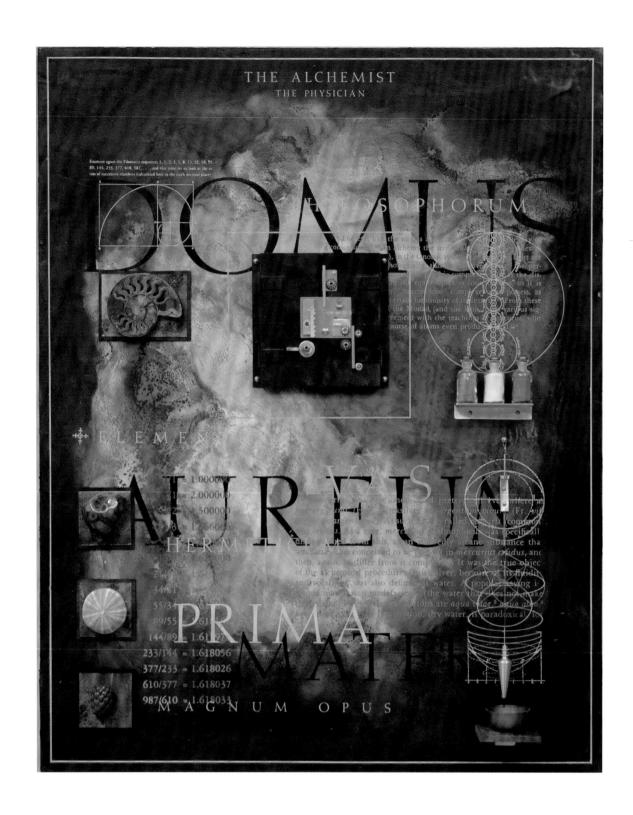

The Alchemist/The Physician, 2008. Encaustic, mixed media on canvas, 48 x 36 x 6 in. Private collection

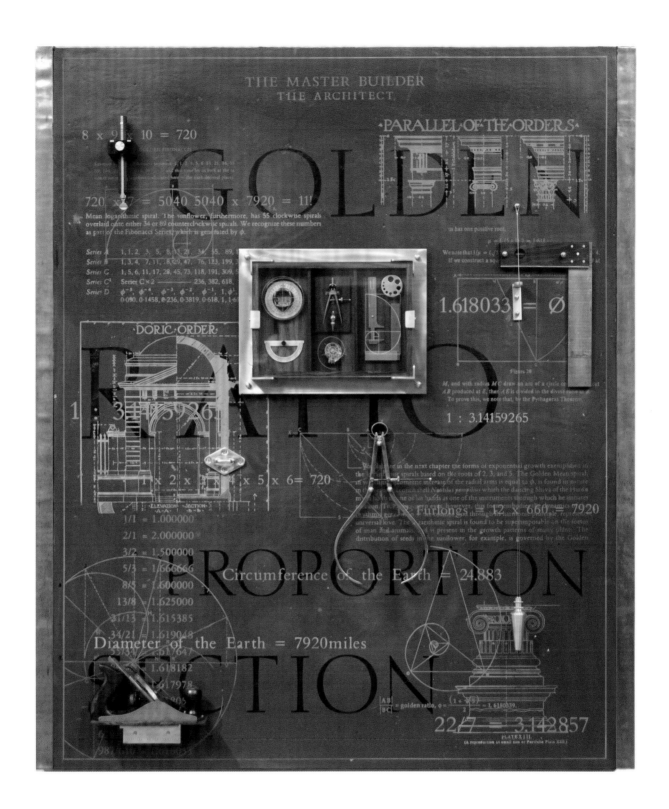

The Master Builder/The Architect, 2008. Encaustic, mixed media on canvas, 48 x 36 x 6 in. Private collection

The Wind Conjurer, 2008. Encaustic, mixed media on canvas, 60 x 42 x 10 in. Private collection

Prospero's Abecedarium, 2015. Fused, slumped and sand blasted glass, mild steel. 44 x 32 x 8 inches

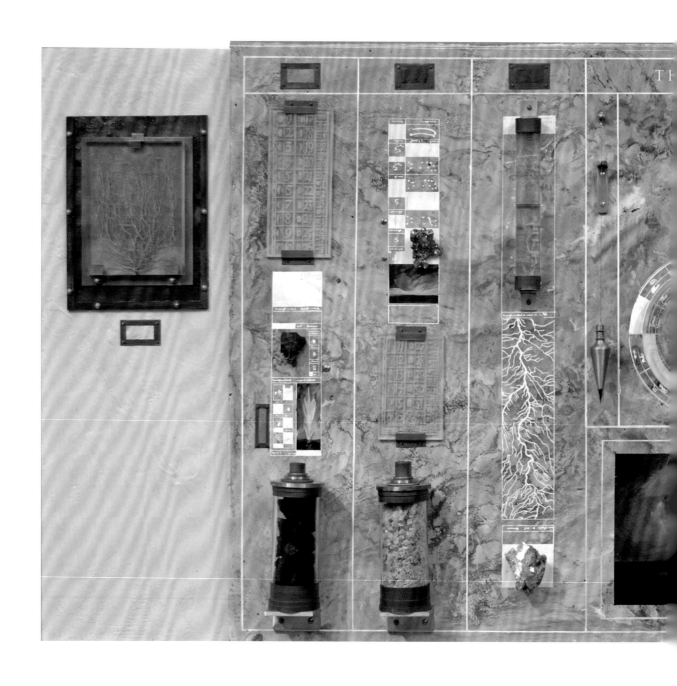

The Lightning Catcher, 2008. Encaustic, mixed media on canvas, 36 x 80 x 7 in. Private collection

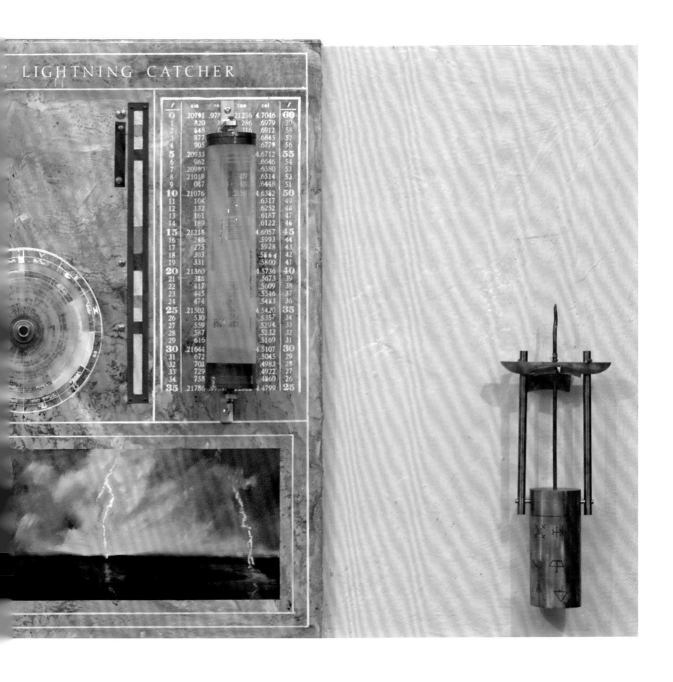

The Navigator, 2008. Encaustic, mixed media on canvas, 72 x 60 x 12 in. Private collection

The Honey Merchant, 2008. Encaustic, mixed media on canvas, 65 x 72 x 12 in. Private collection

SULTAN'S LIBRARY

In 2011, Mee and Evans collaborated on *Sultan's Library*, an exhibition shown at the Friesen Gallery in Ketchum, Idaho.

The artistic conceit for this body of work was that a "sultan or grand emperor" would gather all of his explorers into his newly constructed and empty library of future wonders. He would grandly charge them to disperse out into the world to acquire fabulous and never-before-seen treasures and return them for his collection.

The show presented the fanciful objects that were acquired and shipped back to the fictional library. Many of the objects were shown along with their shipping crates, complete with exotic shipping labels, freight stamps, and fantastic bills of lading. Simulated museum texts were posted on the walls expressing the location and fictitious provenance of the objects.

Installation views of *Sultan's Library*, Friesen Gallery, Ketchum, ID, 2011

Prima Luce, 2011. Encaustic, mixed media on canvas, 68 x 54 x 7 in. Private collection

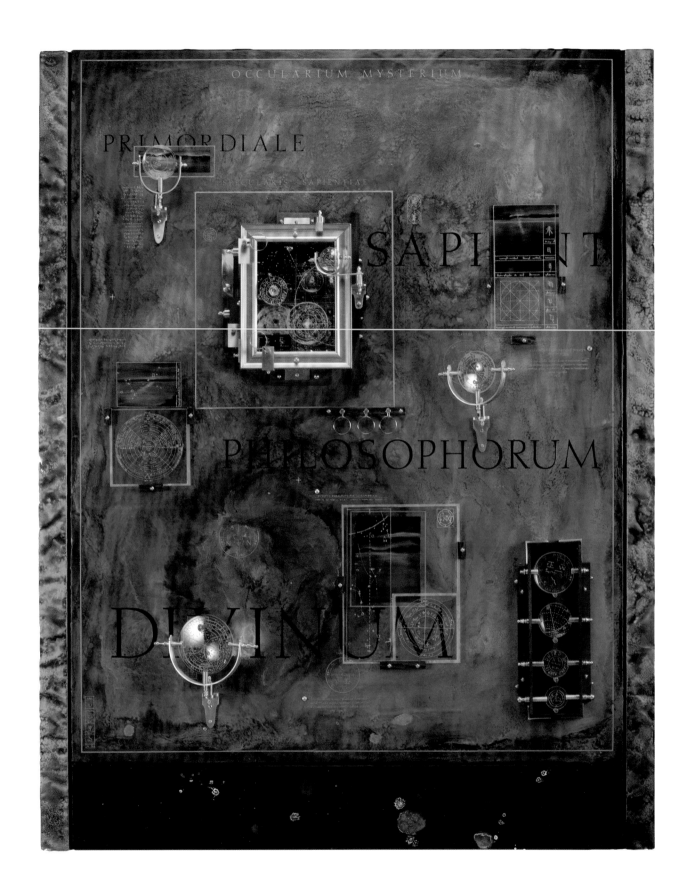

Occularium Mysterium, 2011. Encaustic, mixed media on canvas, 68 x 54 x 7 in. Private collection

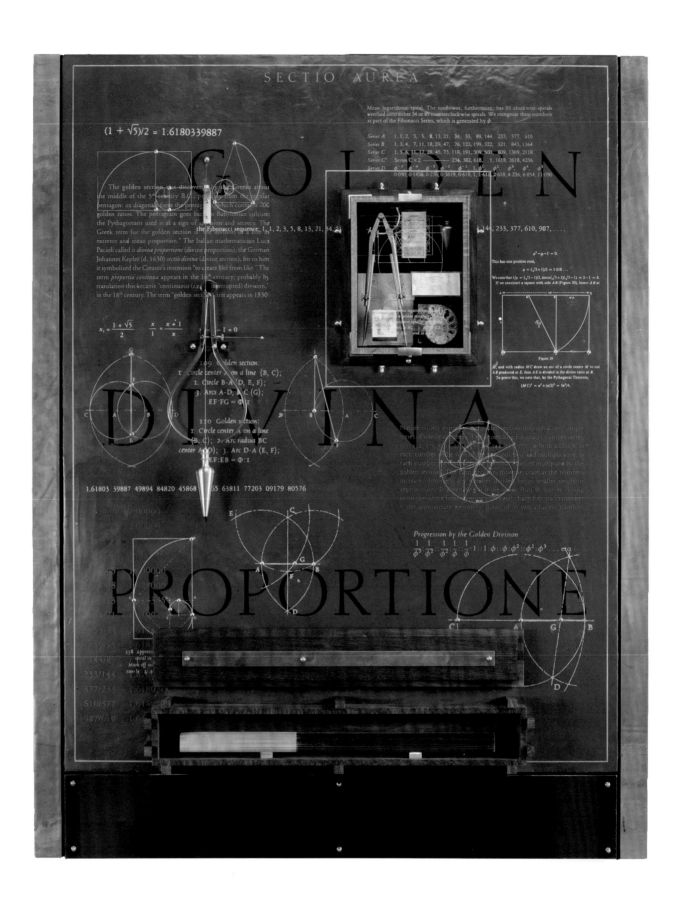

Sectio Aureo, 2011. Encaustic, mixed media on canvas, 68 x 54 x 7 in. Collection of Jon and Judy Runstad

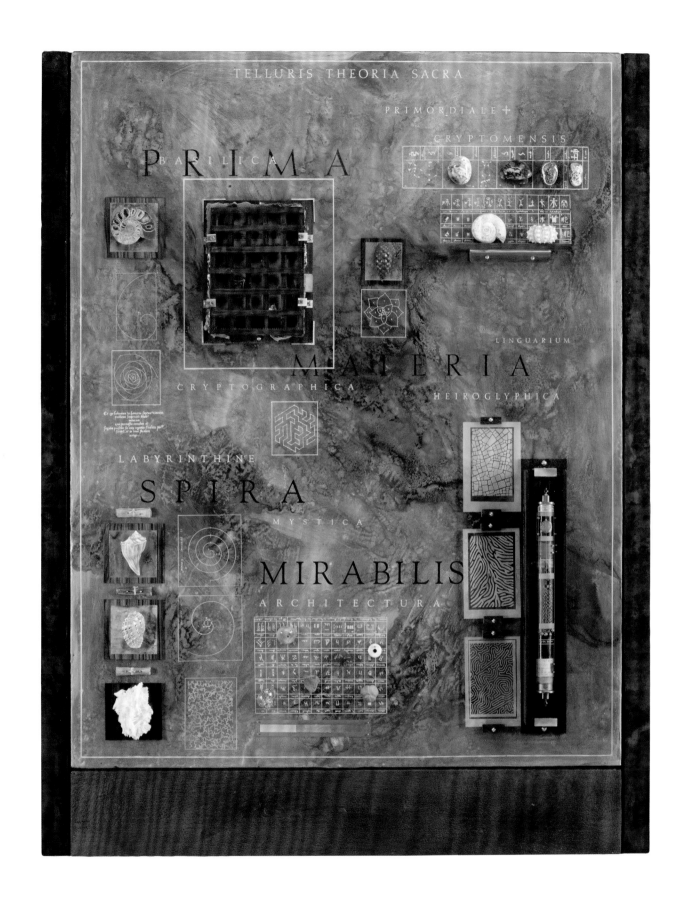

Telluris Theoria Sacra, 2011. Encaustic, mixed media on canvas, 68 x 54 x 7 in. Private collection

Ignis Theoria Sacra, 2011. Encaustic, mixed media on canvas, 33 x 25 x 7 in. Private collection

Novissimi Instrumenti de Venti, 2011. Encaustic, mixed media on canvas, 33 x 25 x 6 in. Private collection

PROSPERO'S BOOKS/PROSPERO'S LIBRARY

These were two incredibly elaborate exhibitions based on ideas found in *The Tempest* by William Shakespeare and secondarily in Peter Greenaway's film *Prospero's Books*.

They were shown both at Freisen Gallery in Ketchum, ID, and Woodside/Braseth Gallery in Seattle in 2015 and 2016, respectively.

Installation view of *Prospero's Books/Prospero's Library*, Woodside/Braseth Gallery, Seattle, 2016

NOTES FROM THE CATALOGUE
NANCY MEE/DENNIS EVANS:
PROSPERO'S LIBRARY

Magician Prospero, rightful Duke of Milan, and his daughter, Miranda, having been stranded for twelve years on an island after Prospero's jealous brother Antonio deposed him and set him adrift with the then three-year-old Miranda. Gonzalo, Prospero's counselor,

secretly supplied their boat with plenty of food, water, clothes and the most prized books from Prospero's library. These books enabled Prospero to find his way across oceans, to combat malignant spirits, to colonize an island, to educate and entertain Miranda and (most importantly) to summon Tempests. The works in these exhibitions imagined what Prospero's Library would have been like.

Installation view of *Prospero's Library*, Woodside/Braseth Gallery, 2016

Un Petite Livre des Étoiles, 2015. Encaustic, mixed media on canvas, 68 x 54 x 7 in. Private collection

Horologium, 2011. Encaustic, mixed media on canvas, 68 x 54 x 7 in. Private collection

Large Tome of Tellurian Topics, 2011. Encaustic, mixed media on canvas, overall 73 x 28 x 12 in. Private collection

The Empire of Signs, 2011. Encaustic, mixed media on canvas, overall 73 x 28 x 12 in. Colorado College

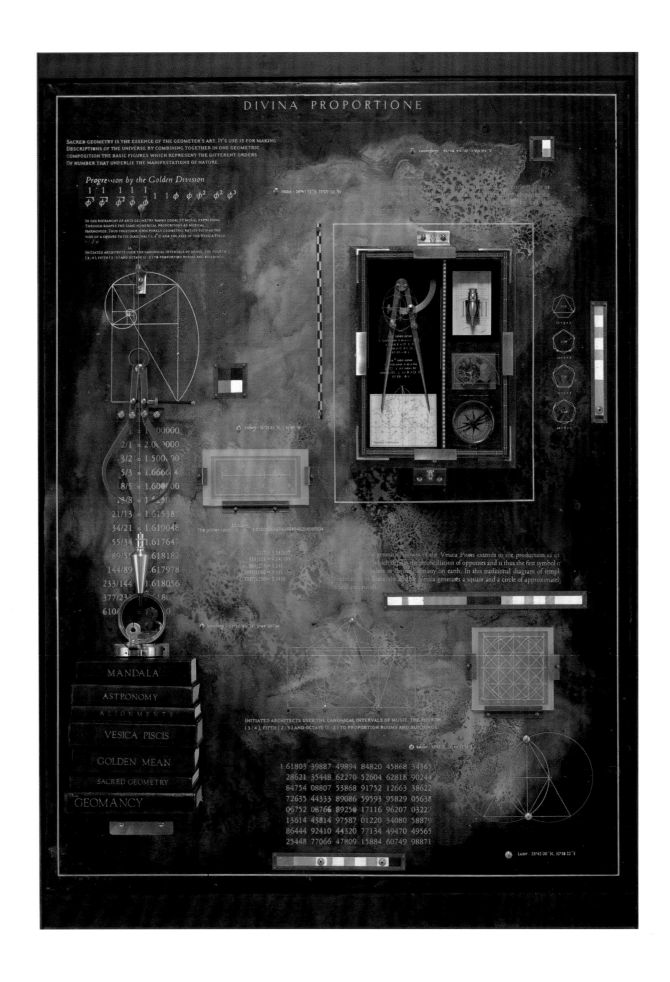

Divina Proportione, 2011. Encaustic, mixed media on canvas, 68 x 54 x 7 in. Collection of Dave Eaton and Kathleen LaFrancis Eaton

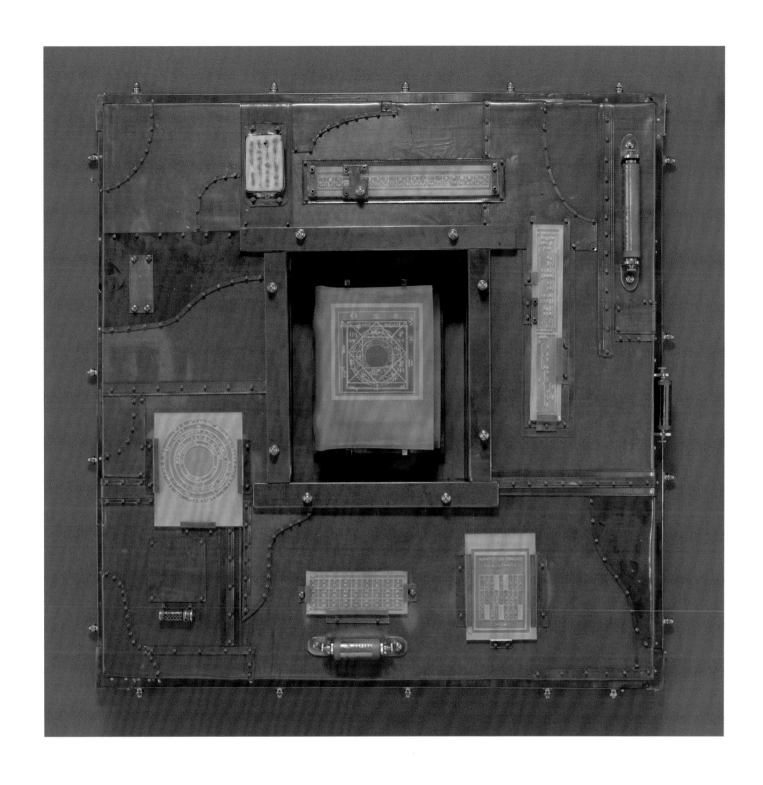

An Atlas of Ciphers, 2011. Encaustic, mixed media on canvas, 26 x 26 x 5 inches. Collection of the artist

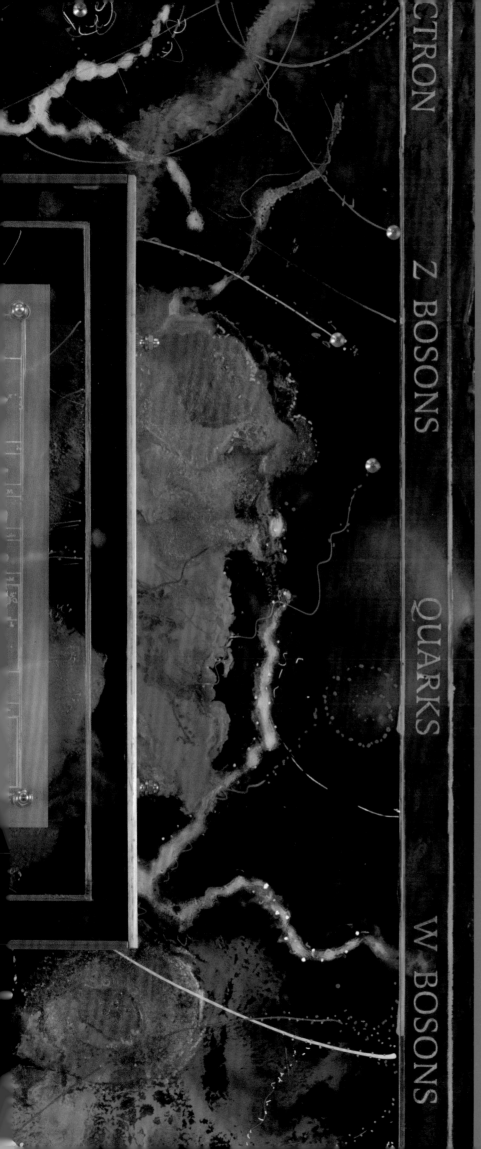

№6 COSMOLOGY

CONTEMPLORIUM

CINTAMANI

THE COSMIC CODE

Detail of *Canto IV* from *The Cosmic Code II*, 2020. Seattle University

CONTEMPLORIUM

In 2009, Evans was invited to create an installation in a private residence. The client was a writer and had a dedicated room in his home for the purpose of writing. Only a desk and computer occupied the room. The client wanted a piece that represented the history of the universe from the point of view of *Homo sapiens*. The resultant artworks covered the entire room—all four walls, corner to corner, beginning with the "Big Bang" and ending at the *end of time*.

This commission was a catalyst for Evans's inquiries into the history of the universe, which, from this project forward, has been the sole focus of his work.

Views of *Contemplorium*, 2009. Multiple panels: encaustic, mixed media, etched glass

CINTAMANI

The paintings in this collection represent an ongoing trajectory of interest for Evans.

On July 4, 2012, the ATLAS and CMS scientists at the Large Hadron Collider at CERN (the European Organization for Nuclear Research) announced they had each observed a new particle in the mass region around 125 GeV. This was a sign that the Higgs boson particle that had been predicted by the Standard Model does exist. This finding threw the scientific community into a frenzy and for whatever existential reason did the same for Evans's work.

This event signaled the beginning of his interest in cosmology.

Multiverses from *Cern Collection*, 2020. Encaustic, mixed media on canvas, 65 x 60 x 10 in. Collection of the artist

Deep Space from *Cern Collection*, 2020. Encaustic, mixed media on canvas, 65 x 60 x 10 in. Collection of the artist

The Standard Model from *Cern Collection*, 2020. Encaustic, mixed media on canvas, 60 x 65 x 10 in. Collection of Nancy Mee

Mysterium Materia from *Cern Collection*, 2020. Encaustic, mixed media on canvas, 60 x 65 x 10 in. Collection of the artist

The Standard Model II from *Cern Collection*, 2020, Encaustic, mixed media on canvas, 60 x 65 x 10 in. Collection of the artist

Origin of Stars from *Cern Collection*, 2019. Encaustic, mixed media on canvas, 54 x 65 x 10 in. Collection of the artist

THE COSMIC CODE

In 2018, Evans continued to expand on the ideas he had developed in the building of the *Contemplorium*. He advanced the story of the History of the Universe in a more detailed and expansive manner. Evans was reading and studying quantum physics and the huge field of Cosmology.

The result was a work of art he called *The Cosmic Code*, which was an array of twenty-one panels, each depicting a particular stage in the evolution of the universe. This version now resides in the University of Washington's Medicine, Karalis Retina Center at South Lake Union.

Shortly after this installation was installed, Seattle University commissioned Evans to create *The Cosmic Code II*, which was another rendition of the above work. This time, the story was depicted using ten larger panels. It is now installed in Seattle University's new Science and Innovation Building.

Canto XI from *The Cosmic Code II*, 2021. Encaustic, mixed media on canvas, 48 x 32 x 2 in. Seattle University

Canto II from *The Cosmic Code II*, 2021. Encaustic, mixed media on canvas, 48 x 32 x 12 in. Seattle University

Canto IV from *The Cosmic Code II*, 2021. Encaustic, mixed media on canvas, 48 x 32 x12 in. Seattle University

Canto X from *The Cosmic Code II*, 2021. Encaustic, mixed media on canvas, 48 x 32 x 2 in. Seattle University

Collider I from *Cern Collection*, 2021. Encaustic, mixed media on canvas, 60 x 60 x 10 in. Collection of MD², Seattle

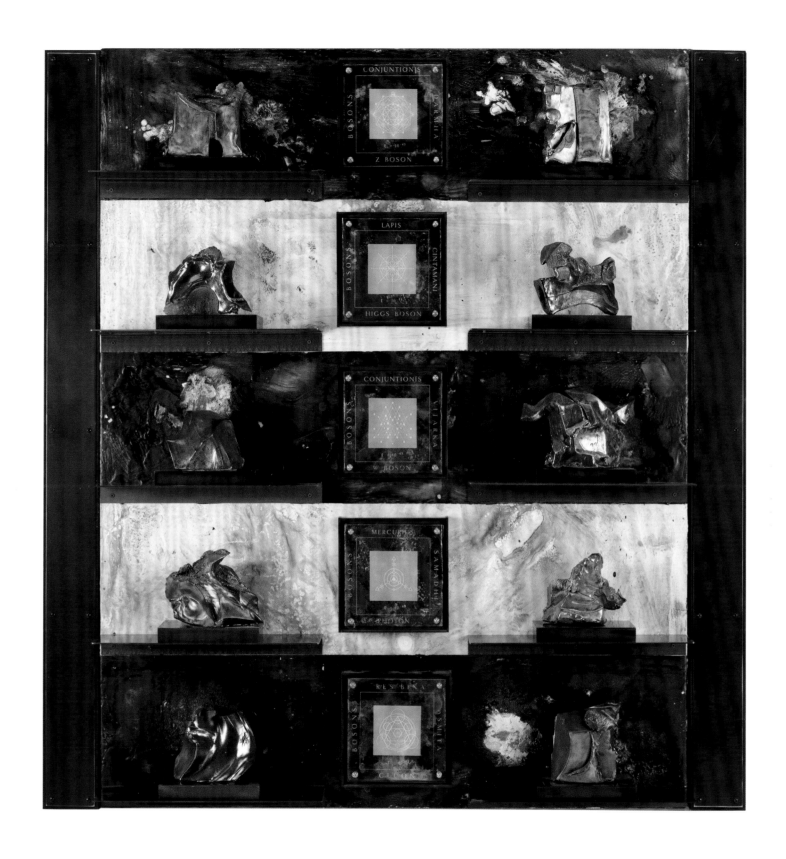

Collider II from *Cern Collection*, 2020. Encaustic, mixed media on canvas, 60 x 60 x 10 in. Collection of Nancy Mee

№ 7 UTOPIAN HEIGHTS

THE GARDEN

THE SHRINE

THE FAMILY

Detail of the entrance to the garden at Utopian Heights

THE GARDEN

The Garden of Souls was begun—inadvertently—on September 11, 2001. It was initially intended to be simply an outdoor garden on the grounds of Utopian Heights, with custom viewing rooms to display and sell Nancy's sculptures.

It evolved during the decades, with Evans planting and shaping and refining the garden and Nancy creating new sculptures, but it still functions as a place for contemplation and reflection, and as a memorial for all souls that were lost—or passed forward, as Dennis and Nancy say—during that single day, September 11.

Evans planted more than forty bright pink Prunus "Thundercloud" trees in the garden and along the adjacent streets, and carefully selected stones and Mee created sculptures to enhance the garden. Bronze plaques with philosophical passages and minimalistic benches offer a place for occasional passers-by and residents of the area to find quiet and contemplation.

(above and following pages) Views of Utopian Heights Garden with Nancy Mee sculptures, 2022

THE SHRINE

In the Utopian Heights garden, Evans and Mee have included a small wooden shrine, inspired by the Shinto shrines they saw in Kyoto, where passers-by can leave their prayers and affirmations. These small notes are gathered and burned every six months, and so joined with the universe. The most private and touching little notes filled the shrine, reminding us of the deep need for spirituality in our daily lives.

Time-lapse photograph of Dennis Evans in his studio, 2018

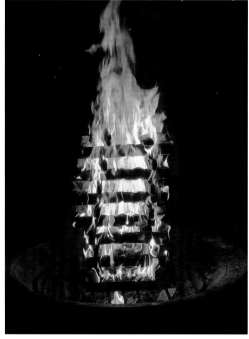

The Solstice Fire, 2021, Utopian Heights Garden

THE FAMILY

Utopian Heights Studios are the primary home and generative workshops for Nancy Mee and Dennis Evans. A long list of young artists, godchildren and occasional helpers have shared the workshops and assisted Nancy and Dennis with their work over the years. This collection of beloved helpers has come to be considered family by Nancy and Dennis.

André Gene Samson, Spike Mafford, Paul Casey at Utopian Heights Studios, 2015

Nancy Mee, Dennis Evans (back to camera), Mary Ann Peters,
Matthew Kangas at a performance of *Twelve Field Us(e)ages/A Passion Play*,
University of Washington Center for Urban Horticulture, 1980

Dennis Evans working in studio, Utopian Heights Studios, 2015

In Utopian Heights Studios: (top) Paul Casey, 2015; (middle, left) Stephanie Shultz, 2015; (middle right) André Gene Samson, 2015; (bottom) Dennis Evans with John Braseth, 2019

(top) Nancy Mee, Utopian Heights Studios, 2015
(above left) Andria Friesen
(above right) Nancy Mee with Dennis Evans

BIOGRAPHY

Born Dennis Eugene Evans, November 16, 1946, Yakima, WA, son of Maurice F. Evans (b. 1915) and
Cecilia La Framboise (b. 1913)
US Marines, 1969–71
US Army National Guard, 1971–75
Married Nancy Mee, 1980
Represented by Friesen Gallery, Ketchum, ID. https://friesenlantz.com

SELECTED AWARDS AND HONORS

Henry Art Gallery Biennial Award, 1975
National Endowment for the Arts Artist Fellowship, 1980

EDUCATION

St. Paul Cathedral School, Yakima, WA, 1956–64
Diploma, Marquette High School, Yakima, WA, 1964
BS, University of Washington, Seattle, 1969
BFA, University of Washington, Seattle, 1973
MFA, University of Washington, Seattle, 1975

TEACHING EXPERIENCE

Helen Bush School, Seattle, 1975–90

EXHIBITION HISTORY

Solo Exhibitions

2022

Dennis Evans: Fractal Contingencies, Friesen Gallery, Ketchum, ID

2019

The Divine Comedy—A Conjuring of the Cosmos, Gallerie C.E.N., Utopian Heights Studios, Seattle

2013

The Humbling of Indra, Woodside/Braseth Gallery, Seattle

2010

The Sorcerers of the River, Woodside/Braseth Gallery, Seattle

2007

Elins and Eagles-Smith Gallery, San Francisco

2006

The Philosopher's Wedding, Woodside/Braseth Gallery, Seattle

2005

22 Kits of Creation, Woodside/Braseth Gallery, Seattle

2003

Writing Lessons/Reading Sessions, Gerald Peters Gallery, New York

2002

Writing Lessons/Reading Sessions, Woodside/Braseth Gallery, Seattle

2000

The Autumn Fires Chronicles, Erickson & Elins Gallery, San Francisco

The Winter Fires Chronicles, Laura Russo Gallery, Portland, OR

The Millennium Fires Chronicles, Woodside/Braseth Gallery, Seattle. Traveled to Simon Edwards Gallery, Yakima, WA

Gail Severn Gallery, Ketchum, Idaho

1999

Cagliostro Library, Simon Edwards Gallery, Yakima, WA

1998

The Book of Hours, Erickson & Elins Gallery, San Francisco

1997

The Library of Babel, Meyerson & Nowinski Gallery, Seattle

The 55 Grammars of Eden, Laura Russo Gallery, Portland, OR

The Anatomy of the Perfect Landscape, Simon Edwards Gallery, Yakima, WA

1996

The Anatomy of the Perfect Language, Erickson & Elins Gallery, San Francisco

1995

The Four Forces of the Universe, Linda Farris Gallery, Seattle. Traveled to Laura Russo Gallery, Portland, OR

1993

The Science of Secrets, Boise Art Museum. Sandy Harthorn, curator

Categories and the Classics, Laura Russo Gallery, Portland, OR

1992

The Critique of Pure Writing, Linda Farris Gallery, Seattle

1991

Altered Altars, Linda Farris Gallery, Seattle

1990

LIBER MUNDI LIBER VITAE, Linda Farris Gallery, Seattle

1989

Northwest Viewpoints: Dennis Evans, Portland Art Museum, OR. John Weber, curator

tHE garden foR remeMbered dEsireS, Linda Farris Gallery, Seattle

1987

Talking Pictures, Linda Farris Gallery, Seattle

1985

Documents Northwest: The PONCHO Series/Dennis Evans, Seattle Art Museum. Bruce Guenther, curator

Syntax: Sintax, Linda Farris Gallery, Seattle

1982

The Chymical Nuptials of Soma and Agni or Rather the Allegory of Corny Agrippa and the Slippery Bath, Linda Farris Gallery, Seattle

1981

Wekel Gallery, Pacific Lutheran University, Tacoma, WA. David Keyes, curator

1980

Seven Garments and Seven Lies for the Passing of Days, Linda Farris Gallery, Seattle

Twelve Field Us(e)ages, Whatcom Museum of History and Art, Bellingham, WA. George Thomas, curator

1978

Eastern Washington University Gallery of Art, Cheney, WA. Hugh Webb, curator

Quay Gallery, San Francisco

Instruments and Diagrams, Linda Farris Gallery, Seattle

1977

Evergreen Gallery, Evergreen State College, Olympia, WA. Paul Sharp, curator

Portland State University White Gallery, Portland, OR. C.E. Licka, curator

Soundings, Linda Farris Gallery, Seattle

FluxFest, and/or, Seattle

1976

Musical Instruments of Dennis Evans, Henry Art Gallery, University of Washington, Seattle. LaMar Harrington, curator

Exhibitions with Nancy Mee

2022

Dennis Evans and Nancy Mee: Cyclopean Binaries, Bainbridge Island Museum of Art, WA. Greg Robinson, curator

2019

Prospero's Library, Woodside/Braseth Gallery, Seattle

2016

Prospero's Books, Woodside/Braseth Gallery, Seattle

2015

Prospero's Books, Friesen Gallery, Ketchum, ID

2011

Sultan's Library, Friesen Gallery, Ketchum, ID

2008–09

Imagine—After the Deluge, Friesen Gallery, Ketchum, ID, and Woodside/Braseth Gallery, Seattle

1998

Evans and Mee: Pillars of Wisdom, Port Angeles Fine Arts Center, Port Angeles, WA. Jake Seniuk, curator

Selected Group Exhibitions

2020

Woodside/Braseth Gallery, Seattle

2019

Woodside/Braseth Gallery, Seattle

2014

FILTERED: What Does Love Look Like?, Friesen Gallery, Ketchum, ID

2013

First Light: Inaugural Exhibition, Bainbridge Island Museum of Art, Bainbridge Island, WA. Greg Robinson, curator

2012

Best of the Northwest: Selected Works from Tacoma Art Museum, Tacoma Art Museum, Tacoma, WA. Margaret E. Bullock and Rock Hushka, curators

2011

The Silver Summit, Friesen Gallery, Ketchum, ID

2009

A Concise History of Northwest Art, Tacoma Art Museum, Tacoma, WA. Margaret E. Bullock and Rock Hushka, curators

Speaking Parts, Tacoma Art Museum, Tacoma, WA. Rock Hushka, curator

2008

eARTh, Woodside/Braseth Gallery, Seattle

Seeds of Compassion, Friesen Gallery, Ketchum, ID

2007

Friesen Gallery, Ketchum, ID

2000

Surface, Gail Severn Gallery, Ketchum, ID

1999

Gail Severn Gallery, Ketchum, ID

1996

Drawing on Chance: *Selections from the Collection*, Museum of Modern Art, New York

Gail Severn Gallery, Ketchum, ID

1995

Only the Shadow Knows: Revelations from the Unconscious, Art Access Gallery, Salt Lake City

1994

Drawings and Sculptures of Joseph Beuys/Contemporary Inspirations, Bellevue Art Museum, Bellevue, WA. Susan Sagawa, curator

Sacred Forms Revisited: *Contemporary Altars*, *Shrines and Icons*, Security Pacific Gallery, Seattle. Chase Rynd, curator

Dreams and Shields, Salt Lake Art Center, Salt Lake City, UT. Frank McIntire, curator

Computer-Generated Art, North Seattle College, Seattle.

1991

Come to Your Senses, Bellevue Art Museum, Bellevue, WA. Susan Sagawa, curator

The War in the Gulf: *From the Artist's Perspective*, William Traver Gallery, Seattle

1990

Sound Visions, Center On Contemporary Art, Seattle. Larry Reid, curator

Art Bound: Artist Handmade, One-of-a-Kind Books, Bumbershoot Arts Festival, Seattle Center. Joyce Moty, curator

Twentieth Anniversary Exhibition, Linda Farris Gallery, Seattle

100 Years of Washington Art, Tacoma Art Museum, Tacoma, WA. Penelope Loucas, curator

Rain of Talent: *Umbrella Art*, The Fabric Workshop, Philadelphia

1988

School of Art 1975–1988, SAFECO Insurance Companies, Seattle. Matthew Kangas, curator

Linda Farris Gallery, Seattle, WA

1987

Bumberbiennale: *Seattle Sculpture 1927–1987*, Bumbershoot Arts Festival, Seattle Center, Seattle. Matthew Kangas, curator

Contemporary Masks, Whatcom Museum of History and Art, Bellingham, WA. George Thomas, curator

Private Visions, *Public Spaces*, Bellevue Art Museum, Bellevue, WA

Culture and Perception: *Surface*, NBBJ, Seattle

Inside Information, The Art Gym, Marylhurst University, Lake Oswego, OR. Terri Hopkins, curator

1986

15th Avenue Studio, Henry Art Gallery, University of Washington, Seattle. Chris Bruce, curator

Northwest Artist's Books, Carolyn Staley Gallery, Seattle

Artist Boxes, Museo Rufino Tamayo, Mexico City

1985

Seeing Double, Bumbershoot Arts Festival, Seattle Center, Seattle. Ron Glowen, curator

1984

Id, Bette Stoler Gallery, New York

Little Fictions, *Little Romances*, Hodges/Banks Gallery, Seattle. Ron Glowen, curator

Seminary, Whatcom Museum of History and Art, Bellingham, WA. George Thomas, curator

1983

Linda Farris Gallery Artists, Pritchard Gallery, University of Idaho, Moscow, ID

Outside New York: *Seattle*, The New Museum, New York. Ned Rifkin, curator. Traveled to Seattle Art Museum, Seattle

X-Change: *Five L.A. Artists and Five Seattle Artists*, Karl Bornstein Gallery, Los Angeles

1982

Six Story Tellers North of Tukwila, Wekel Gallery, Pacific Lutheran University, Tacoma, WA. Greg Bell, curator

1980

Eight Seattle Artists, Los Angeles Institute of Contemporary Art, Los Angeles

Raconteur: *A Private View*, Henry Art Gallery, University of Washington, Seattle, WA. Harvey West, curator

Seattle Drawing Invitational, Seattle Pacific University, Seattle. Michael Caldwell, curator

1979

Another Side to Art: Ceramic Sculpture of the Northwest 1959–1979, Seattle Art Museum, Seattle. LaMar Harrington, curator

1979 Biennial Exhibition, Whitney Museum of American Art, New York. Barbara Haskell, Richard Marshall and Patterson Sims, curators

Sound: *An Exhibition of Sound Sculpture, Instrument Building and Acoustically Tuned Spaces*, Los Angeles Institute of Contemporary Art. Richard Armstrong, Ivor Darreg and Peter Frank, curators. Traveled to P. S. 1, Long Island City, NY

The Washington Open, Seattle Art Museum, Seattle. Barbara Haskell and Charles Cowles, jurors

Some Seattle Drawing, and/or, Seattle. Anne Focke, curator

1978

Crafts '78, Bellevue Art Museum, Bellevue, WA

Harmonious Craft: *American Musical Instruments*, Renwick Gallery, National Collection of Fine Arts, Smithsonian Institution, Washington, DC. Lloyd Herman, curator. Traveled to American Craft Museum, New York

New Ideas #1, Seattle Art Museum. Charles Cowles, curator

1977

Fluxfest, and/or, Seattle.

Northwest Craftsmen's Exhibition, Henry Art Gallery, University of Washington, Seattle. LaMar Harrington, curator

Northwest '77, Seattle Art Museum, Seattle. Charles Cowles, curator

Seattle Sculpture Invitational, Seattle Pacific University, Seattle. Michael Caldwell, curator

1976

Drawing 1976, Bellevue Art Museum, Bellevue, WA

In Touch: *Nature, Ritual and Sensuous Art from the Northwest*, Portland Center for the Visual Arts, Portland, OR. Lucy R. Lippard, curator

Linda Farris Gallery, Seattle

1975

Northwest Craftsmen's Exhibition, Henry Art Gallery, University of Washington, Seattle. LaMar Harrington, curator

Seattle Sculpture, Seattle Pacific University, Seattle. Michael Caldwell, curator

Seattle/7 Printmakers, Town Hall Gallery, University of Alabama, Tuscaloosa, AL

Washington Crafts Invitational, State Capitol Museum, Olympia, WA

1974

4 x 4/Seattle Video, and/or, Seattle

1973

Northwest Craftsmen's Biennial, Henry Art Gallery, University of Washington, Seattle. LaMar Harrington, curator

58th Annual Exhibition of Northwest Artists, Seattle Art Museum, Seattle

SELECTED COLLECTIONS AND COMMISSIONS

4Culture, King County Public Art Collection, Seattle

AT&T Gateway Tower, Seattle

Boise Art Museum

Bristol-Myers Squibb

City of Seattle Office of Arts and Culture, Portable Works Collection

Colorado College, Colorado Springs, CO

Davis Wright Tremaine LLC, Seattle

Eastern Washington University, Cheney, WA

Henry Art Gallery, University of Washington, Seattle

Junior League, Seattle

Kittredge Gallery, Pacific Lutheran University, Seattle

Metropolitan Museum of Art, New York

Microsoft, Inc., Redmond, WA

The Museum of Modern Art, New York

PathoGenesis Corp., Seattle

Philip Morris USA

Physio-Control, Redmond, WA

Portland Art Museum, OR

Rare Books, University of Washington Libraries, Seattle

Renwick Gallery of the Smithsonian American Art Museum

Seattle Art Museum

Seattle University School of Law

Sheraton Seattle Grand Hotel

Swedish Hospital First Hill Campus, Seattle

Stanford University Center for Advanced Studies in the Behavioral Sciences, Palo Alto, CA

Stohl Rives LLP, Seattle

Tacoma Art Museum

University of Delaware Library, Newark

University of Washington Medical Center, Seattle

Whatcom Museum, Bellingham, WA

BIBLIOGRAPHY

Newspapers, Magazines and Journals

Albert, Fred. "The Art of Living." *Seattle Magazine*, March 1995, 28–33.

Albright, Thomas. "At the Galleries: Invasion of the Shamen." *San Francisco Chronicle*, October 28, 1978: 37.

Ament, Deloris Tarzan. "Dennis Evans: A Career Based on Magic." *Seattle Times*, January 11, 1989: C1, 5.

Appelo, Tim. "Short Reviews." *The Weekly* (Seattle), May 15, 1980.

Berger, David. "Museum Piece Plays Well on Several Levels." *Seattle Times*, May 17, 1985.

———. "Works by Dennis Evans." *The Weekly* (Seattle), September 27, 1978.

———. "Dennis Evans Shrines . . . ." *Artweek*, September 30, 1978.

Campbell, R.M. "Art Pavilion Show—Small is Beautiful." *Seattle Post-Intelligencer*, March 15, 1978: D13.

———. "The Elegant Sound of Rain Falling on a Sponge." *Seattle Post-Intelligencer*, February 19, 1977.

———. "Evans: It's Not Your Standard Gallery Show." *Seattle Post-Intelligencer*, September 29, 1978: 18.

Dalton, Marcie. "PA Library Pieces Unveiled at Fine Arts Center." *Peninsula Daily News*, July 2, 1998: D4.

Downey, Janice. "Arts Center Books Duo." *Peninsula Daily News*, July 30, 1998.

Faber, Nancy. "Arts," *People*, July 16, 1979.

Glowen, Ron. "Altered States." *Artweek*, September 25, 1982, 16.

———. "Seminary." *Vanguard* 13, no. 3 (April 1984): 46–47.

———. "Surveying Seattle, A New Image." *Artweek*, November 19, 1983.

Hackett, Regina. "Artist Eulogizes Ritual He Knew As a Catholic Farmboy." *Seattle Post-Intelliigencer*, January 14, 1989: C1.

———. "Dennis Evans Creates an Art Web." *Seattle Post-Intelligencer*, September 11, 1982.

———. "Four Gallery Exhibits Highlight the Strengths of Northwest Diversity." *Seattle Post-Intelligencer*, October 14, 1992: C5.

———. "Seattle Artists Come Home in N.Y. Show." *Seattle Post-Intelligencer*, October 19, 1983: C12.

———. "Seattle Artists Picked for N.Y. Show." *Seattle Post-Intelligencer*, December 22, 1982: D6.

———. "She Strives for 'Pure' Response in Her Work." *Seattle Post-Intelligencer*, May 11, 1980: G6.

———. "Smoke Screen is Essential to Evans' Mysterious Works." *Seattle Post-Intelligencer*, May 16, 1985: C9.

———. "Snubbed in NY: Seattle Art show Gets No Respect." *Seattle Post-Intelligencer*, October 12, 1983.

Kangas, Matthew. "Ceramic Dematerializations." *Artweek*, September 20, 1980.

———. "A Decade of Excellence at Linda Farris." *Argus*, August 10, 1979.

———. "Is the Art Museum's 'Open' Really Closed?" *Argus*, August 3, 1979.

———. "L.A. X-Change/Linda Farris Gallery/Seattle/June 9–July 5." *Vanguard*, September 1983.

———. "Little Romances/Little Fictions." *Vanguard*, May 1984.

———. "Modern Ideas: Abstract Artists Appear to Know No Boundaries." *Seattle Times*, October 12, 1995.

———. "Neel, Noah & Chew Featured in Pioneer Square Galleries." *Argus*, October 26, 1979.

———. "Part of the Way Up From Verbosity-as-art." *Argus*, March 10, 1978, 8.

———. "Review: Dennis Evans and Nancy Mee at Woodside/Braseth." visualartsourceweeklynewsletter.com, September 17, 2016.

———. "School for Sculptors: Sizing up the Graduates of the University of Washington Art Department." *Seattle Weekly*, September 6, 1989.

———. "Scientific Mumbo-Jumbo at Luce Show." *Argus*, April 13, 1979.

———. "Sculpture in Seattle Since the 1962 World's Fair." *Northwest Arts*, May 26, 1978.

———. "Seattle Atelier." *Artweek*, March 8, 1990.

———. "SEATTLE: 'Northwest Impressions' at Henry Art Gallery." *Art in America*, May 1987.

———. "'Shocking Gaps' in Current SAM Display." *Argus*, December 28, 1978.

———. "Three Important Artists: Dennis Evans, Mary Ann Peters, Robert Maki." *Argus*, Fall 1978.

———. "Two Northwest Traditions." *Art in America*, September 1979.

Kelly, Claire C. "Sense and Sensuality in Northwest Art." *Artweek*, October 23, 1976, 1.

Kendall, Sue Ann. "Divergent Styles Mark Two Artists' New Shows." *Seattle Times*, September 18, 1982.

Larson, Kay. "Uncommon Visions." *New York* 16, no. 20. May 16, 1983: 60–61.

"Library Art." *Peninsula Daily News*, June 29, 1998: A5.

Lincoln, Brad. "Library's Art Fuels Debate/Art: About 200 Attend Meeting to Discuss Religious Overtones of Panels." *Peninsula Daily News*, May 30, 1997: A1.

———. "Library Opts for Art Work." *Peninsula Daily News*, June 11, 1997: A1.

———. "Library Sparks Anger from Pastors/Art: Thursday Meeting to Air Concerns." *Peninsula Daily News*, May 28, 1997: A3.

Lippard, Lucy R. "Northwest Passage." *Art in America* (July-August 1976).

Logan, Dave. "The Library Board Voted to Display 9 Glass Etchings of the Muses." *Peninsula Daily News*, June 11, 1997: A1.

Muchnic, Suzanne. "An Assault from Seattle." *Los Angeles Times*, July 6, 1980: 89–90.

Seniuk, Jake. "Below Olympus," *On Center* 10, no. 4 (July/August 1998), 1–3.

Smallwood, Lyn. "Dennis Evans," *ARTnews* (January 1985), 179.

Szymanski, Jerry. "You are Art: The Idea as Art," *Bellingham Herald*, January 20, 1984.

Tarzan, Deloris. ["Dennis Evans, in his Alter Ego Ubu Waugh, Has an Installation of Tuned Sponges"]. *Seattle Times*, February 11, 1977.

———. "Evans Explores Art as Apparatus." *Seattle Times*, October 1, 1978: M7.

———. "Farris Gallery Celebrates 13 Years of Success." *Seattle Times*, May 27, 1983.

———. "Four Artists Present 'New Ideas'/Art Ain't What It Used to Be." *Seattle Times* [1978].

———. "Has Success Spoiled Bright, Young Dennis Evans?" *Seattle Times*, May 14, 1980: D1.

———. "Washington Artists Get Fellowships." *Seattle Times*, August 6, 1980.

Taylor, Barbara. "Dennis Evans." *Insight*: *A Journal* of *the Henry Gallery Association* (Spring 1980).

Thorpe, Keith. "New Glass Art Panels Placed in Library." *Peninsula Daily News*, June 29, 1998: A5.

Wihman, Liisa. "The Garden of Souls in the Utopian Heights Neighborhood." *The Intercontinental Gardener*, May 3, 2011.

Winn, Steven. "Galleries: Artists are still better as artists," *Seattle Weekly* [1978].

Books and Catalogues

Allan, Lois. *Contemporary Art in the Northwest*. Roseville East, New South Wales, Australia: Craftsman House, G+B Arts International, 1995: 80, 218–19.

Armstrong, Richard, Ivor Darreg and Peter Frank. *Sound*: *An Exhibition of Sound Sculpture, Instrument Building and Acoustically Tuned Spaces*. Los Angeles: Los Angeles Institute of Contemporary Art, 1979.

Bullock, Margaret E., and Rock Hushka. *Best of the Northwest*: *Selected Works from Tacoma Art Museum*. Tacoma, WA: Tacoma Art Museum, 2012, 96–97, 224.

Dennis Evans: *The Critique of Pure Writing*. Seattle: Linda Farris Gallery, 1992. Essay by Cameron Martin.

Guenther, Bruce. *Documents Northwest: The PONCHO Series/ Dennis Evans*. Seattle: Seattle Art Museum, 1985.

———. *50 Northwest Artists: A Critical Selection of Painters and Sculptors Working in the Pacific Northwest*. San Francisco: Chronicle Books, 1983, 40–41.

Grosshans, A., ed., *Hindsight I*. Seattle: and/or, 1977.

———. *Hindsight II*. Seattle: and/or, 1978.

Handhardt, John, Barbara Haskell, Richard Marshall, Mark Segal and Patterson Sims. *1979 Biennial Exhibition*. New York: Whitney Museum of American Art, 1979, 28.

Harrington, LaMar. *Ceramics in the Pacific Northwest: A History*. Seattle: University of Washington Press, 1979.

Heagerty, Ned, and Bill Ritchie. *Twelve Field Us(e)ages*. Bellingham, WA: Whatcom Museum of History and Art, 1980.

Herman, Lloyd. *Harmonious Craft: American Musical Instruments*. Washington, DC: Renwick Gallery, National Collection of Fine Arts, Smithsonian Institution, 1978.

Kangas, Matthew. *Bumberbiennale: Seattle Sculpture 1927–1987*. Seattle: Bumbershoot Arts Festival, 1987, n.p.

———. *Relocations: Selected Art Essays and Interviews*. New York: Midmarch Arts Press, 2008, 13–16, 128–29, 202–27, 228–32, 234, 454.

———. *School of Art 1975–1988*. Seattle: SAFECO Insurance Companies, 1988.

Lippard, Lucy R. *In Touch: Nature, Ritual and Sensuous Art From the Northwest*. Portland, OR: Portland Center for the Visual Arts, 1976.

———. *Overlay: Contemporary Art and the Art of Prehistory*. New York: The New Press, 1983, 192–93.

Nineteen Artists in Seventy-Nine: An Exhibition in Two Parts. Seattle: Linda Farris Gallery, 1979.

Outside New York: Seattle. New York: The New Museum and Seattle: Seattle Art Museum, 1983. Essay by Ned Rifkin.

Seniuk, Jake. *Strait Art: An Anthology of Exhibitions from the Upper Left-hand Corner*. La Conner, WA: Marrowstone Press and Museum of Northwest Art, 2019.

Taylor, Barbara. *Eight Seattle Artists*. Los Angeles: Los Angeles Institute of Contemporary Art, 1980.

Weber, John. *Northwest Viewpoints: Dennis Evans*. Portland, OR: Portland Art Museum, 1989.

West, Harvey. *The Washington Year: A Contemporary View, 1980–1981*. Seattle: The Henry Gallery Association, 1982.

PUBLICATIONS BY THE ARTIST

Cintamani: Dennis Evans, Works from 2010 to 2018. Seattle: artist's studio, 2018.

Dennis Evans: The (55) Grammars of Eden. Seattle: artist's studio, 1997.

Dennis Evans: The Book of Hours. Seattle: artist's studio, 1999.

Dennis Evans: The Humbling of Indra/Works from the Book of the Cosmos. Seattle: artist's studio, 2013.

Dennis Evans: The Seven Libraries of Babylon. Seattle: artist's studio, 1998.

Dennis Evans: The Sorcerers of the River. Seattle: artist's studio, 2010.

Dennis Evans: Writing Lessons/Reading Sessions. Seattle: artist's studio, 2002.

Evans, Dennis, and Carmine Chickadel. *The Canticle of Hours*. Seattle: Neo Vatikan Press, 1995.

——————. *Dark Matter*. Seattle: Neo Vatikan Press, 2015.

——————. *The Seven Cardinal Virtues*. Seattle: Neo Vatikan Press, 1991.

——————. *The Seven Deadly Sins*. Seattle: Neo Vatikan Press, 1990.

——————. *Thaumaturgy*. Seattle: Neo Vatikan Press, 1999.

Nancy Mee/Dennis Evans: Imagine—After The Deluge . . . Works from the 15 Masters of a New Utopia. Seattle: artist's studio, 2009.

Nancy Mee/Dennis Evans: Prospero's Library. Seattle: Utopian Heights Studios, 2016.

Nancy Mee/Dennis Evans: Sultan's Library. Seattle: artist's studio, 2010.

The Science of Secrets. Seattle: artist's studio, 1994. Essays by Basil Valentine, Sandy Harthorn, Susan Sagawa and John Weber.

INTERVIEWS

Dennis Evans, as Ubu Waugh, "Interview with Ubu Waugh" [with Charles Grimes], *Le Jardin de Monde: The Journal of International Casafundada*, Summer 1977: 32–41.

Hackett, Regina. "Artist eulogizes ritual he knew as a Catholic farm boy," *Seattle Post-Intelligencer*, January 14, 1989: C1, 3.

INDEX

Page numbers with an *f* refer to a figure or a caption; *n* refers to an endnote. Work titles without an artist's name are by Evans. Museums, galleries, and venues not otherwise identified are in Seattle, WA.

ARTIST'S ACKNOWLEDGMENTS

All books are the product of many minds. This project is no different. It is a story of my transformation from a know-nothing farm boy to a mature older artist. The notion of making this book has been lingering on the fringes of my mind for the last ten years. The motivation for doing it now came from one source, my wife and studio mate, Nancy Mee. She has for years been needling me about starting this project. Her long, unconditional belief in me, my work and the value of my vision has been steady and constant. She is my rock.

This project had many false starts in search of a perfect writer. Finally, I settled on Matthew Kangas. My choice mystified many people as Matthew and I had been on opposite sides of ideas about my work for many years.

The fact that Matthew had been viewing and writing about my work since 1977 was significant. He and I often did not agree but we continued to have respect for each other's point of view and opinion. Most importantly, Matthew was present pretty much from the beginning; he viewed many of my performances and reviewed many of my exhibitions. He has seen almost everything that he has written about in this monograph. He has given an enormous amount of time and done much research for this project, and I have nothing but the deepest respect for his ideas and thoughts and hard work. I would like to thank him for his honesty, enthusiasm and insights.

The second magician and member of our team who deserves a great amount of thanks is Sheryl Conkelton, our scrupulous editor. She brought a skilled eye to our story with the clarity and precision of a heart surgeon. She made us all better.

And the last member of our book team, Phil Kovacevich, embodies the phrase, "a picture is worth a thousand words." His elegant style and good humor made the design decisions a pleasure, and our book "*Magnificent.*"

A special thanks goes to Patterson Sims, who so graciously agreed to interview me and allow our interaction to be a jump-start for this project.

However, there would be nothing to write about if not for the art. The enormous number of art works created in the nearly fifty years of studio practice could not have been accomplished without a small army of helpers and assistants who supported both Nancy and myself in multiple ways.

First on the list is André Samson, who began assisting me in 1982 and who now is my Watson, my Sancho Panza, always championing the "practical over the ideal." Andre is our studio's lifeguard and tractor mechanic and jack-of-all-trades. He continues to assist us in every way. It is hard to imagine Utopian Heights Studios without him. Another significant assistant was Stephanie Schulz; she was with us for thirteen years. And, Paul Casey spent twenty-three years with us in the studio. They each have added a powerful dimension and breadth to our studio practice. John Brooks and Cameron Martin had shorter times with us but each in their own way contributed in special ways. They all brought unique qualities to our work and studios.

In a special category are the printers, photographers and performers who worked with me throughout the years: David Bethlamy, Sheila Coppolla, Tim Heitzman. As are the performers, Mary Ann Peters, Andy Bateman, Catherine Mee and Marcia Dillon.

And the inimitable Mother Art, Margery Aronson, who belongs in a category all her own.

And, lastly, the Light Catchers: Spike Mafford and Nancy Mee.

And acknowledgments would be incomplete without the ever faithful Whitey—Whitey Ford, the 1999 white Ford Econoline van that hauled manure for the gardens and fine art for the marketplace.

I want to thank some of the gallerists who gave me the opportunity to show my works to the greater public. Their function was to exhibit and transform the base materials of art into gold. Without them, most artistic enterprises would collapse due to the heavy cost of production.

A special thanks must go to Linda Farris, who plucked me out of my MFA exhibition and unquestioningly gave her gallery space and support for twenty years. John Braseth and Gordon Woodside also championed and sold my work for another twenty years in Seattle. Andrea Friesen and Yanna Lantz still represent and exhibit my work in Sun Valley. David Austen brought Nancy's and my work to the desert, in Palm Desert and Palm Springs, California. They all had a significant impact on my professional career. There were many more, but this group includes the dealers who had a major impact on my work and career.

And then there are what I still refer to as my spiritual grandparents and creative guides: Carl Jung, Joseph Campbell, Italo Calvino, Jorge Luis Borges, Milorad Pavic, Umberto Eco, Thomas Pynchon, James Joyce, Thomas Lopez (the creator of Moon over Morocco) and Peter Greenaway. Their ideas taught me how to trust my own inner voice and the unlimited and unbounded borders of my creative imaginations.

And, lastly, the intangible—those special souls and teachers who touched me and directed me at crucial forks in the road: Lorene Samuelson and Christos Papadopoulos, who saw innate talent in a young yet-to-be artist and encouraged and blessed me and sent me along the path; Bill Ritchie and Jan van der Marck, who further educated me and continued to support me with great enthusiasm.

And, in Stephen Sondheim's words from *Do I Hear a Waltz:*

> *Did it go by so quickly?*
> *Really, it seems a crime.*
> *But thank you so much*
> *For something between*
> *Ridiculous and sublime.*
> *Thank you for such*
> *A little but lovely time.*

Dennis Evans, Seattle 2022

AUTHOR'S ACKNOWLEDGMENTS

Allan Ament, Freeland, WA; Skye Bassett, Registrar, Boise Art Museum; David Berger, Seattle; Rena Bransten, San Francisco; Jonna Chissus, King County Library System; Sheryl Conkelton, editor, Houston; Jade D'Addaro, Librarian, Special Collections, Seattle Central Library; Diana Edkins and Joyce Faust, Art Resource, New York; Sandy Esene, Civic Art Collection, City of Seattle Office of Arts and Culture; Meghan Finch, Detroit Institute of Arts; Judi Gibbs, Write Guru, Ltd., Seattle; Anne Grosshans, Richmond Beach, WA; Regina Hackett, Seattle; Lloyd E. Herman, Seattle; Jordan Howland and Andy Le, 4Culture | Public Art, Seattle; Estate of Walter F. Isaacs, Special Collections, University of Washington Libraries; Sherri Jackson, Bridgeman Images; Sarah Jane, Gallery and Program Director, Port Angeles Fine Arts Center, Port Angeles, WA; Anne Jenner, Librarian, Special Collections, University of Washington Libraries; Andrew Keating, New York; Sheila Klein, Edison, WA; Phil Kovacevich, graphic designer, New York; John Kucher, Seattle; Charles B. Luce, New York; Sherry Markovitz, Seattle; Nancy Mee, Seattle; John Moilanen, Port Angeles, WA; Metropolitan Museum of Art, New York; Allee Monheim, Special Collections, University of Washington Libraries; Virginia Mosklevskas, Getty Research Institute, Los Angeles; Museum of Modern Art, New York; The Hon. David Olson and Dayle Nelson, Cathlamet, WA; Mary Ann Peters, Seattle; Ann Poulson, Henry Art Gallery, University of Washington; Greg Robinson, Bainbridge Island, WA; Kim Tischler Rosen, Artists Rights Society; Andre Samson, Seattle; Norie Sato, Seattle; Stephanie Schulz, Seattle; Pepper Schwartz, Vashon, WA; Fredericka Foster Shapiro, New York; Erin Shield, Port Angeles Branch Library, North Olympic Library System; Joanna Spurling, Librarian, Vancouver Art Gallery Library, British Columbia; staff librarians for the Hugh and Jane Ferguson Seattle Room, the Mixing Chamber, the Periodicals Department, the Carlo and Eulalie Scandiuzzi Writers' Room, and the Northwest Art Archives of Seattle Central Library; staff of the Seattle Public Library Ballard Branch US Bancorp Quiet Room; Valerie Stenner, Special Collections, Morris Library, University of Delaware, Newark; Josef Venker, S.J., Collections Curator, Seattle University.

My greatest debt of gratitude goes to Dennis Evans whose art, dedication and determination have made this publication an exciting challenge from beginning to end.

Published by Utopian Heights Studio, Seattle, Washington
©2022 Dennis Evans

Essay ©2022 Matthew Kangas

Designed by Phil Kovacevich
Edited by Sheryl Conkelton
Proofread by Barbara Kindness
Index by Judi Gibbs

ISBN: 979-8-9869685-0-6

Printed in Italy

SITE A

B

SITE F

SITE E

SITE C

SITE D

SECONDARY HEXAGON STRUCTURE

BOTH MAGNITUDE and
POSITION (B° — A°)